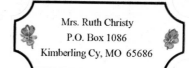

A HISTORY OF
THE AMISH

Steven M. Nolt

Good Books
Intercourse, Pennsylvania 17534

Photography Credits

Covers: front and back, Doyle Yoder

Beth Oberholtzer, 1, 38; Jan Gleysteen, 7, 10, 14, 19, 22, 23, 26, 33, 83; *Mirror of the Martyrs* (copyright 1990, Good Books, Intercourse, PA 17534), 12; The People's Place, 28, 57, 63, 208 (right); Mennonite Historical Library, 42 (both), 45, 58, 79, 85; *A Modest Mennonite Home* (copyright 1990, Good Books, Intercourse, PA 17534), 43; Richard Reinhold, 48, 239, 283; Jonas Yoder, 61; Doyle Yoder, 69; *Pennsylvania Mennonite Heritage*, 76, 180 (both) 183; Stephen E. Scott, 89, 104, 194, 215, 246; J. Lamar Mast, 94; Archives of the Mennonite Church, 98 (Edwin J. Yoder Collection), 108, 186 (C. Henry Smith Collection), 135, 160 (Historical Committee Collection), 178 (both, Michael Richard Collection), 247 (Mennonite World Conference Collection); Steven R. Estes, 118 (*A Goodly Heritage: A History of the North Danvers Mennonite Church*, copyright 1982, p. 56), 146, 150, 222 (*Living Stones: A History of the Metamora Mennonite Church*, copyright 1984, p. f); "Courtesy of the Illinois State Historical Library," 148; Harold Thut, 156; James Burkett, 167; Della (Bender) Miller, 171; Nelson Springer, 177; Horst Gerlach, 184; *The Amish in America: Settlements That Failed, 1840-1960* (Pathway Publishers, Aylmer, ON), 189, 200; Ivan H. and Alice Stoltzfus, 205; *A Craftsman's Handbook: Henry Lapp* (copyright 1991, Good Books, Intercourse, PA 17534), 208 (left); Lancaster Mennonite Historical Library, 214; Family Life (Pathway Pubishers, Aylmer, ON), 227; Kenneth Pellman, 231; William D. Lewis, 232; *Hutchinson News*, 236; Ed Sachs, 255; "BERRY'S WORLD reprinted by permission of NEA, Inc.," 256; *Des Moines Register and Tribune*, 257; Wide World Photos, 258, 271; Toronto (ON) *Globe and Mail*, 272.

Design by Dawn J. Ranck

A HISTORY OF THE AMISH
Copyright © 1992 by Good Books, Intercourse, Pennsylvania 17534
International Standard Book Number: 1-56148-072-X
Library of Congress Catalog Card Number: 92-29684

Library of Congress Cataloging-in-Publication Data

Nolt, Steven M., 1968- .
    A history of the Amish / Steven M. Nolt.
        p. cm.
    Includes bibliographical references and index.
    ISBN 1-56148-072-X : $9.95
    1. Amish—History. I. Title
BX8129-A6N65   1992
289.7'3—dc20
                                       92-29684
                                           CIP

Table of Contents

Acknowledgements

This book is written to serve as an introduction to Amish history in at least two ways. First, those unfamiliar with the shape and movement of the Amish experience will discover the outlines of that story here. Second, readers may dig further into specific areas of the Amish past by using the book's notes and bibliography as a point of departure. Hopefully this volume will nudge its readers to continue exploring the Amish experience beyond these pages.

An important theme in Amish history is the presence of community and the practice of mutual aid. This book is itself a product of such mutuality and sharing. I received a great deal of help and advice from so many people while preparing the text. The staff of the Lancaster Mennonite Historical Society, the Archives of the Mennonite Church, and the Mennonite Historical Library (Goshen College) were very helpful. The Heritage Historical Library, Aylmer, Ontario, was also a most significant resource. Its vast holdings coupled with the broad knowledge of its director make it a necessary stop for anyone on the trail of Amish history. A number of Amish persons from Indiana, Ohio, Ontario and Pennsylvania reviewed all or parts of the manuscript and offered important suggestions and corrections. Their help was invaluable. Although they wish to remain anonymous here, they each have my thanks. Others offered thoughtful criticism, encouragement and assistance all along the way. Especially helpful were Steven R. Estes, Donald B. Kraybill and Joe A. Springer. Jan Gleysteen, J. Craig Haas and Perry A. Klopfenstein also reviewed the text or relevant portions thereof and provided useful comment. Perhaps more than anyone else, Steve Scott worked with me on every step of this project. His significant contribution to this book cannot be measured. Steve researched the North American maps found in this volume. I also thank Elizabeth Weaver Kreider for her careful editing, and Merle and Phyllis Good for supporting a first book. Finally, special thanks is due Rachel, who patiently listened to more talk of history and writing than she probably cared to during our engagement and first months of marriage.

Steven M. Nolt

The Reformation Heritage of the Amish

"We have been united to stand fast in the Lord."
— *Anabaptist leaders, 1527*

The Amish Story

The twentieth century dawned bright and clear in America. A pervasive spirit of optimism buoyed hopes for a better, brighter future. The advances of science and the wonders of technology which had amazed Americans at the 1892 World's Fair disappointed no one in the decade that followed. On the international stage, the United States was fast becoming a "great power," and at home its efforts turned more and more toward social and urban reform and renewal. Western civilization offered itself as the world's salvation for the arriving hundred years. And with the moral and emotional catastrophe of world wars and a Great Depression still several decades away, even America's churches were confident that 1900 marked the beginning of a new "Christian Century."

In McVeytown, Mifflin County, Pennsylvania, sixty-four-year-old Amishman Jonathan K. Hartzler was not so sure. Hartzler was a rather progressive-thinking man himself, but as he thought about the state of his own Amish people at century's end, his progressivism could not chase nagging questions out of his mind. Would his people survive the next hundred years? Why, he wondered, were a number of Amish congregations close to his home declining almost to the point of extinction? And why, he also asked himself, were some members of his church so prone "to look upon the dark side" of their own people and "upon the bright side of churches in other denominations"? Such "unfavorable comparisons" were driving some Amish to predict the doom of their own group.[1]

Mustering all of his own optimism, Hartzler decided "to get at

Very few Old Order Amish construct church buildings; virtually all gather for worship in the homes of members (Lancaster County, Pennsylvania).

the truth" and "seek for the causes of the decline, and by the help of God, remove them." Carefully, he gathered detailed information on Amish church membership and migration, bracing himself for whatever conclusions he would discover. Happily, he found that the Amish churches in his home state—far from declining—had actually grown by nearly three-quarters in the last half of the 1800s. Now Hartzler, too, could be optimistic about the coming century.

As he reflected on the drama of God's activity in the world, Hartzler began to see in Amish history more than a human story. "Persecution drove our forefathers from their homes," he remembered. But despite the difficulties of those days, "they became one of God's means to carry the gospel from the old world to the new." As later generations of Pennsylvania Amish moved westward, they, too, "probably far more than they were aware" were "led by the hand of God," he concluded.

Yes, Hartzler could also see his people playing a part in a God-ordained manifest destiny, as many American politicians saw their own nation. Yet Hartzler's bright vision was also tinted with typical Amish humility—a distraction which never bothered the leaders in Washington. God's "goodness has been so great," the old man realized, while his Amish church had been "so wayward and so unworthy." But therein lay Hartzler's faith: God would be as faithful in the twentieth century as he had been "in Bible times. His compassions fail not; they are new every morning."[2]

Nearly a century later the Amish remain an alive and growing group in North America. Studied and observed by millions of tourists and academics each year, the Amish are the world's fascination. Rejecting automobile ownership, public utility electricity, and the fads and fashions of Madison Avenue, the Amish at first glance appear to be timeless, frozen in the past. In fact, the Old Order Amish are a dynamic, vibrant people, a committed Christian community whose members have taken seriously the task of discipleship and group witness. From their background in the Protestant Reformation, to their 1693 beginnings in the Swiss and south Rhine Valley, and from their immigration to North America, to their struggle to remain a people in the midst of incredible social and cultural pressures, the Amish have persevered through an amazing past. Migrating, dividing, struggling and standing together, the Amish people have lived a story which is rich and deep.

Still firmly rooted in the same faith which encouraged Jonathan K. Hartzler, the Amish have persisted and changed and continued their story. Like Hartzler's turn-of-the-century progressive musings on westward expansion, the Amish story at times seems to be a very North American tale. But it is also a different story from that of its host societies, as the Amish faith has led its communities on a strikingly divergent path through modern Canada and the United States.

Understanding the Amish story requires the breadth of vision of Jonathan K. Hartzler. Hartzler understood that he needed to look both to his people's faith and to their European origins in order to make sense of their life in 1900. That Hartzler remembered the persecution of his people in Europe is no surprise. The Amish are one of several spiritual heirs of the Protestant Reformation's Anabaptist[3] movement and the strength of Hartzler's faith had its roots deep in turbulent sixteenth century Europe.

The Turbulent Sixteenth Century

In the early 1500s a number of political and economic woes troubled Western European society. For more than fifty years a population explosion had outstripped the Continent's ability to feed itself. Inflation of prices and rents drove many land-owning peasants into poverty, while in the towns and cities a growing group of powerful and wealthy merchants and craftspeople challenged the rule of hereditary nobles. University scholars grew sharply critical of state corruption.

Nations felt threatened by the growing power of the Turkish Empire to the East. Kings struggled not only to wrest power and authority from their local nobles, but also against their rival monarchs across Europe. The conditions grew all the more intense and frightening as the printing press shrank the European world. No longer were events in Paris and Vienna so distant; the printed page relayed messages of doom, destruction and social unrest from city to city in a matter of days. Free from direct state control, the new European press circulated ideas and arguments in a way that often increased anxiety and discontent.

Amid the turbulence of early sixteenth-century European life, the church still held the social fabric together. For more than a thousand years western Europe had been united in "One Holy Catholic and Apostolic Church." During the fourth century, through the support of the Roman emperors, Christianity had changed from a persecuted movement to the only officially tolerated religion in the Roman Empire. Under the presumably Christian empire, bishops and priests received special privileges, and eventually the bishop of Rome was accorded particular prestige. The church and the Roman state were linked in building a common, unified, "Christian" civilization. Dissent against the One Church was also a crime against the state.

In time, the western half of the Roman Empire crumbled, but the church remained to pick up the pieces. Throughout the Middle Ages the Pope, as bishop of Rome, led Christians in building a holy civilization in Western Europe. The church offered God's salvation to all who sought divine grace through participation in the sacraments (especially the Holy Communion), which the church regulated carefully.

But the church did much more than oversee the way to heaven. The church mediated national conflicts, crowned rulers, patronized the fine arts, supported higher education, and encouraged trade and exploration. The church had led Europe through the centuries, but now, in the early sixteenth century, society was splintering, and the church itself was breaking up—a fact which

The Grossmünster (Great Church) in Zurich, Switzerland. The Anabaptist movement in Zurich began in 1525.

frightened people more than political or economic woes.

Indeed, some popes had been pawns of French kings and German emperors, and often church councils and activist priests had cried out for church reform. But after 1517 the trouble in the church was different. The Roman Catholic Church was actually losing its moral and political authority in some parts of Europe. In that year the Wittenberg monk and lecturer Martin Luther (1483-1546) had proposed a whole series of changes, not only of church structure—as many reformers had done before— but also of key church doctrines.[4]

Luther and the Protestant Reformation

Luther proposed revolutionary challenges to some of Rome's most basic teachings. Luther taught "salvation by grace through faith alone," that God's saving grace comes to each Christian individually through each one's *faith*, rather than through the church's sacraments. Such thinking undercut the church's importance and authority. By the time he officially broke with Rome in 1521, Luther was also championing church decision-making based solely on Bible study instead of tradition and canon law, and the use of the German language instead of Latin to make worship more understandable to the lay people.

Luther's ideas were promoted widely by printers across Germany. A number of German princes also supported him, for both religious and political reasons. Church leaders in other (mostly German) cities began introducing many of Luther's reforms into their own parishes. An important fellow-reformer was Huldrych Zwingli (1484-1531), the priest of the Great Church in the city of Zurich, Switzerland. Like Luther, Zwingli preached salvation by grace through faith alone, rejected the doctrine of Purgatory and advocated the marriage of clergy. Zwingli also taught the symbolic, rather than physical, presence of Jesus' body and blood in the bread and wine of communion.

As early as 1518, Zwingli's teaching attracted reform-minded younger men and women in the Zurich area. By 1522 small groups of these students and craftspeople began meeting in private homes for Bible study and prayer.[5] They were excited by the ideas of the Reformation, but troubled because they feared that Zwingli's reforms were losing momentum and might even be reversed. Zwingli, like Luther, relied on the government to put his reforms into place. Luther and Zwingli could not imagine a society without a strong leader; when they removed the pope from their social scheme, they replaced his power and authority with that of a local prince or city council.

Radical Reformers in Zurich

That state-church strategy troubled the reform-minded Zurich youth who felt that the church was now being controlled by the Zurich City Council. When Zwingli's reforms strengthened the Council's power (such as his rejection of Rome's authority over Zurich), the city fathers readily agreed. But when the changes involved the Council's own sacrifice (such as relaxing the unjust tithes which the city extorted from the surrounding rural villages), the Council stalled.

Moreover, because the church routinely baptized all infants, the church by definition continued to include *all* of the state's citizens, and morality sank to an intolerable low. Everyone was officially a member of the church, but not all were committed. The church could not demand the high ethics of Christ's Sermon on the Mount from those who were "Christians" only because they were citizens. The church settled for the lowest commonly held personal and social ethics. New Testament teachings were disregarded in the face of political realities.

This government-guided church reform bothered the young Zurich dissenters. If the Word of God was to form the church, then no human government should stand in the way, they believed. In 1524, when Zwingli concluded that unbiblical parts of the Catholic mass should be discarded, the City Council balked. Zwingli conceded to the Council, irking the young dissenters.

Gradually the dissenters realized that the recovery of the church as the New Testament described it could only occur on radically different grounds than either Rome or the Reformers were using. These more radical reformers had a very different concept of the church itself. For them the church was a community of Christians voluntarily committed to Christ and to each other. Baptism—the sign of church membership and commitment—could only be received by adults who chose to join the fellowship. The state could have no part in controlling or directing the activities and doctrines of the church. The church must be free of state control.

Salvation came by grace through faith, these radicals believed, but it was more than a future ticket to heaven. It transformed one's life with God and with other people. Since Christ taught peaceful nonviolence and nonresistance to worldly enemies, radical Christian obedience prohibited participation in either the military or the judicial arms of the state. The New Testament church demonstrated sharing of personal goods and the practicing of mutual aid among Christians, and the dissenters took those teachings seriously as well.

Anabaptism Is Born

Before long the ideas of the voluntary, "free" church radicals clashed with the Zurich Council, which demanded a unified church and state on its own terms. Some dissenters refused to have their infant children baptized because the children were not

Anabaptists met secretly for worship in this Swiss cave.

yet old enough to understand Christ's call of discipleship. The city demanded that the radicals stop meeting, have their children baptized and expel the non-Zurichers from among them. Snubbing the Council, the dissenters met on January 21, 1525, and baptized one another, signaling their own conscious decision to follow Christ and form a church apart from the state. Since they had been baptized as infants, this new adult baptism was a second baptism (in Latin, *anabaptismus*). These Anabaptists (as they were now called) wanted an adult baptism because they felt that their infant baptisms had been meaningless.

Such disobedience to the state church was intolerable in Zurich. Both Zwingli and the Council knew that the Anabaptist ideas challenged the unity of the church and the state. Anabaptism was socially subversive. In rejecting infant baptism, the Anabaptists separated the political tie between church membership and citizenship. By challenging the unity of the church, the Anabaptists tore the fabric of the society in two. In rejecting the state's authority in matters of religion, the Anabaptists threatened anarchy. By refusing military service, the Anabaptists made the city vulnerable to foreign attack.

The Anabaptists were imprisoned and exiled, fined and threatened. Meanwhile their ideas, already present in the rural countryside around Zurich, spawned a number of Anabaptist fellowships beyond the town walls. Even the threat of the death penalty could not halt the growing movement. Within several years, Anabaptist groups existed throughout Switzerland, southern Germany, the Austrian Tyrol and into Moravia. Always their purpose was the same: by God's grace to work diligently at being the church, with a strong emphasis on ethical discipleship and without state interference.

Persecution and Its Effect

During the next century, the Anabaptists were ferociously persecuted. Anabaptists were jailed, tortured, burned, beheaded or sold as galley slaves to row themselves to death on the Mediterranean. Some of the Swiss city-states employed "Anabaptist hunters" who tracked down suspected citizens and were paid by the head. When Anabaptist groups sprang up in northern Germany and the Netherlands, authorities there also reacted harshly. Hundreds of Anabaptists were killed in the decades after the first baptisms in 1525.[6]

Anabaptist meetings often took place at night, in the woods or among small groups. Leaders traveled secretly and had to hide precious—but illegal—Anabaptist tracts and devotional materials. Many members lived in fear and some recanted their beliefs and returned to the state churches.

The century of intense persecution left lasting marks on the Anabaptist movement.[7] The re-baptizers often developed a deep distrust of the larger society and a negative view of government. Generations later, Anabaptist descendants still recounted the stories of those who suffered (see "Ausbund," p.21 and "Martyrs Mirror," p. 16).

In addition to fostering a tendency to withdraw, the fierce persecution further encouraged the simplicity and piety which the Anabaptists already saw in the Bible. The line dividing the suffering church and the cruel world became all too clear. The world was arrogant, wealthy, proud and violent. The Anabaptists saw themselves as meek, simple, humble and nonresistant. While some of these characteristics may have been typical of

During the sixteenth century, hundreds of Anabaptists were executed for their faith. Etching by Jan Luyken.

rural Swiss and south German people generally, the experience of persecution accentuated them among the Anabaptists.

Anabaptist organization reflected the desperate times as well. Local congregations were self-governing, and often each had its own preaching minister and sometimes also a deacon who collected and distributed money for the poor. Regional elders (later, in North America, they came to be called "bishops") served several congregations by leading in baptisms, communion, ordinations and marriages. The most important role which elders (bishops) and ministers played was that of modeling Christian discipleship and guiding church discipline. Administering the rites of the church was secondary. In fact, the Swiss Anabaptists allowed lay members to lead worship and teach meetings if no ordained leader was available.

Toward Unity of Belief and Practice

Persecution did not stop the spread of the movement. Just two years after it began, Anabaptism was so widespread that some of its leaders sensed a need to more precisely outline what held them together. Gathering in the village of Schleitheim on the Swiss-German border, the Swiss and south German Anabaptists, who called themselves simply "Brethren" or "Swiss Brethren," declared their definition of the church. "We have been united to stand fast in the Lord," they announced, "as obedient children of God, sons and daughters, who have been and shall be separated from the world in all that we do and leave undone, and . . . completely at peace."[8]

The Swiss Brethren then agreed on several foundational points of Anabaptist church life and practice. They began with adult baptism and church discipline. Discipline was a key issue for the Swiss Brethren and would remain so for their spiritual descendants. The Swiss Brethren themselves were being "disciplined" by government executioners for leaving the state churches. The church discipline advocated by the Anabaptists, however, was wholly nonviolent. The Anabaptists excommunicated and barred from fellowship those who fell into unrepentant sin.

While milder than its execution-style state church equivalent, church discipline for the Swiss Brethren was nevertheless extremely important. Since they affirmed both the voluntary nature of the church and the high ethical standards of personal discipleship, the Swiss Brethren also had to grapple with what to do when persons decided to stop following Jesus. Establishing a pure church required marking definite boundaries. While the New Testament was clear that Christians should avoid "the world," it was unclear what such avoidance involved. For the time, the Swiss Brethren themselves avoided the question; but they seem to have felt that barring the unrepentant from the communion table kept church integrity pure enough.

Trouble in the North

The Anabaptists in northern Europe soon had to wrestle with church discipline in a situation which was more urgent and less theoretical than their south German and Swiss brothers and sisters. Anabaptism arrived in northern Germany in 1530 and spread immediately to the Netherlands, where it grew rapidly. This northern Anabaptism had some different emphases from the movement in Switzerland and the southern Rhine Valley. Most notably, there was great enthusiasm for the imminent Second Coming of Christ, with bold predictions about impending events before that Great Day. Some Anabaptists were uncom-

Anabaptist leader Menno Simons.

fortable with the fanaticism often associated with these predictions, and preferred a "quiet and peaceable life" of obedience to Jesus' teachings. Others, however, set out with force to usher in the new Messianic Age. Ironically, these Anabaptists took up the sword in order to create an Anabaptist church-state. Capturing the city of Münster in 1534, these violently-inclined Anabaptists turned the tables on the state churches and began to persecute and punish anyone who refused to be baptized as an adult!

Within a year an army jointly raised by Catholics and Protestants crushed the Münster takeover. But the after-shocks of the struggle pounded the northern "peaceful" Anabaptists who had rejected the actions at Münster from the start. Fearful state authorities connected the actions at Münster with *all* the Anabaptist groups, even those which denounced every form of violence. Persecution of the Anabaptists became severe in the Netherlands and northern Germany following Münster, since officials now considered all Anabaptists to be violent and militant revolutionaries.

Scattered, discouraged and scared, nonviolent Dutch Anabaptism struggled to re-define itself. Into this disorganized movement came a former Dutch Catholic priest named Menno Simons (c.1496-1561).[9] (So important was his influence that within a few decades many of the northern Anabaptists were called "Mennonites.") Menno had secretly sympathized with the Anabaptists for years. In 1536 he denounced the violence of Münster and openly joined the nonviolent Anabaptist group. For the next quarter century, until about 1560, Dutch Anabaptist leaders, including Menno, worked to re-build the peaceful Anabaptist fellowships across northern Europe.

Menno needed to distance himself and his fellow believers from the debacle of Münster. No longer was it possible to simply refuse communion to the fanatical Anabaptists of the Münster stripe; biblical, peaceful Anabaptists could not even risk *associating* with them. The unrepentant, excommunicated Anabaptists who espoused violence needed to be avoided in any and all social and personal relationships, Menno taught.

Other questions began to plague the Dutch Anabaptists. Some European theologians and church reformers began to teach that the church was only "spiritual" and "other-worldly," so that Christian relationships and ethics in this life did not matter much. In a corrective reaction to such teaching, Menno and the "Mennonite" Anabaptists placed even more emphasis on the rejection of sin in the church, and the separation of believers from those who had left the church. Christians needed to avoid, or "shun" the unrepentant.[10]

The Question of Shunning

In the course of a few years, some northern Anabaptists became more and more extreme in their practice of shunning

Martyrs Mirror: Anabaptist History Among the Amish

In the late sixteenth century, the Dutch government began to tolerate the Mennonites. Now socially accepted, Dutch Mennonites soon worked their way into mainstream culture. By the middle of the 1600s Dutch Mennonite merchants, physicians and artisans were becoming quite wealthy.

A Dutch Mennonite minister, Thieleman Jansz. van Braght (1625-1664) feared that his people were becoming too acculturated. Would they not forget the New Testament teaching on simplicity, humility and the suffering church as they became more secure in this life? Braght believed that one way to call the church to faithfulness was to remind it of its martyr past. He began collecting tales of Anabaptist martyrs from court records, stories and other books. In 1660 he published them in a 1,478-page tome entitled *The Bloody Theater or Martyrs Mirror*.

The book included explanations of traditional Mennonite beliefs (including shunning) as well as hundreds of gripping martyr stories. About one hundred of the tales were made all the more graphic in the book's second edition when the Dutch Mennonite artist Jan Luyken (1649-1712) provided 104 copper engraved illustrations.

Many church leaders felt that the book implicitly taught nonresistance to enemies, since the stories told of those who chose the way of suffering over fighting. In 1748, faced with the threat of oncoming frontier wars, Pennsylvania Mennonites had the book translated into German.

In 1780 Amish Elder Hans Naffziger (c.1712-c.1791) of Essingen, Germany, made arrangements for that Pennsylvania edition to be reprinted in Europe for his own Amish congregations in the Palatinate and Alsace. The Amish Naffziger worked together on the project with Peter Weber (1731-1781), a Mennonite minister. In war-torn Europe the stories would do their people good, too, they thought. Meanwhile the Amish in North America were also reading the German *Martyrs Mirror*. Several decades later in 1849, Mifflin County, Pennsylvania, Amishman Shem Zook (1798-1880) issued a new German-language edition of the *Martyrs Mirror*. An Amish publisher still keeps a German edition of the martyr book in print.

Today the *Martyrs Mirror* is found in most Amish homes. References to it are common in Amish circles. The book has, in many ways, supported the idea that the world is not to be fully trusted. The themes of separation, suffering and faithfulness ring from its pages. No doubt the faith, piety and experiences of sixteenth-century Anabaptist martyrs have greatly influenced and shaped Amish thought even into the late twentieth century.

See Thieleman J. van Braght, *The Bloody Theater; or Martyrs Mirror of the Defenseless Christians*. (Scottdale, Pa. and Waterloo, Ont.: Herald Press, 1990). See also John S. Oyer and Robert S. Kreider, *Mirror of the Martyrs* (Intercourse, Pa.: Good Books, 1990).

excommunicated members (the practice was known as *Meidung* in German). Some would have nothing at all to do with former church members. Others even called for the suspending of the marriage relationship when the church excommunicated one of the partners. Menno seems to have tried to play a more mediating role between those who called for strict and more mild excommunication, but in the end Menno sided with those who called for social avoidance.[11]

The issue of shunning repeatedly stifled church unity among the Anabaptists. In 1554, when the Dutch and northern European Mennonites finally formulated a specific statement on avoidance of the excommunicated, the Swiss and south German Mennonites rejected it as too harsh. Three years later a well-attended conference of Swiss and southern leaders sent a delegation up north to visit Menno and to suggest that the Dutch practice of shunning was going too far.

Eventually, however, the Swiss and south German Mennonites agreed to practice social avoidance in some way. Perhaps they made this concession to their Dutch brothers and sisters for the sake of church unity. Or perhaps the Swiss and south Germans actually were persuaded that the New Testament called on Christians to end their social contacts with wayward believers. Either way, in 1568 and again in 1591, the south German Mennonites adopted church rules which called for socially avoiding those members who left the church.[12] To what extent the south Germans actually practiced what they preached is unclear. Meanwhile, in the north, decades of harsh church discipline were beginning to tear the Dutch Mennonites apart.

Finally Unity?

By 1632, however, the long struggle over shunning in the north seemed to be resolved. In an historic meeting held in the Dutch city of Dort (Dordrecht), Dutch and northern Mennonite leaders drew up a church unity agreement, the *Dordrecht Confession*.[13] The confession became one of the longest-lasting and most influential Mennonite confessions of faith. It outlined Mennonite doctrine from creation to Christ's second coming. The next-to-last of its eighteen articles dealt with avoidance. The article recognized the value of ending business and social relationships with those who left the church. Christians could not conscientiously support the life and lifestyle of those who gave up the way of discipleship, it argued.

But *Dordrecht* also called for "Christian moderation" in the use of avoidance. The church was still to feed, clothe and otherwise help excommunicated members who were in need, "according to the love and teaching of Christ and the apostles." The church could not view the shunned as "enemies," it cautioned, but rather should ask the erring to amend their lives and "be reconciled to God" and the church.

The *Dordrecht Confession* seemed to strike a balance by presenting a moderate form of shunning which aimed at keeping clear the boundaries of Christian ethics, while urging those who had left the church to return. Accepted by many congregations in the north, the document circulated among the Mennonites in south Germany and Switzerland as well, as did many of Menno's writings which advocated social avoidance. A generation later, in 1660, Alsatian Mennonite ministers and deacons representing congregations recently emigrated from Switzerland officially adopted as their own the *Dordrecht* statement with its article on shunning. At least one of those signers did not approve of the article on social avoidance.[14] Even though other Swiss Anabaptist leaders also rejected shunning, they offered the *Dordrecht Confession* when the government in Bern demanded an outline of their doctrine.[15]

After more than one hundred years of debate and argument among the Anabaptist-Mennonites, the controversy over social

A prison cell at Trachselwald, Switzerland, in which Anabaptists were imprisoned.

avoidance finally seemed to be dying down after 1660. By then all the Mennonites seemed to officially sanction the shunning of unrepentant former church members. Had the Mennonites finally achieved "unity in the Lord," or was the issue still unresolved?

Staying Alive

While the south German and Swiss Mennonites were trying to resolve their internal disagreements over shunning practices, they also faced the continued external threats of state and state-church persecution. After 1614 Swiss authorities avoided creating religious martyrs. Instead of public executions, state leaders tried to imprison, fine and exile the Anabaptists to discourage the group's growth. Beginning in 1635, Swiss city councils, especially the one which governed the area around Bern, tried to systematically rid their lands of the Swiss Brethren.

In 1648, the Anabaptists and all of Europe hailed the end of the terribly destructive Thirty Years War. Fought over political ambitions and alliances which were often complicated by Protestant and Catholic rivalries, the war had taken the lives of more than half the inhabitants of some areas. The waste of human life was phenomenal, even by twentieth century standards. Just as frightening, farmland which had laid untilled in the midst of years of war was reverting to forest and threatened to kill the war's few survivors by famine.

In the dire conditions left by the war, princes hurried to find anyone who would farm their war-ravaged acres. The situation was so desperate that many even considered Anabaptist tenants. By at least 1653, persecuted Swiss Brethren began to move down the Rhine River into the devastated lands on its west bank known as the Palatinate. Eleven years later one of the Palatinate's dukes issued a special offer of toleration to the Swiss Brethren (he called them "Menisten," correctly associating them with their fellow Mennonites in the North). The Mennonites would receive full religious freedom for themselves, the duke promised, but they could not proselytize, meet in large groups nor construct church buildings. Despite these restrictions and heavier taxes, some Mennonites saw the offer as better than the harassment and threat of deportation they faced in Switzerland.[16]

Simultaneously, several French nobles invited the Swiss Brethren to move into lands just north of Switzerland on the west bank of the Rhine. Known as the Alsace, this region was governed by religiously tolerant French aristocrats, but most of its citizens were German-speaking Alsatians. Small numbers of Anabaptists had lived in both the Palatinate and the Alsace for generations, but the large migrations after 1670 changed Mennonite church life there.[17] The new immigrants came in large numbers and were still very interested in what was happening in Switzerland. The Mennonite congregations in Switzerland, the Palatinate and the Alsace were now even more closely connected than they had been before.

Building the church had been hard work for the Anabaptists. Opposition and persecution had come from all sides. Still they had pressed on with their New Testament vision of a free church made up of voluntarily committed disciples of Christ who had experienced God's salvation and were living witnesses to a new way of life. At times, this vision itself had been a stumbling block, as the Anabaptists struggled with how the church relates to those who are not disciples. The tension of being "in" the world, but not "of" it, had sometimes been too great. But the Anabaptists had not and would not give up living in that tension, choosing rather, they said, "to persevere along the path we have entered upon, unto the glory of God and of Christ His Son."[18]

Ausbund: Anabaptist Hymnal of the Amish

In 1535 a group of Anabaptists traveling from Moravia to southwestern Germany were captured on the Bavarian border. Placed in the prison of a Passau castle, some of these Anabaptists spent nearly five years there before authorities set them free. Others died in the dungeon.

During their imprisonment, to occupy their time and to encourage each other spiritually, the prisoners wrote fifty-three hymns. Most of the lyrics spoke of sorrow, loneliness and imminent death. The hymns were also hopeful, since the authors believed that their suffering and tribulation were to be expected in this life and were nothing compared with the glory of heaven.

By at least 1564 the hymns were printed as a book. The book proved popular, and soon other favorite Anabaptist hymns (for the most part lengthy martyr ballads with dozens of stanzas) joined the Passau collection. Only nineteen years after its first edition, the prison hymn book was re-issued again, this time with 130 songs. The hymnal's second edition was the first to receive the title *Ausbund*, probably meaning "selection."

The hymns often stressed Anabaptist themes, such as believers' baptism, nonviolence and the suffering of Christ's followers. Many times the tunes were popular secular ones now set to Christian lyrics. The *Ausbund* was the Anabaptists' most frequently used worship book, second only to the Bible. German-speaking European Mennonites and Amish continued to use the *Ausbund* some three hundred years after the first words were sung in the Passau dungeon.

In North America, Mennonites used the book regularly until about 1800. The Amish continued to use the book into the next century and today nearly all Old Order Amish congregations still use it, or adaptations of it. Today's *Ausbund* contains 140 hymns, a brief doctrinal statement and a short collection of Swiss Anabaptist martyr biographies. No printed music is included in the volume; all the tunes have been passed on orally through the years. While some of the tunes have been forgotten and others greatly embellished, the Amish have accurately preserved many of the melodies for centuries.

Contemporary Amish church life has been enriched and influenced by the singing of *Ausbund* hymns. The stories of martyrdom and persecution strengthen the Amish sense of humility and total dependence upon God. The Amish have preserved a valuable piece of Reformation-era hymnody.

See *Ausbund, Das ist: Etliche schöne christliche Lieder.* . . . (Lancaster, Pa.: Lancaster Press, 1991). For more information, see Paul M. Yoder, et al., *Four Hundred Years With the Ausbund* (Scottdale, Pa.: Herald Press, 1964).

The castle at Passau on the Danube. Anabaptists imprisoned there wrote hymns which became the nucleus of the Ausbund *hymnal.*

— 2 —
Amish Beginnings, 1693-1711

"There you have it."
— *Peter Zimmerman announcing the*
beginning of the Amish church

Uncertain Times

In 1690, the Swiss and south Rhine Mennonite world was still one of trouble and persecution, reminiscent of the early days of Anabaptism. By that year, probably at least one thousand Swiss Brethren had emigrated to the Palatinate alone, as Swiss harassment continued. The next year Bernese authorities began yet another round of arrests and imprisonment, this time because

The Emme River Valley in Switzerland, home to many Swiss Brethren (Mennonites), including Hans Reist.

the Anabaptists refused to bear arms.[1]

Those Mennonites who had left Switzerland for the Alsace and Palatinate had not escaped difficulty either. The Mennonites' unwillingness to participate in local Alsatian militias, for example, caused some problems for the new arrivals there. Also, local French Catholic priests resisted any further religious competition in the region. The resentment of the Alsatian locals might have been as much ethnic as religious, since the Mennonites were Swiss. Later, both the Alsatian natives and the French state church officials were concerned that the new Swiss arrivals "enjoyed all of the best land"—a complaint not grounded in doctrinal differences.[2]

Beginning in 1688, the decade-long War of Palatinate Succession disturbed and destroyed life for the Swiss Mennonite refugees in the Palatinate. The troubles from which they had fled Switzerland were now following them down the Rhine. Successors of the Palatinate rulers became more fickle and autocratic in dealing with the Mennonites.[3]

Troubling Issues

The continued harassment of the Swiss Brethren/Mennonites in Switzerland, Alsace and the Palatinate led to some heated church discussions. Not all neighbors of the Mennonites discriminated or protested against the Anabaptists. Many were friendly and helpful. Additionally, some Anabaptist families had relatives who had left their fellowships and re-joined the local state churches. These state church converts often looked out for their harassed family members and made important social or political contacts for them.

Sometimes these sympathetic friends and relatives were known as Half-Anabaptists (*Halbtäufer*) or True-Hearted (*treuherzige*) People—names which suggest some of the Mennonite ambivalence towards them. At the same time, plagued by discrimination and social stigma, many Mennonites turned to the True-Hearted for help and aid. The alliance was especially strong in Switzerland where official opposition was harshest and the Mennonites had lived enough generations to have extended family connections with the True-Hearted. In the Palatinate and Alsace, the more recent Mennonite immigrants had few relatives in the state church, so connections with the True-Hearted in those areas were not as important.[4]

How were the Mennonites to relate to these sympathetic friends and relations? In an era when all churches—Catholic, Anglican, Lutheran and Reformed—branded nearly everyone outside of their own group as heretical, the Mennonites were not alone in viewing ecumenical relations as problematic. For the Anabaptists, the difficulty was all the more perplexing since they advocated adult baptism and separation from sinful, worldly social structures as a mark of true Christian discipleship. Were the True-Hearted saved? They had not been voluntarily baptized as adult believers. If they were saved, then the practice of adult baptism was meaningless. The True-Hearted also refused to leave their respectable and socially-secure state church member-ships and continued through their tithes and offerings to support the very apparatus which persecuted the Mennonites. Were not the True-Hearted inconsistent and hypocritical? But could the Mennonites condemn the True-Hearted, especially when they exhibited such Christ-like ethics as "giving a cup of cold water" to their persecuted neighbors? Indeed, many True-Hearted peo-ple had put their own reputations and property on the line when they befriended the outcast Mennonites. How could the Men-nonites criticize them? How could some Mennonites have sur-vived without them?

An old Anabaptist perspective on the problematic relationship was that Mennonites just could not know whether or not the True-Hearted people were saved; only God knew. The Menno-nites should pray for the True-Hearted and be grateful for their friendship, but there was no need to cut off relations with them or condemn them. This view was held mostly in Switzerland.

Another equally traditional line of reasoning also circulated among the Mennonites, especially in the Alsace and Palatinate. This tradition drew on the strict Anabaptist distinction between the church and the world. For those who held this world-view, there was little or no middle ground—the True-Hearted were not saved and the Mennonites should not rely on their help in times of trouble. God alone would see the persecuted through.

Mennonites who held to this more dualistic view also made much of the Anabaptist practice of shunning those who recanted and joined the state church. Accepting the aid of True-Hearted family members who had returned to the state church violated the principle of social avoidance. Drawing on wide streams of earlier Mennonite thought, those who held to this perspective had plenty of biblical and historic Anabaptist support for their call for separation and avoidance. In each generation, Mennonites were compromising more and more with larger society, they claimed; the fellowships needed reform and renewal.

Jakob Ammann

As the seventeenth century came to a close, stirrings of spiritual renewal surfaced among the south Rhine and Swiss Mennonites. One of the voices calling for reform in church life was a young Swiss elder named Jakob Ammann (see "Jakob Ammann," p. 34). Ammann later moved north to the Alsace to shepherd congregations there. He may have already lived there when he began agitating for changes in church life—at the least he had connections and support in that area. Most of the controversial events surrounding him, however, took place in Switzerland. Ammann's first call for reform was his proposal of more frequent communion services.[5]

In striving for literal obedience to the Bible, Swiss Mennonites had observed communion once a year because the first Lord's Supper instituted by Jesus had been a part of a once-yearly Passover meal. By at least 1693, Ammann suggested that church life would be strengthened if congregations communed

The Alsatian village of Markirch (today Sainte-Marie-aux-Mines), home of Jakob Ammann.

twice a year. Since the Mennonites had stressed preparing for the Lord's Supper by closely examining their lives and relationships with God and other people, having communion more often might cause members to be more diligent in their Christian life.

Also, the Anabaptists had always excluded those living in open sin from the communion table. A more frequent observance would also force congregations to more often deal with situations which required church discipline. Since Ammann represented those who believed that Mennonites were becoming too lax, he welcomed more attention to church order.[6]

Ammann's congregations instituted a more frequent communion, and apparently some other fellowships asked their own leaders to make the same change. A number of these other elders and ministers, notably Elder Hans Reist, balked at the idea of introducing a new practice (see "Hans Reist," p. 30). Perhaps threatened by the challenge of Ammann's strong personality or popular appeal, Reist and several other elders rejected more frequent communion. They admitted that Ammann and those who agreed with him could do as they wished, but Reist and his associates made it very clear that they considered the change quite unnecessary.

To Avoid or Not To Avoid

Ammann sensed that Reist represented the weakening of Mennonite church life and resolve, which Ammann abhorred. Reist was a friend of the True-Hearted and held out the possibility that they might be saved even without publicly confessing God's grace and receiving baptism. Also, Reist did not practice social avoidance against those who left the church or who refused to confess their sins; he was comfortable with merely excluding such from the once-a-year communion table. So when some in Reist's congregation continued to clamor for more frequent communion and Reist called fellow ministers Niklaus Moser and Peter Giger for counsel, Ammann decided to open the debate further. Ammann asked Moser and Giger to find out what Reist really believed about shunning.

Reist answered with the words of Jesus, replying that, "What enters the mouth does not defile the man, but what comes out of the mouth" (Matthew 15:11).[7] The message to Ammann was clear: Reist believed that avoidance of sin was only a spiritual, not a physical, possibility. Reist had no intention of practicing

The confrontation between Jakob Ammann and Hans Reist as carved by Aaron Zook, a member of the Beachy Amish church.

literal social shunning of errant members as an attempt to win them back to the church.

Ammann now believed that renewal in the church was all the more urgent since it was clear that even seasoned leaders like Hans Reist did not uphold a strict separation from the world. In 1693 Ammann and three other like-minded ministers began to travel through the Swiss Mennonite communities, preaching social avoidance and questioning elders and ministers on their teaching.

The party soon found that Reist's friend, Niklaus Moser, agreed with them that shunning was important, and also rejected the idea that the True-Hearted were saved. In the next town, Reist's other advising minister, Peter Giger, apparently also confessed the practice of shunning. Buoyed by their new-found sympathy, Ammann's group traveled down into the Swiss Emme River Valley, with its heavy Mennonite population, and summoned Hans Reist himself. The exchange between Reist and Ammann was heated. Reist rejected Ammann's call for shunning on the grounds that Jesus ate with known sinners and yet had kept himself pure. Christians in the late seventeenth century could do the same, Reist claimed.

But, Ammann counter-charged, Reist was not keeping the church pure. A woman who had lied, and then repeatedly lied about her lying, was still considered a member in good standing of Reist's congregation. Even though her untruth had been revealed, Reist had not practiced even the *spiritual* discipline which he espoused. Here was proof for Ammann that Reist was drifting from the Anabaptist teachings of church purity and Christian ethics.

Ministers in a neighboring town suggested that Ammann call a general meeting of all the Swiss church leaders and settle the matter publicly and completely. Niklaus Moser's barn served as a meeting place. Many of the elders and ministers did not attend—among them, Hans Reist. Sensing a growing tension between Ammann and Reist, Moser and Giger backed away from their earlier acceptance of shunning. At the meeting, they told Ammann that they would like to decide the issue only with the counsel of all of the ministers and thorough Bible study. After some discussion, those present decided to invite all leaders and lay members to meet again in two weeks. Hopefully all could reach an understanding then.

The next fourteen days were filled with personal meetings and letters. Through emissaries, Ammann tried to contact Reist, who still refused to say that the True-Hearted were not saved. Reist also wrote a letter criticizing Ammann, saying that "in matters concerning doctrines and church rituals, not too much attention should be given younger men [i.e., Ammann]."[8] Reist's authoritarian, condescending attitude seriously hurt efforts at reconciliation, as did another letter, written during those two weeks by Peter Giger, who was now less than sympathetic toward Ammann. The Reist party's aloofness was begging for a confrontation.

Days of Division

When the day of the second general conference arrived, Hans Reist and several other area ministers who were sympathetic to him did not appear. In the long moments of that very tense situation, Ammann assured everyone that he did not want to cause any schism in the church, but he reminded them that matters could not be settled until Reist arrived. One of the women who was waiting for the discussion to get started left the meeting to go and find Reist, to tell him that the rest of the group was waiting.

But Reist had no intention of meeting with Ammann or debating the issues under consideration. He sent word back to those at the Moser barn that he and several other church leaders were involved in harvesting and were too busy to be bothered.

Hans Reist

Hans Reist (also known as Heusli Hans) was a Mennonite elder in the Emme River Valley east of Bern, Switzerland. Very little is known about his life aside from the information which has been preserved in letters chronicling his disagreements with Jakob Ammann. He was married to Barbara Ryser.

Reist knew persecution first-hand. In 1670 authorities expelled Hans and Barbara, penniless, from their home village of Rotenbaum because the couple were Anabaptists. The Bern government confiscated the Reists' house and sold most of their grain, animals and furniture—including a loom. Reist must have had few debts, because after the state paid them off with the profits of the sale, quite a bit of money remained.

Like many expelled Mennonites, Reist broke exile in a few years and returned home, hoping to once again live in peace. State records mention his name in 1686. In 1701, officials again arrested Reist and he promised to attend the state church and take the holy sacraments. Probably Reist had no more intention of keeping that promise than he had of remaining in exile thirty years earlier. Reist was an elder who knew how to survive tough times and who understood his own weaknesses and ability to compromise. He apparently sympathized with the failings of others and allowed his own congregation and the True-Hearted a lot of spiritual latitude.

One small collection of Reist's writing remains in the form of a sixteen-page booklet which contains one prayer and one hymn. Supporting Ammann's charge that Reist taught salvation for the True-Hearted, Reist's prayer petitions God "on behalf of all those peoples who do so much good unto us with food and drink and house and shelter, and who produce and show unto us great love and loyalty. Lord God, be their rich rewarder here and in the life eternal."

Reist's prayer also reveals the deep pain he must have experienced during the struggle with Ammann. "Draw us together," the elder prayed, "in Thy great love and let no dissension or scattering come among us any more, but rather let us see, O Lord of Harvest, how great the harvest, but how few Thy faithful workers are." Reist went on to ask God to "rouse up" ministers and elders among the Mennonites.

Reist's hymn was a forty-six stanza ballad which told the biblical story of Abraham and Isaac.

For more information, see Samuel Geiser's entry "Reist, Hans" in *The Mennonite Encyclopedia: A Comprehensive Reference Work on the Anabaptist-Mennonite Movement* (Scottdale, Pa.: Mennonite Publishing House, 1956-59); Isaac Zürcher, "Hans Reist House and the 'Vale of Anabaptists,'" *The Mennonite Quarterly Review* 66 (July 1992): 426, 427; and Robert Friedmann, *Mennonite Piety Through the Centuries: Its Genius and Its Literature* (Goshen, Ind.: The Mennonite Historical Society, 1949), pp. 184, 185.

Upon hearing this, Ammann "nearly became enraged" and denounced Reist on six counts.[9] Not stopping with the pronouncement of charges, Ammann immediately excommunicated Reist. The startling course of events left onlookers "fairly horrified" and several people begged Ammann to be patient and let his temper cool.[10] Instead Ammann turned and questioned five other men as to their views on shunning. When their answers were somewhat conditional, Ammann expelled them from the church as well. Shocked at the apparent break-up of the church before their very eyes, the gathered Mennonites waited for someone to speak a word of peace—some word to undo all the harsh words that had just torn the church apart.

Instead, as if to validate all that had just happened, Ammann's associate, Peter Zimmerman, said, "There you have it," and the meeting broke up quickly and in confusion with neither side offering the customary handshake.[11]

In the hours following that painful encounter, a number of leaders tried to resolve the crisis. Two of the ministers whom Ammann had excommunicated offered to hold a discussion to try and work out the groups' differences. After some hesitation, Ammann and his supporters agreed to attend the forum, which included Peter Giger and his congregation. The sides consented to one basic guideline: "that while one was speaking the others should remain attentive, and listen to him."[12]

Ammann addressed the group first. When Giger next took his turn to present the views of the Reist group, Ammann got up to walk out. Angry that Ammann would not offer the same hearing which he had just received, Giger grabbed Ammann's shirt sleeve and said, "Let me present my words also." But Ammann "jerked his arm away, and left the room," dramatically bringing the meeting to a premature end.[13]

Although the division had not yet spread to Anabaptist communities beyond Switzerland, it was clear that there were now two distinct groups: the larger Mennonite community represented by Hans Reist, and the reforming "Ammann-ish" faction led by Jakob Ammann.[14] If before this encounter the Swiss church leaders had underestimated Ammann's resolution or the seriousness with which he regarded purity in church life, they could do so no longer. Ammann intended to establish a disciplined church even if it meant leaving behind most of his fellow Anabaptists.

The Division Spreads

The story of what had transpired in Switzerland during 1693 soon spread to the other south Rhine Mennonite communities, and eventually to the Dutch and North German Mennonites. Thereafter letters flew back and forth, with all parties advising, scolding, questioning and challenging both the Reist/Mennonite and Amish groups. Some Palatinate ministers wrote to the Amish and counseled them to be reconciled with the Reist people. They also wrote to the Alsatian congregations and warned them not to listen to Jakob Ammann any longer.

Alsatian church leaders, however, claimed that Reist was the one to ignore. They were confused as to why Reist thought that social avoidance was a "new" teaching. The Alsatian congregations thought that the Swiss Mennonites had accepted the biblical teaching of shunning some thirty years ago! Why had Reist not practiced it, they wondered? Most Alsatians agreed that Ammann was the true reformer in the controversy—restoring classical Anabaptist doctrines that the Swiss had somehow let slide. Earlier, Ammann had excommunicated several members of the Alsatian Mennonite congregation at Markirch who would not stop attending the services of the state church. The expelled had evidently tried to win some small bit of social acceptance by going to their local parish church. Ammann and other Alsatian leaders would allow no such compromise of faith for personal gain.

Returning to his home in the Alsace, Ammann responded to the past months' events with a long letter. He reminded those who called him a troublemaker that he had merely followed the three-part practice of church discipline outlined by Jesus in

The mill at Ohnenheim in the Alsace. In 1660 Alsatian Mennonites met here and adopted the Dordrecht Confession *as their own statement of faith. Later, during the Ammann-Reist controversy of 1693-94, the Palatinate Mennonites called a unity conference at the mill. That gathering failed to bring peace, however, and the two groups remained divided.*

Matthew 18. Ammann privately confronted those who were erring and asked them to mend their ways. When they refused admonition, he visited them with several witnesses and only finally, as a last resort, was he forced to excommunicate those who would not reform. But Ammann also had words for those who as yet were not involved in the Reist-Ammann division. Ammann sent a "Warning Letter" to the Mennonite churches in the south Rhine and Swiss regions in which he demanded that "both men and women, ministers and lay members" declare by February 20, 1694 whether they supported him or supported

Jakob Ammann
(1656?-before 1730?)

Sources on Jakob Ammann are nearly as rare as those for Hans Reist. Apparently Ammann was a native of Erlenbach, a village in the Simme Valley, Switzerland, south of Bern and Thun. Just before and after 1690, an Ammann family from that area was questioned and censured on the suspicion that they were Anabaptists. Whether or not this was the family of Jakob Ammann is unknown, but the events do indicate some of the stigma which Anabaptism held in the region.

Sociologist John A. Hostetler has presented some strongly suggestive evidence that Ammann was a convinced convert to Anabaptism from the Swiss Reformed (state) church. Such a personal background would help to explain his zeal for traditional Anabaptist thought as well as his assuming and exercising strong leadership. Converts are often more committed to a group's ideals than later-generation members, and Reformed congregations credited pastors with a good bit more authority than did the Anabaptists.

Around the time when the controversy with Hans Reist erupted, Ammann moved to the Alsace to serve as elder for a congregation in the village of Markirch (today the town is known as Sainte-Marie-aux-Mines). Ammann instituted reforms there, such as forbidding members to attend the neighboring state church.

On February 27, 1696, Ammann appeared before Markirch's local magistrate "in the name of all those of his religion" to declare that the Amish would not serve in the local militia nor as town guards or public property custodians. Their religious nonresistance would not permit them to participate, but they would be willing "to pay a few signs of good will each year for being relieved." The official accepted the payment of the extra tax in lieu of military drilling.

In 1713 governing authorities decided that they had had enough of the Anabaptists and ordered the Amish out of Markirch. Many of the Amish left, although the congregation there did continue to function throughout the eighteenth century. What happened to Ammann after 1713, or where he went, is unknown.

Ammann's daughter asked to join the Wimmis Reformed Church near Bern in 1730. She told authorities at that time that her father had been a Swiss Anabaptist minister, but that he was no longer living and had died outside of the territory of Bern. Since she had no close relatives, the state itself became the daughter's godfather and paid her to join the state church.

Today few Amish persons know much of anything about Ammann. Hostetler notes the comment of two Pennsylvania Amishmen in 1830: "The birthplace of Jacob Aymen [sic] we have not ascertained, nor yet the exact place of his residence—having never considered him a man of note, we do not deem the place of his nativity a matter of consequence." Nevertheless, more than 135,000 people today call themselves "Amish."

For more information, see Sam Steiner's entry "Ammann, Jakob," in *The Mennonite Encyclopedia: A Comprehensive Reference Work on the Anabaptist-Mennonite Movement*, vol. 5 (Scottdale, Pa. and Waterloo, Ont.: Herald Press, 1990); Delbert L. Gratz, "The Home of Jacob Amman [sic] in Switzerland," *The Mennonite Quarterly Review* 25 (April 1951): 137-39; John A. Hostetler, *Amish Society*, third ed. (Baltimore: The Johns Hopkins University Press, 1980), pp. 41-47; and Jean Seguy, Mervin Smucker, trans., "The Bernese Anabaptists in Sainte-Marie-aux-Mines," *Pennsylvania Mennonite Heritage* 3 (July 1980): 2-9.

Reist.[15] Although Ammann said that he was still open to someone showing him his error with scripture, he served notice that the Amish would shun ("according to my instruction and creed") those congregations which did not decide by March 7.[16]

In response to events which seemed more and more out of control, the Palatinate Mennonites called a conference of reconciliation at a mill in the Alsace. The Palatinates proposed a compromise. They suggested that Reist had, in fact, been negligent in exercising church discipline and in teaching that the True-Hearted might be saved, but the Palatinates rejected Ammann's teaching on shunning the excommunicated. Grudgingly, the Swiss Mennonites—including Reist himself—agreed to the compromise.

The Amish, however, would not accept the proposed solution. The social avoidance of those who left the church, even to the point of not eating common meals together, was one of Ammann's major reforms; it was also the historic understanding of many Anabaptists. The only Amish response to the meeting at the mill was Ammann's banning and shunning of most of the Palatinate ministers along with a large group of other people whom he had apparently not met.

The Church at Risk

The Swiss and south Rhine Mennonite communities had remained surprisingly united in faith and life for more than a century and a half. Within several months spanning 1693-94, the fellowships were torn apart and broken in deep pain and resentment. Were the issues trite items of no lasting concern? Was the whole schism the result of personality conflicts blown out of proportion? While personality differences more than likely contributed to the disagreement, the issues involved were quite significant. The stakes were high. From the viewpoint of both sides, the church itself was at risk.

For Ammann, the danger the church faced was compromise. The Anabaptist reformers of 150 years before had given their lives for a church which would be an alternative to sinful society. Now many Mennonites were moving more and more into mainstream culture. The Dutch and north German Mennonites were becoming wealthy and respected citizens—would the same thing happen to the south Rhine and Swiss fellowships? Emphasizing humility and simplicity, Ammann and others were requiring male members to wear untrimmed beards and to use hooks and eyes to fasten their coats, instead of buttons. Fashionable styles which represented frivolous spending or resembled military uniforms were clearly forbidden by the biblical injunction to avoid even the appearance of evil.

Moreover, if the Anabaptists had really believed that salvation was given by grace through faith, then the True-Hearted, who had not publicly accepted such grace and submitted to its accompanying symbol of water baptism, could not be saved. The same was true for what Ammann saw as the clear New Testament teaching of social avoidance: there was just no middle ground.[17]

In those regions in which persecution was relatively light and compromise was a greater threat—the Alsace, parts of the Palatinate and the mountains south and west of Bern—Ammann received most of his support. He championed strict doctrinal interpretations and an activist approach which appealed to Mennonites who needed a strong group identity.[18]

For Reist and the ancient Mennonite communities in the Emme River Valley and the Palatinate, the threat was anything *but* lost identity. Their identity as outcasts was all too clear. For the Reist group, the threat to the church was a cold legalism. They already faced enough external threats. Shunning or stricter dress standards which would further divide them from within were the last thing they needed.

Reist could additionally claim, probably quite accurately, that the Swiss Anabaptists had never really practiced social avoidance, even though they had agreed to it in principle during unity discussions with their northern European Mennonite cousins. Ammann's insistence on implementing it now only stirred up trouble. Physical avoidance was simply not taught in the New Testament, as Reist read it. And as for the True-Hearted, Reist thought that it was presumptuous for humans to declare whether or not a person was saved, baptism notwithstanding. But for all their emphasis on openness and opposition to avoidance, it was the Mennonites who seemed to practice shunning when the time for reconciliation came.

The Amish Ask for Forgiveness and the Mennonites Refuse

A few years after the Mennonite and Amish division, several of the Amish leaders felt that they had acted too quickly in excommunicating more than half the church. They especially wondered if their actions were justified because they had not counseled with their own congregations before expelling the Reist group. Several Amish leaders—including Ammann himself—then excommunicated themselves from the church, symbolically demonstrating that they were repentant and wanted to rejoin the larger group of Mennonites. The response of the Mennonites was disappointing at best. Some of the Reist group revelled in the Amish admittance that they had been too quick. Some Mennonites even went so far as to equate Jakob Ammann with several symbolic biblical figures of evil and doom.

Again the question of social avoidance came up and ended the unity talks. One Amish minister, Uli Ammann (no known relation to Jakob), later wrote that the Amish had hoped to come to some agreement, "but it was all in vain."

"Our labor had no consideration with them," Uli Ammann lamented. "When they [the Mennonites] spoke of the affair they commenced with our errors, but would not acknowledge to having erred themselves . . . and from thenceforth there was wrangling and a division among the people."[19] In 1711 a forgiving

Today Amish and Mennonite people cooperate in several church-related projects. Here Amish and Mennonite women attend an auction held to raise money for the international relief and service group Mennonite Central Committee, an organization supported by both churches.

Alsatian Mennonite fellowship received Uli Ammann and another Amish minister as fellow members with their congregation, but most Amish were not so fortunate.[20]

In 1699 and 1700 Mennonite leaders rebuffed repeated Amish attempts to seek peace, even after some Amish again excommunicated themselves in self-humiliation. The Mennonites reasoned that the Amish had earlier acted unjustly and that they continued to claim that the practice of shunning was biblical. Additionally, the Amish observed a literal footwashing service as a part of their communion, following the example of Jesus who had washed his disciples' feet during the first Lord's Supper (John 13). Most of the Swiss Mennonites thought that literal footwashing was an unnecessary ritual, even though it, like avoidance, was a part of the old Mennonite *Dordrecht Confession.*

Two Groups

Throughout the turbulent years of Swiss and south Rhine Mennonite division, the War of Palatinate Succession ravaged both the Alsace and the Palatinate. Meanwhile, the Bern government in

Switzerland also became more determined to drive the Mennonites from its lands. Amid so much hardship along the Rhine, and persecution in the Alps, the small group of Mennonites split.

Four days before Christmas 1697, the north German Mennonite patriarch, 85-year old minister and ship owner Gerrit Roosen of Hamburg, wondered about the connections between the larger events of the European world and the church life of the Mennonites. Roosen "worried" over the war and its effects on people, and over the new political division created by France's complete take-over of the Alsace. He was also deeply saddened by the Mennonite-Amish division, well known as it was to northern Mennonites. Although the Dutch and north German Mennonites of Roosen's region had originally advocated shunning, they had recently practiced it less and less often. Roosen rejected Ammann's conservative clothing and appearance regulations. "In all of Paul's letters," the old minister wrote, "we do not find one word in which he has given believers regulations concerning the forms of clothing they should have."[21]

Roosen's ideas represented a growing consensus among European Mennonites. In the north an emphasis on inner piety over outward appearance meant that simple lifestyle patterns and physical-social separation from the world were not so important as long as a person's heart was right. In the south, the Mennonites' very struggle to survive had brought the need to rely on the True-Hearted People and to often define identity in ethnic, rather than disciplinary, terms.

Ammann's position represented a different approach. The church as a physical and social reality needed boundaries equally physical and social. The separation from the world was not merely a matter of inner feeling, nor even the result of being a persecuted minority group. Church renewal came by way of commitment and strict discipline. In the end, though, both the Amish and the Mennonites were trying to safeguard the church.

Despite its uniqueness, the Amish church shared some things in common with the rest of Western Europe. After 1700 the Amish caught the beat of "New World" immigration. North America beckoned the Amish as persuasively as it called the rest of northwestern and central Europe. Separate though they wanted to be, Jakob Ammann's people were soon caught up in colonization as were their worldly state church neighbors. The lure of the Atlantic escaped no one.

Church Discipline and Matthew 18

The Anabaptists believed that, with the grace of God, Christians voluntarily followed Jesus in life and death. Having made a commitment to God and the church, however, occasionally a believer would "fall away" from the gospel by living in unrepentant sin or succumbing to false doctrine. It was the responsibility of the rest of the congregation (and especially of the leaders) to plead with erring ones to change their ways. Eventually, if members refused to repent or acknowledge wrongdoing or wrong believing, the church would excommunicate them from the fellowship. Hopefully, being cut off from the church would jolt the erring one into repentance, a changed life and reunion with the church.

For the Anabaptists, the key scriptures addressing excommunication were Jesus' words to his disciples in Matthew 18: 15-18:

> "Moreover if thy brother shall trespass against thee, go and tell him his fault between you and him alone: if he shall hear thee, thou hast gained thy brother. But if he will not hear thee, then take with thee one or two more, that in the mouth of two or three witnesses every word may be established. And if he shall neglect to hear them, tell it unto the church: but if he neglect to hear the church, let him be unto thee as a heathen man and a publican. Verily I say unto you,Whatsoever ye shall bind on earth shall be bound in heaven: and whatsoever ye shall loose on earth shall be loosed in heaven."

According to these verses a three-step process (private warning, warning with witnesses and public warning) must take place before a member is put out of the church. This process ensured that church leaders did not excommunicate arbitrarily. More importantly, the three stages gave the erring member several opportunities to repent, ask forgiveness and reform.

How exactly these verses were applied in the actual life of the congregation was one of the most significant points of disagreement between the Ammann and Reist groups. Both appealed to scripture and Anabaptist-Mennonite history in support of their interpretations.

Ammann argued that Reist had not followed the Matthew 18 scriptures closely enough. Reist had not excommunicated a member of his congregation who had told a series of serious lies—in spite of the fact that the larger congregation knew the situation and the member had refused to repent.

The Reist group, on the other hand, thought that it was Ammann who was not taking Matthew 18 seriously enough. They reminded Ammann that he had excommunicated fellow members without offering them the three opportunities for repentance since he expelled numerous Palatinate Anabaptists whom he had never met—not to mention never having addressed privately or with witnesses.

The second major argument involving church discipline centered on what excommunication itself involved. Ammann believed that the Bible clearly required the church to socially avoid the excommunicated. Reist, to the contrary, felt that merely excluding the expelled member from communion was enough. Ammann could have found support in scriptures such as Romans 16:17; 1 Corinthians 5:9-11; 2 Thessalonians 3:6, 14, 15; 2 Timothy 3:2-5; and Titus 3:10. Reist alluded to passages like Matthew 9:10-13 and 15:11.

Personality issues aside, the Ammann-Reist controversy had at its heart a disagreement regarding a very significant issue: interpreting and applying the important text in Matthew 18.

— 3 —
Maintaining the Church:
The Amish in Europe,
1693-1801

"It is our desire to continue steadfast."
—*Amish leaders in a pastoral letter, 1781*

The Push for Emigration

The first century of Amish life in Europe was marked by both the scattering of the church and the persistence of its vision. In 1693 the Amish were a small group of Christians concentrated in the Alsace, the Palatinate and Switzerland. Partial expulsion from those regions, the lure of North America and opportunities to settle in eastern Europe all scattered the Amish church. On Sunday mornings in 1801, Amish were meeting for worship from

Anabaptiste Suisse.

Anabaptiste.

Swiss Anabaptists, eighteenth century.

During the eighteenth century many Amish left Europe by traveling down the Rhine River to the port of Rotterdam, and from there to Pennsylvania.

western Pennsylvania to Russian Volhynia.

Despite the far-flung settlements of these people, the purpose of the group remained clear. The Amish were still taking seriously the call to be a people of God, committed to lives of individual and group discipleship as they migrated together, worked together and helped each other.

An early challenge to Amish survival was the push of emigration from Europe. Soon after the Amish began as a distinct group, forces that moved people halfway around the world began to affect the population of Western Europe. The Amish were by no means the only folks to be pushed out of their homes and pulled elsewhere during the 1700s. The Amish were one small part of a general population movement out of the south Rhine Valley.

The stakes were somewhat higher for the Amish, though. The wide and general dispersion of the Amish—so soon after their beginning—could have easily diluted their faith and life and led to rapid blending into their new surroundings. However, the Amish sense of Christ's call to be "in" the world but not "of" the world kept their new home communities from completely assimilating them during the eighteenth century.

The forces that pushed many Germans (including the Amish) out of their homes in the Rhine Valley included economic and political hardship. Groups of people from the Palatinate, the Alsace and central Germany left Europe because, as one immigrant simply put it, "I do not know how to make ends meet here anymore. . . . I won't be able to subsist here much longer."[1] Heavy taxes, inflation and rising rents caused many to abandon what they had in the hope of what they might find. Wars and rumors of wars also harassed families into leaving. Especially in Switzerland, where the local city-states paid their bills by hiring out Swiss soldiers to fight in other nations' wars, was there real resentment against the military. All of these conditions affected the Amish as well as their neighbors.

Religious persecution also pushed the Amish from Switzerland and the Rhine Valley. Again, the Amish were not the only people to suffer intolerance. In 1699 the government of Bern expelled the pastor of the city's largest state church because he had held unauthorized Bible study meetings.[2] In many places both Catholics and Protestants—if they were minority members of their home territories—often felt unwelcome.

During the first seventy years of the eighteenth century, all of these conditions encouraged many Rhine Valley Germans to leave their homes; the Amish felt the same pushes. Additionally, though, some Amish were pushed harder: many of the Swiss Amish and Mennonites were told outright to leave (into the eighteenth century there were posted commissions for citizens who betrayed Anabaptists to the Bern authorities).[3] And in parts of the Palatinate, military training conflicted with Amish teachings on nonresistance to violence.

Eventually, most Amish were forced out of the very areas in which they had originated. Only three small Amish congregations survived in Switzerland. All three were close to the Alsatian border.[4] In the Alsace itself, some Amish communities, like Ammann's home congregation at Markirch, were expelled (although some of the Amish later returned). Some Alsatian Amish then moved south, into the French-speaking territory of Montbeliard, where they were allowed to live in relative peace.[5] By 1750, and especially under the able leadership of Elder Hans Rich (1730-1798), Montbeliard developed into a thriving Amish community. Meanwhile, other Alsatian Amish moved northwest into the French Lorraine. And some remained in the Alsace. Increasingly, the various pushes of emigration scattered the Amish in more directions.

To the Netherlands

Settling in the Netherlands was the first of many Amish moves out of the south Rhine Valley. In 1711 the Swiss Bernese government decided to entirely rid its lands of all Anabaptists. Already in 1699 the Bern government had asked the Dutch East India Company if they would ship Swiss Anabaptists to islands in the Pacific Ocean.[6] The shipping company never responded and the Swiss drew up their own plans to export the Amish and Mennonites to North America. A number of attempts to ship the

An Amish couple from Kampen, the Netherlands, late eighteenth or early nineteenth century.

Anabaptists out of the Alps failed, but in the summer of 1711 the Bern government was set to try again. On this occasion another nation, the Netherlands, intervened and promised the Swiss Mennonites and Amish safe passage from Switzerland to Dutch territory. Once there, the refugees could decide for themselves where they wanted to go.[7]

But problems troubled this scheme as well. First, the Swiss could only round up enough Anabaptists to fill four of the five ships they had contracted. Then, to the chagrin of the Dutch ambassador, the Mennonites nearly refused to ride on the same boats with the Amish.[8] The deep division of 1693-97 was apparently still too sore. Finally the Mennonites were persuaded to go along, although many jumped ship at a number of points down the Rhine and tried to make their way back to Switzerland. In August, the boats arrived in the Netherlands with an almost entirely Amish cargo. (The few Mennonites who did stick it out to Dutch territory grumbled and complained and eventually headed back south toward the Palatinate.)

Upon arrival in Holland, the Amish were invited to settle in Prussia (now northern Poland), but decided to remain in the

An Atlantic Crossing

The passage to America was a frightening experience. Storms could delay arrival by weeks, while disease and death could make even a relatively quick voyage seem to take forever. One eighteenth-century traveler noted that children under age seven often perished in the crossing. For adults, the passage was often no less deadly.

In 1737 the ship *Charming Nancy* brought a number of Amish families to America. A journal probably kept by one of the ship's Amish passengers records these sad voyage details:

"The 28th of June while in Rotterdam [in the Netherlands] getting ready to start my Zernbli died and was buried in Rotterdam. The 29th we got under sail and enjoyed one and a half days of favorable wind. The 7th of July, early in the morning, Hans Zimmerman's son-in-law died.

"We landed in England the 8th of July, remaining 9 days in

port during which 5 children died. Went under sail the 17th of July. The 21 of July my own Lisbetli died. Several days before Michael's Georgli had died.

"On the 29th of July three children died. On the first of August my Hansli died and the Tuesday previous 5 children died. On the 3rd of August contrary winds beset the vessel and from the first to the 7th of the month three more children died. On the 8th of August, Shambien's Lizzie died and on the 9th Hans Zimmerman's Jacobli died. On the 19th, Christian Burgli's Child died. Passed a ship on the 21st. A favorable wind sprang up. On the 28th Hans Gasi's wife died. Passed a ship 13th of September.

Landed in Philadelphia on the 18th and my wife and I left the ship on the 19th. A child was born to us on the 20th—died—wife recovered. A voyage of 83 days."

From S. Duane Kauffman, "Miscellaneous Amish Mennonite Documents," *Pennsylvania Mennonite Heritage* 2 (July 1979): 12. On the diary's authorship, see the article's note 3.

Netherlands instead. They formed several congregations and established themselves in farming with the financial help of the generous Dutch Mennonites. To the more culturally refined Dutch, the traditional dress and untrimmed beards of the Amish were somewhat peculiar. The Amish use of a Swiss-German dialect also set them apart in the Netherlands. An old story has persisted that Amish church services seemed so unique to their Dutch neighbors that at times civil guards needed to keep curious crowds away from Amish worship meetings![9]

Onward to Penn's Woods

While the Bern government was trying to forcibly move Amish and Mennonites to North America, some Mennonites had been voluntarily immigrating there for some time. Indeed, ten years before the Mennonite-Amish division itself, a Mennonite couple, Jan and Mercken Schmitz Lensen, had been the first Mennonites to settle in what would be the oldest continuous Mennonite community in America—Germantown, Pennsylvania. For the next eighty years, Mennonites, primarily from the Palatinate and from Switzerland, felt the pull of Penn's Woods. In the eighteenth

Duke Maximilian Joseph invited Amish families to settle in Bavaria because they were considered superior farmers. Today the Amish continue to be known for their agricultural skill.

century, Pennsylvania was the destination of virtually all Mennonites who left Europe. It would be the Amish destination as well.

In 1681 the Englishman William Penn had received the land that would become Pennsylvania, and planned his "holy experiment." Penn was a member of the Religious Society of Friends (Quakers), a church which was itself a persecuted, minority group in England and Germany. In Pennsylvania, Penn established a colony in which religious toleration would be the order of the day.[10] He particularly advertised in the German Rhine Valley for immigrants to settle in his province. Pennsylvania became one of the New World's great havens for persecuted European religious minorities, including Quakers, Moravians, Schwenkfelders, Mennonites and Amish.

Exactly when Amish families first left Europe to seek a better life in North America is not known. Perhaps no Amish left until 1736 (information on Amish who emigrated before that time is sketchy). In 1737 Amish emigration began in earnest when the *Charming Nancy* sailed for Pennsylvania with twenty-one Amish families aboard.[11] Once the Amish began to emigrate, they did so relatively quickly. Within about three decades, more than one hundred households left for the New World. Amish immigration followed the general pattern of German New World immigration— many Amish came to Pennsylvania during the peak years of German arrival in Philadelphia.[12] Some ships carried groups of Amish, others only a family or two. Sea travel was, of course, terribly dangerous and could take months (see "An Atlantic Crossing," p. 46).

The European exodus was also expensive. By 1710 the generous Dutch Mennonites had established a Commission for Foreign Needs to help both their fellow Mennonites and the Amish with immigration costs. In 1742, though, one Mennonite pastor complained that the Dutch Commission was partial to the Amish. His own Mennonites were not getting as much financial help from the Dutch as some Amish had received, he thought. Perhaps that was because the Amish needed less help than the Mennonites. The Dutch seemed more willing to offer aid to those families or groups who were making an effort to help themselves. The Amish, according to one Mennonite historian, "seem to have been better able to finance their own emigration" than were many Mennonites. Perhaps the "reason may well have been a more close-knit group structure"[13] and a stronger commitment to mutual aid among the Amish.

Other New Homes

As Amish families immigrated to the freedom promised by Pennsylvania, other Amish migrated within Europe itself in search of peace, freedom and more land. A number of families moved northeast and southeast from the Alsace and Palatinate into other German territory. As early as 1730, Amish had moved into Hesse. Within several decades, congregations existed around Wittgenstein, Waldeck and Marburg. Hessian territory eventually hosted a sizable portion of the European Amish population.[14]

In 1799 a German noble encouraged an Amish migration from the Palatinate, Alsace-Lorraine and Hesse to Bavaria. The nobleman had inherited the Bavarian crown that year and invited Amish and Mennonites to settle in his new lands because of their excellent farming reputation. Once expelled, the Amish were now invited residents! A French official was even disturbed when his Amish population began moving to Bavaria. "The emigration of the Anabaptist farmers would be disastrous," he lamented, "for they are the most competent, and in general they are obedient to the law." Within about a year of the original invitation three Amish congregations formed near Regensburg, Ingolstadt and Munich. In Hesse, Bavaria and elsewhere in Europe, the Amish rarely owned land. Most often they rented farms from nobles. Many nobles were short on cash, but long on land, and were quite happy to see good Amish tenant farmers moving into their territories.[15]

The Amish in Eastern Europe

A third migration took Amish families into Polish territory and eventually, Russian Volhynia.[16] In 1781 the Austrian emperor invited German farmers to settle in Galicia (now southeastern Poland). Galicia had been a part of Poland, but as a result of the constant change and exchange of national real estate, the territory was then under Austrian control. Three years later twenty-eight Mennonite and Amish families were among the 3,300 German households who responded to the invitation.

Within a short time, the division between and distinctions among the Amish and the Mennonites began to plague the families. Also, the local Galician population was not too happy with the sudden influx of foreign settlers, and pressured the newcomers to leave. So in 1796, eleven Amish families (probably the entire Galician Amish population) left the settlements and moved into western Russia where they joined a Hutterite community.

Like the Amish and Mennonites, the Hutterites also traced their beginnings to the Anabaptist movement of the sixteenth century Reformation. While holding similar beliefs with the Amish and Mennonites, the Hutterites led a distinctive communal lifestyle. Unlike the Mennonites and Amish, whose families lived on individual farms, the Hutterites lived in large "colonies" with many families holding joint property ownership, eating common group meals and performing group-assigned tasks and trades.[17]

The Amish and Hutterites, although both stemming from a common religious tradition, were probably more different than alike. The new combination Amish-Hutterite group lasted only about a year. Unfortunately, neither group really knew enough

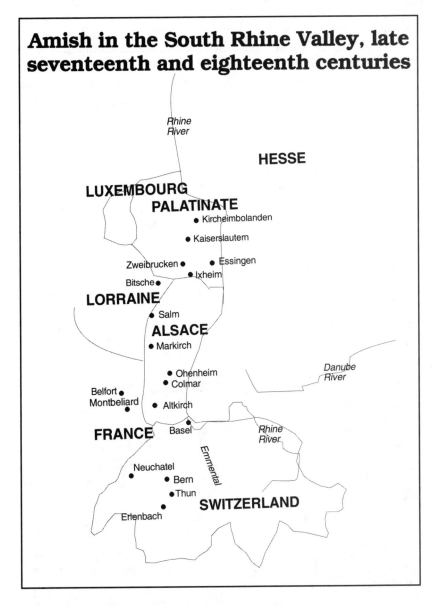

Amish in the South Rhine Valley, late seventeenth and eighteenth centuries

Rhine River

HESSE

LUXEMBOURG

PALATINATE

● Kircheimbolanden

● Kaiserslautern

Zweibrucken ●   ● Essingen

Bitsche ●   ● Ixheim

LORRAINE

● Salm

ALSACE

● Markirch

Danube River

● Ohenheim
● Colmar

Belfort ●
Montbeliard ●   ● Altkirch

FRANCE   Basel

Rhine River

Neuchatel
●   ● Bern

Emmental

● Thun

● Erlenbach   SWITZERLAND

about the other to make the merger of the two peoples work. A few doctrinal differences emerged and some old traditions of both groups clashed. Moreover, the Amish were not prepared for the strenuous work ethic and hard labor which was a part of that particular Hutterite colony. Claiming that the Hutterites were much too interested in material gain, the Amish left in disgust. Two young Amish women remained and married

Hutterite men.

In 1801 these wandering Amish families eventually settled in Russian Volhynia (now northwestern Ukraine). Eventually other Amish joined them there. A group from the French Amish congregation of Montbeliard had left their homes in 1791 and also moved eastward until they, too, ended up in Volhynia. The Volhynian Amish church adhered to the same Amish church discipline generally used by their fellow members in western Europe, and also apparently sang from the *Ausbund* hymnal. Traditional Amish garb, the wearing of beards and the use of hooks and eyes rather than buttons on men's coats were also characteristic of these Volhynian settlements.

Still a Separate People

If European nobility regularly overlooked questions of theology when inviting the Amish to settle on landed estates, that did not mean that the Amish church itself was any more accepted. The beliefs and practices of adult baptism, separation of church and

An Amish Baptismal Service, 1781

A document which seems to have served as a church discipline and statement of doctrine and practice for the European Amish includes a section describing baptismal services. According to the document, the elders and ministers were to instruct applicants for baptism by beginning with the biblical account of the creation. Next, the leaders told of the sin of Adam and Eve and their consequent expulsion from Paradise. The ministers were then to preach "the gospel of grace . . . with repentance and improvement of life, unto faith in the Holy Gospel."

Following this instruction, the applicants entered into an undetermined number of weeks of study during which the congregation was "admonished to diligently watch over" them "and support them by their good example."

If the candidates proved faithful and the whole congregation agreed that they were sincere in their confessions and repentance, the applicants would be baptized. Sermon texts were to include John 3, Acts 2 and Romans 6, after which the account continues:

"With these words the applicants are requested to come before the ministers and when they [the applicants] have fallen on their knees the story of Philip and the Ethiopian eunuch is told them, how he was reading the prophet Isaiah but did not understand it and how then Philip preached the Gospel to him, so that he desired to be baptized, and Philip baptized him. Then the applicant for baptism is asked: Do you believe from your whole heart that Jesus Christ is the Son of God? Answer, yes. Do you also believe that God raised him from the dead, and are you willing to be obedient to God and the Church, whether to live or die? Answer, Yes.

". . . The bishop [elder] places his hands on the head and a fully ordained deacon pours water on his [the bishop's] hands, whereupon the bishop calls him [the baptismal candidate] by name and says: On this confession of faith which thou hast confessed, thou art baptized in the name of God the Father and of the Son and of the Holy Ghost. Then the bishop gives him [the new member] his hand and raises him up, pronounces peace and says: The Lord continue the good work which he hath begun in you and complete it unto a blessed end through Jesus Christ. He then dismisses him in the name of God."

Excerpted from "An Amish Church Discipline of 1781," *The Mennonite Quarterly Review* 4 (April 1930): 140-48.

state, and nonresistance to violence were still suspect in most of the Continent. In 1744, when Nicholas Stoltzfus (c. 1719-1774), a Lutheran hired hand on an Amish farm, asked to marry an Amish woman, state authorities permitted the nuptials only if the couple agreed to move away from the area after the wedding. They consented and left. Later widowed, Nicholas ended up in North America.[18]

Other opposition surfaced elsewhere. In 1780, when the Montbeliard Amish petitioned for permission to build a church meetinghouse, authorities rejected the request.[19] Among the Amish living near Zweibrücken in the Palatinate, the occupation by French troops in 1793 and the establishment of universal military training forced a number of Amish to leave that area.[20]

Some thirteen years earlier, to the west of Zweibrücken, the Amish Elder Hans Naffziger was convicted of baptizing two young women who had not been raised Amish. The two had been taken from their mother and put in a state orphanage after their father had died. After coming of age and leaving the orphanage, the young women returned to live with their mother, who was a member of the Amish church.

For a time the two continued attending the services of the state church as they had been taught at the orphanage. But they soon found that they felt more at home among their mother's congregation. When the women asked to be baptized as young adults and join the Amish, Elder Naffziger resisted, warning them that it was illegal to leave the state church and join the Amish. The women persisted and eventually Naffziger baptized them (see "An Amish Baptismal Service, 1781," p. 52). Authorities found out and sentenced the young women to death. Probably because of his advanced age, Naffziger was only fined and banished from his home and congregation forever. Apparently the sentences were never carried out.[21] Clearly, though, much of the larger world was still maintaining the boundary between itself and the Amish.

The Amish Faith

Testing of the Amish faith came from within the fellowships as well as from state persecution and restriction. In 1765 church life among the Amish in the Netherlands was fraught with disagreements. Three church leaders from Hesse and the Palatinate mediated the troubles that divided the congregations, and the correspondence of one of those mediators offers insight into what was important to the Amish during the mid-eighteenth century.[22]

The Amish were apparently still holding tightly to an Anabaptist understanding of the church as the people of God. For the Amish, meeting for worship, hearing Bible reading and participating in a communion service held meaning only if the participants were at peace with one another. "Church" only existed as the members were united with one another in Christ. Thus, the Amish in the Netherlands had not celebrated the Lord's Supper during their six years of argument because to do so amid the disagreements dividing the group would have only made a mockery of the service.

The fact that the Amish in the Netherlands had invited other ministers to help them resolve their difficulties also illustrates the structure of the Amish church. Congregations were largely autonomous with leaders selected from among the members of the congregation. There was no church hierarchy beyond the local congregation. When issues needed discussion or problems needed resolution, leaders from different areas would gather and address them in a rather informal way. In 1752, for example, a region-wide general Amish leadership conference met at Steinseltz. In 1759 and again in 1779, Amish leaders gathered in Essingen and reaffirmed traditional Amish beliefs and practices.[23]

Without hierarchy or modern organizational structure, however, the Amish did maintain a felt unity. When the *Palatinate* Amish heard that discord in the Netherlands "had caused many young people to go into the world," the Palatinates *themselves* felt "much sadness."[24] And when an Amishman in America received news that his brother in Europe had married a non-Amish woman and "joined the worldly people," the Pennsylvanian was "much grieved."[25] The Amish sense of peoplehood followed them and tied them together wherever they went.

To their non-Amish neighbors, the Amish wearing of beards and hook-and-eye coats gave the group some physical distinction. Also, the practice of shunning members who left the church clearly marked the boundaries of the group. The decades of expulsion and emigration had not destroyed the Amish sense of peoplehood.

"We greet you once more and commend you to God," a group of Amish ministers wrote in a pastoral letter toward the end of the eighteenth century. Certainly greetings to the scattered Amish church needed to travel much farther than when Jakob Ammann was able to personally visit all of his like-minded ministers. On two continents and in many countries, the Amish had spread far beyond the south Rhine Valley. Yet the church had remained faithful to its biblical understandings; indeed, the first issue addressed in the pastoral letter was baptism. Echoing Ammann's own pastoral wish the leaders wrote: "It is our desire to continue steadfast by the grace and help of the Lord in spite of our weakness."[26] That same desire to continue steadfastly was persisting in America.

— 4 —

Settlement and Struggle in the New World: The Amish in Eighteenth Century Pennsylvania

"In this country is a very good living."
— *Amishman Hans Lantz*

Early Settlements

The first known Amish settlement in America was located in north-central Berks County, Pennsylvania. In 1736 the Detweiler and Sieber families arrived, perhaps the first of the approximately 500 Amish who immigrated to the New World in the 1700s. Hans Sieber and another early immigrant, Jacob Beiler, quickly bought land in the Northkill Creek and Irish Creek areas of Berks County. This original settlement grew until it included perhaps nearly 200 people. By 1750 such common twentieth century Amish surnames as Fisher, Hershberger, Hertzler, Hochstetler, Kauffman, King, Lantz, Miller, Speicher, Troyer, Yoder and Zug (Zook) were already represented in Berks County.[1]

A second settlement, nearly as old as Northkill, began when several Amish immigrant families chose Lancaster County, rather than Berks, as their new home. Sometimes called the Old Conestoga settlement, it lasted through most of the eighteenth century before its families moved to other locations. Scattered Amish households may also have lived in northern Lancaster County's Cocalico region for a time, and later in the far eastern part of the county, near Cains.

Although Lancaster County later developed a sizable Amish population, the majority of early Amish settlers lived outside of its boundaries during the colonial period. Amish families gathered in Berks County's Cumru Township (Maiden Creek) and on the Berks-Lancaster border along the Conestoga Creek (Morgan-

During the eighteenth century Amish immigrants to North America entered the port of Philadelphia. This scene was carved by Aaron Zook.

Ruins of the building used by the Chester County, Pennsylvania, Amish as a place of worship during the late eighteenth and early nineteenth centuries.

town). Also beyond Lancaster's borders was the Tulpehocken-Lebanon Valley Amish settlement which extended from Berks into what would become Lebanon County. By 1767 Amish arrivals, along with already established families, were heading west to Somerset County, Pennsylvania. During the eighteenth century three Amish congregations formed there.[2] Beginning in 1791, also to the northwest, was the Amish settlement in Mifflin County.[3]

While some Amish moved west, others headed east. By 1768 another congregation formed—this time closer to Philadelphia. Several families moved from established Amish settlements into the so-called Great Valley of Chester County. The Chester County Amish were a somewhat unusual group. The congregation built a schoolhouse and then apparently began to use the building as a meeting place for Sunday morning church services.[4] While the Amish in some places in Europe may have used meetinghouses even as early as the Ammann-Reist division, by-and-large the Amish had met only in the homes and barns of members.[5] Perhaps out of frugality, perhaps out of necessity or perhaps to emphasize that *people* (and not the building) were really the church, the Amish rejected special physical structures for worship. In another innovative move, Chester County Amish Bishop Christian Zook (1752-1826) likely issued a printed hand-

Lewis Riehl (1746-1806)

While North America was the land of opportunity for some Europeans, not all who crossed the Atlantic came of their own free choice. When Lewis Riehl was about eight years of age he was exploring in and around a European harbor where ships were preparing to sail for the New World. Someone persuaded young Lewis to board a ship, and once the boy was on deck he was not allowed to go back to shore. Thus, against his will, Riehl was on his way to America. In order to pay the cost of his free ride, the ship's captain legally bound Lewis as a redemptioner to a family in Chester County, Pennsylvania. According to Riehl family tradition, the farmer which owned Lewis' services did not treat him well. As soon as Lewis had finished his required years of service, he left and found a welcome home among the Malvern, Chester County, Amish. Lewis later joined the Amish church and married Amishwoman Veronica Fisher (1750-1825). The Riehls were among those Amish families that left the older Chester County settlement and moved to Mifflin County, Pennsylvania.

See David Luthy, "New Names Among the Amish, Part 3," *Family Life* (November 1972): 22.

bill during the War of 1812, urging the Amish and other nonresistant churches to elect public officials who stood for peace and an end to the war.[6] The Chester County Amish were also well known for their generous hospitality and mutual aid offered to fellow Amish immigrants who traveled westward through Chester. Apparently their young people rather often married non-Amish, perhaps one reason the group eventually died out.[7]

In the later 1700s, a few Amish may have been among those Pennsylvania Germans who moved south into Virginia and North Carolina. Records of settlers with typical Amish surnames in those states are suggestive, but inconclusive. In neither place did Amish congregations form, so if several Amish did move south, they apparently blended with their neighbors and surrounding Protestant denominations. Throughout the eighteenth century, the Amish church in North America grew roots in Pennsylvania soil.[8]

Because of their well-organized and -financed immigration to

America, the Amish, as a group, were well suited to begin purchasing land in the New World. Some Amish bought heavily and then resold to their children, to other Amish families or to non-Amish neighbors. When describing the land holdings of early settler Christian Beiler (c.1729-1812), a twentieth century Amish historian simply says, "All in all Christian had so many land grants that it is doubtful if we can name them all."[9] Along with farm purchases, Amishman Christian Rupp was one of five Lancaster Countians who received a deed for land on which to build a community school.[10]

In contrast to many Mennonite farmers who purchased unimproved property, the later Amish immigrants often bought partially cleared land from non-Amish owners. Despite the benefit of taking over somewhat-improved farms, these Amish were generally buying cheaper, thinner soil on the frontier, rather than the more productive Mennonite-held acres in central Lancaster County. Even in the Old Conestoga settlement where Amish and Mennonites lived side-by-side, tax records show the Mennonites to have been generally wealthier than the Amish.[11]

For the most part, though, the Amish did not settle very near the Mennonites, many of whom had preceded them to the New World. While the Mennonites had strong communities in Philadelphia, and Montgomery and Lancaster Counties, the Amish began buying elsewhere, and only later moved into Lancaster in great numbers. The Mennonites in Philadelphia and Montgomery County likely had little contact with the Amish. In a 1773 letter to their fellow believers in the Netherlands, the Philadelphia Mennonites wrote, "As to the Amisch, they are many in number; but they are not here near us, and we can give no further information concerning them except only this, that they hold very fast to the outward and ancient institutions."[12]

The Church in the New World

The Amish had purposely established those "outward and ancient institutions" of church life in the New World. While many Amish emigrated to better their economic lot—and the Amish migration within Pennsylvania during the mid-eighteenth century usually continued this pattern of economic self-help—religious freedom was still a prime reason the Amish had crossed the Atlantic. The first well-known Amish bishop (elder) in America was Jacob Hertzler (1703-1786), immigrant of 1749 and

Bible of Bishop Jacob Hertzler. The 1744 book contains Hertzler's inscription and signature.

Northkill settler.[13] More than likely, one or several other bishops or ministers actually preceded Hertzler as a church leader, but no firm record of their service exists.

During the colonial period, the frequency of Amish worship services was rather irregular (as were the services of frontier churches of all denominations). The few church leaders in Pennsylvania traveled extensively to serve all the Amish communities. Eventually the church ordained a resident bishop in each

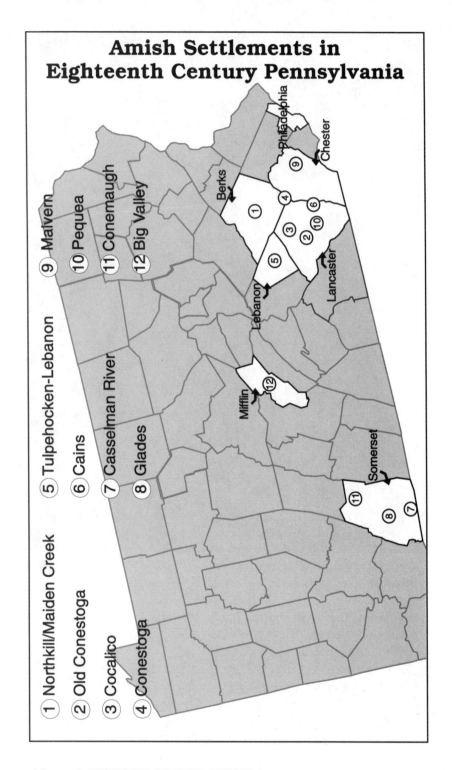

Amish Settlements in Eighteenth Century Pennsylvania

1. Northkill/Maiden Creek
2. Old Conestoga
3. Cocalico
4. Conestoga
5. Tulpehocken-Lebanon
6. Cains
7. Casselman River
8. Glades
9. Malvern
10. Pequea
11. Conemaugh
12. Big Valley

Jacob Hochstetler stops his sons from shooting at hostile Indians surrounding the family's cabin, in this carving by Aaron Zook.

settlement and charged him with performing baptisms and marriages, serving the Lord's Supper and carrying out church discipline. Ministers assisted in holding preaching services on a more regular basis, and the deacons administered the alms distribution to the poor and kept almsbook records.

Hertzler himself provided stability for the Amish congregations in a century swept up in competing political and religious opinions. Hertzler family tradition holds that the old bishop was "very sociable and talkative." Even in his old age he seems to have preferred walking rather than riding horseback as he traveled, trekking many miles on foot.[14]

The everyday life of Pennsylvania's Amish revolved around survival and producing an honest living as much as it did around Sunday worship services. Most of the Amish were farmers, although several, like the Lebanon Valley's Hans Gnage and the Old Conestoga community's Michael Garber, were millers. Jacob Beiler of the Northkill settlement was a tanner. And Hans Blank, of the Lebanon Valley (and later eastern Lancaster County), was said to have been a physician, converted to the Amish church in Switzerland.[15] For those who farmed in Lancaster County, wheat was the chief cash crop of the eighteenth century.[16] Data from Amish wills drawn up in several settlements show that other typical farm products included flax (linen) and apples. Homemade spirits were also common. These same wills also made specific provisions for Amish widows. The children who took over managing the farm were directed to supply their mother with ample produce from garden and field.[17]

How Different From Their Neighbors?

How much were colonial Amish settlers like their non-Amish neighbors? When it came to moving westward, the Amish appear not to have been much different. Many of the early Amish immigrants were among the first to settle in the areas in which they chose to live. At least that was the case in much of Berks and what became Lebanon Counties. In Somerset County, Amish communities probably appeared by 1767—two years before the region was even officially open for settlement.[18] By moving into frontier areas, some of which had only recently lost their Native American populations, the Amish participated with their neighbors in the vanguard of expanding European settlement in Pennsylvania.

One way in which the Amish were *not* like their neighbors was that the Amish refused to own slaves. Slavery was a legal part of Pennsylvania life until 1780, and even after that year only a gradual program of emancipation freed human-property. No records exist of any Amish family ever owning slaves. Probably the refusal to own African-American workers stemmed as much from the Amish insistence on Christian simplicity as it did from Christian humanitarianism. Studies of colonial Pennsylvania slave-owning practices show that slaves were often not so much an economic necessity in Penn's Woods as much as a status symbol which announced their owner's financial success. Among a people who shied away from even fancy and decorative clothing, the ownership of human ornaments of wealth was naturally taboo.[19]

Some Amish families did purchase redemptioners, however.[20] Redemptioners were skilled European immigrants who could not afford their own way to America, and so traveled to the New World in the hope that someone would pay their passage for them in return for a certain number of years of work. Amish farmers bought redemptioners because their labor, unlike that of slaves, was not a sign of unnecessary expense. Occasionally a redemptioner may have even joined the Amish church as a result of contact with Amish employers or neighbors (see "Lewis Riehl," p. 59 for one example). A testimony to the practice of mutual aid, Amish church almsbook records also show that established

Pennsylvania Amish sometimes paid outright the immigration costs of fellow Amish families, thus sparing the newcomers the need of becoming redemptioners.[21]

Frontier Fires

As frontier settlers, the Amish found themselves affected by the politics of provincial warfare. Western Pennsylvania was one of the major battlegrounds over which the British and French fought for imperialistic New World control. The English, settling from the Atlantic coast westward, and the French, claiming lands from the Great Lakes southeastward, clashed over rights to the Appalachian Mountain region. After 1756, the ensuing military conflict which became known as the French and Indian War (or Seven Years War), spread death and destruction even into eastern Pennsylvania. Many of the Native American tribal nations sided with the French against the English and attacked frontier settlers' farms. Thus, Berks County, and what became Lebanon and Dauphin Counties to the west, felt the heat of international politics.[22]

The frontier Amish were not immune from these attacks, and at least one Amish family, the Hochstetlers, suffered the death and captivity which the war brought (see "The Hochstetler Incident," p. 66). Other Amish families may also have been affected. One Hans Lantz of the Northkill Amish settlement wrote that his family had "been obligated to flee" their home "on account of the war." The Lantzes had returned home only after the English "gained the upper hand . . . [and] fought back the French and the Indians. . . ."[23]

Fear of attack by the French and Indians perhaps balanced the fear of losing religious freedom from the English. After the Pennsylvania government declared war on the Delaware and Shawnee nations in the spring of 1756, the province moved to institute a militia law to raise defense troops. The "peace churches"—the Religious Society of Friends (Quakers), Mennonites, Amish, German Baptist Brethren (Dunkers)—appealed for some exemption from this program. The Quakers were already exempt to some degree, and the Mennonites and others agreed to supply material aid to frontier war refugees, or even to the military itself.

Although the war had died down by 1760 for the most part, the conflict had tested Amish identity on a number of fronts.

The Hochstetler Incident

One of the most popular and well-worn stories in Amish family history is that of the Native American attack on the family of Jacob Hochstetler (1704-1775). The Hochstetlers lived in the Northkill Amish settlement in Berks County, Pennsylvania. Frontier settlements like Northkill suffered a number of such incidents from 1755-58.

Folk tradition holds that during the night of September 19, 1757, Jacob Hochstetler, Jr., opened the family's cabin door to see why the farm dog was barking so intently. Thereupon, he was shot in the leg by a group of Indians stalking the house. The wounded boy and his two brothers, Christian and Joseph, all reached for their hunting guns in order to defend the family against the Natives. But their father Jacob would not allow them to shoot, and made the boys put the weapons away. As a devout Amishman, his commitment to nonretaliation and Jesus' teaching to "turn the other cheek" would not permit him see his sons resort to violence.

The Hochstetlers instead hid in the cellar below the house, but the attackers then set fire to the cabin itself. Trying to escape through a cellar window opening, the family was caught. The Indians killed Jacob Jr., his mother and sister. Jacob Sr., Joseph (c.1744-1812), and Christian (c.1746-1814) were taken captive. Separated from his sons, Jacob was taken into French-controlled western Pennsylvania. The Native American group which had taken the Hochstetlers was apparently working closely with the French. The attack was more likely provoked by regional politics and war than by anything the Hochstetlers themselves had done, despite a family legend that Mrs. Hochstetler had earlier angered Natives by turning away a number of their hungry.

The following spring, Jacob Hochstetler's captors gave him the privilege of hunting in the woods by himself. Hochstetler fled. After fifteen days he made his way by canoe and raft to Shamokin, Pennsylvania, and eventually back to an Amish community. Four years later, his two sons were still captives and he had issued an appeal to the province's lieutenant governor asking for help in finding them. Several years later, both sons were freed and re-united with their father.

Family tradition carried the Hochstetler story through the generations in a rather embellished form. But the general outline of the events, deaths, captivity and escape match what surviving documents from the time report.

The traditional tale is told in Rev. Harvey Hostetler, ed., *The Descendants of Jacob Hochstetler, the Immigrant of 1736* (Elgin, Ill.: Brethren Publishing House, 1912), pp. 26-45. Actual historical reports documenting the incident are found in Richard K. MacMaster, et al., *Conscience in Crisis: Mennonites and Other Peace Churches in America, 1739-1789, Interpretation and Documents* (Scottdale, Pa. and Kitchener, Ont.: Herald Press, 1979), pp. 122-27.

Despite the attacks, the frontier Amish communities stayed where they were. Northkill, a settlement hit hard by the fighting, remained the strongest Amish congregation into the 1780s. Then the availability of better soil in the west—not Native American hostility—brought it to an end. Moreover, even after the war Amish settlers continued to move into areas known to be subject to violent attack. The militia law could have tested the Amish resolve to be a nonresistant people, but apparently both the church and the state could compromise without incident. By 1776, however, a new "war for independence" would nearly push the Amish church to the breaking point.

The Threat of Revivalism

One of the greatest threats to the continued existence of the Amish church came not from chiefs and generals, but from preachers. Beginning in the mid-eighteenth century the Amish church lost many members to other "evangelical" denominations. During this time, a powerful and wide-ranging religious revival movement spread throughout the mid-Atlantic colonies and energetic evangelical preachers took their brand of revivalist faith into areas which included Amish settlements.[24] The religious freedom, toleration and equality among church groups in Pennsylvania created a spiritual open-market in which pastors and evangelists spread their wares and sold their products as freely and easily as any merchants. Not only were the Amish reticent to verbally broadcast their faith, but their unique understandings of salvation and church made them prime targets of other groups' proselytizers.

The Amish believed that Christians experienced salvation in everyday living. This was not salvation earned by individuals; it was the free gift given by God's grace. But that gift was realized as one's life was transformed day by day into the image of Christ. *Nachfolge Christi*—daily following after the way of Jesus—was one way in which Amish forebears, the Anabaptists, had described the Christian life. To the Amish mind, being faithful to Christ's commands was a visible indication of faith. The Amish did not down-play Christian "conversion," as such—in fact Amish writings stressed the need for regeneration, or the new birth, which would result in a new way of life. They saw quite clearly a marked difference between the Christian and non-Christian life. But that difference—when lived out—was sharp enough to authenticate itself without needing to be confirmed by an extraordinary conversion "experience."

The revivalism of the so-called evangelical churches stood in noticeable contrast to Amish faith understandings. For the revivalists, salvation was primarily an instantaneous experience—very often preceded by a deep, inner-personal struggle and culminating in an emotional release interpreted as forgiveness. Not that the revivalists put no emphasis on ethics or the Christian's daily life, but for the evangelicals these things were secondary: the singular, emotional experience of conversion was the only sure sign of one's being right with God.

Additionally, the Amish view of the church was different from that of the revivalists. The Amish thought of church in community terms. Church members were mutually accountable to each other even for decisions about personal lifestyle choices. The church itself, as a *body* of believers, shared in communion as a sign of their unity with Christ *and* with one another. Baptism in the Amish church symbolized a commitment to both God *and* fellow believers. In the revivalist understanding, emphasis on individual salvation weakened the importance and authority of the church. Communion and baptism were rites between the individual and God; that the larger congregation was somehow involved was almost incidental. Furthermore, group accountability broke down. If a prior, single "experience of conversion" had permanently validated one's faith, there was hardly need for the church to address issues of pride, wealth or worldly lifestyle which might come up later.

To some of the revivalist groups such as the Methodists,

Amish buggies outside a Somerset County, Pennsylvania, meeting-house (white building) and horse barn (unpainted building). Amish have lived in Somerset County since 1767. They are one of the only groups of Old Order Amish who worship in church buildings.

Baptists and (later in the century) United Brethren, the Amish seemed stuck in formal traditionalism. The Amish church service seemed "cold" to circuit-riding preachers and itinerant evangelists who sought to bring a "warm" spirituality to the Amish. Exactly how many Amish left their church and joined the revivalist groups is unknown, but the numbers seem to have been large. In one famous case, Abraham Drachsel (Troxel), Jr. (1753-1825), an Amish bishop in what became Lebanon County, Pennsylvania, made "too much of the doctrine of regeneration." His congregation silenced him from preaching and he left the Amish church. Apparently a sizable number of the congregation followed him, and one Amish historian believes that defection to other church groups led to the ultimate demise of the Lebanon Valley Amish settlement.[25]

Even more threatening were the German Baptist Brethren (also called "Dunkers," today the Church of the Brethren). While sharing many of the revivalists' emphases, the Brethren were much closer to traditional Amish understandings of church than were other evangelicals. Thus, the similarity of the Brethren to the Amish made the German Baptists attractive to some Amish.

Like the Amish, the Brethren preached in German, emphasized plain dress (including the wearing of beards) and the footwashing rite, and were nonresistants. Vigorous Brethren preaching drew many Amish members and members' children into the Brethren camp.[26]

Perhaps one of the reasons some Amish families moved west into Somerset County was to escape the influence of eastern revivalist churches, but the popular evangelicals won converts from among the Amish there, too. Evangelists were eager to win Amish followers, but the Amish themselves were slow to put divine faith into human words. They preferred to let their lives speak for themselves and let their responses to life be their clear witness. Events in Pennsylvania soon tested that Amish response and challenged a clear witness.

Tories, Rebels and Pacifists

The storm of the French and Indian conflict had hardly cleared for a dozen years when new clouds of war gathered on the horizon. The outbreak of what came to be known as the American Revolution had a profound impact on the young Amish communities in Pennsylvania.[27] The Amish were caught in the midst of political and military turmoil.

To American patriots living in seaport towns and cities, the trade policies and taxes of the British Empire seemed both unfair and intolerable. To many southern planters and a few frontier farmers, the government of King George III was burdensome. But for perhaps as many as a third of the thirteen colonies' citizens, the British crown was the object of loyal devotion. For these folks, scattered up and down the Atlantic seaboard, the patriots in Boston and Philadelphia were nothing but illegal rebels who deserved death as traitors. Those loyal to the government of London were called "Tories" and they fought and worked for king and empire.

For the Amish and other Christian peace churches, the political choice offered by the patriots on the one hand, and the Tories on the other, was not enough. The peace churches represented a third option—peaceful neutrality. They believed that God had commanded Christians to live in love with everyone—a clear call of discipleship that put even state-sanctioned military violence off limits. Thus the Amish (and other pacifists) could not really support either side in their bloody battle for control of the colonies.

At the same time, the Amish had taught that Christians were

to be subject to government. To their non-Amish neighbors, such teaching probably made the official Amish peace position seem somewhat sympathetic toward George III.[28] As the war dragged on, other issues also complicated the political picture for the Amish. Since 1727, in order to settle in the British colonies, all German immigrants had signed a declaration of loyalty to the British crown. While some of the Germans may have signed without much thought, the declaration was, for the Amish, a matter of ethics. If they had promised loyalty to London, then Christian honesty required them to keep that pledge, they believed. And what of taxes? The Amish had always paid taxes to their authorities, but during the Revolution two groups—patriots and Tories—both claimed to be the sole authority to whom tribute was due.

War-time events did not wait on theological reflection. Already by mid-1775, energetic Pennsylvania patriots organized Committees of Observation and Safety and Committees of Correspondence, which served as local patriot watch-dog groups. The Committees tried to force men to join local militias and families to stop buying British goods. Using social intimidation and physical force, the Committees attempted to have all Pennsylvanians fall in line behind the revolutionary cause. Those who refused to join were publicly labeled "Tories." Neither the patriots nor the Tories accepted the peace church position of neutrality. As one diary entry recorded, "If one objects with the merest word, one is told 'You are a Tory!' Those on the other side say, 'You are rebels.'"[29]

On July 1, 1775, as the war's first weeks rapidly evaporated any middle ground between patriots and Tories, a small group of Mennonites, Amish and Brethren met with and tried to appease the Lancaster County Committee of Correspondence. According to the meeting's official minutes, Christian Rupp and Michael Garber, "Representatives of the Society of people called Amisch Menonists," were among those peace church leaders who were present. Rather "than by taking up of Arms, which we hereby declare to be against our Consciences," the Amish and other petitioners asked if they could instead contribute money to a general fund "to assist the Common Cause." They were conscious of the fact that the war had brought "Calamities & Misfortunes" to many Americans and they wished to offer humanitarian aid.[30]

An Amish Folktale: "Strong" Jacob Yoder (c.1726-1790)

"Once upon a time, so the story runs, a certain strong man in Virginia who had heard of this 'Strong' Yoder had a desire to meet him and test his strength. He left his home on horseback and journeyed to Pennsylvania. When he came into the community he met a neighbor of 'Strong' Jacob's and inquired about him. He said that he was the strongest man in his own community, and he had come to whip this man, who was his rival. The neighbor told the stranger that Yoder was a peaceable man and that he had better let him alone. But the Virginian went on, arriving at 'Strong' Jacob's home after dark. The man made all the noise he could on the porch. When 'Strong' Jacob opened the door, the stranger, to get the advantage of 'Strong' Jacob, took hold of him, but Yoder was more than his equal and at once thrust him onto the floor, holding him and calling for a rope. He tied him securely, dragged him beside the fireplace, and let him lie there until morning, then released him and sent him home. The stranger was convinced that he had found a man who was superior to him in physical strength, and went home a wiser, though disappointed man."

From C. Z. Mast and Robert E. Simpson, *Annals of the Conestoga Valley in Lancaster, Berks, and Chester Counties, Pennsylvania. . . .* (Elverson, Pa. and Churchtown, Pa.: C. Z. Mast and Robert E. Simpson, 1942), p. 267.

The Committee agreed and the churches set out to collect funds in lieu of military service. Where records have survived, it seems that the Amish and Mennonites did contribute to the fund even though the Committee kept the purpose of the collection unclear. As historian Richard MacMaster has pointed out, many peace church people "thought they were giving for nearby poor families or to help refugees from British-occupied Boston; in fact, most of the money went for military expenses."[31]

Not all Amish were so accommodating to the patriots' Committees. In the fall of 1779, in Berks County, Amishman Isaac Kauffman (1718-1802) was tried, convicted and jailed as a Tory. Earlier that year a militia officer had demanded to use Kauffman's horse. Kauffman refused and retorted, "You are Rebels and I will not give a horse to such blood-spilling persons." Both Kauffman's opinion and his refusal to hand over his animal clearly revealed to the court that he was "a person of evil and seditious mind and disposition." Despite his having "eight young Children" and his apologizing for his "improper Expressions," Kauffman's sentence was the forfeiture of half of his land and goods as well as imprisonment for the duration of the war.[32]

The War Continues

Already in 1777, the Amish were among those who would not deny their past pledges to George III nor take new oaths to the revolutionary government. They lost the right to vote as a result. Beginning the next year all who were not sworn supporters of the patriot state had to pay double taxes. On one Berks County tax list from 1779 a patriot wrote the word "Tory" after the names of nine Amish heads-of-household. On that list, Amish families represented more than a quarter of all Tories in the county. Oral tradition among the Amish has kept alive the story that several of these Amish tax-list-Tories spent time in jail and were freed only when a kind-hearted Reformed Church pastor interceded on their behalf.[33]

The Amish community in Chester County was close to some of the war's combat action. The September 1777 Battle of Brandywine probably involved British and American troop movements across Amish farms. Several Amish farmers lost livestock to foraging Crown soldiers returning to Philadelphia. Washington's men from nearby Valley Forge took all of Amishman Christian Zook's fences for lumber—and, legend holds—his wife's freshly baked bread.[34]

If their patriot neighbors thought that the pacifist Amish were Tories in disguise, perhaps a few almost were. Amishman Hans Lantz praised George III in a private letter, and then confided: "I also hate and despise with all my heart treachery, rebellion and assassinations. . . . I am also heartily disposed . . . to prevent such as much as possible." Either way, Lantz hoped that the kings's "throne might be well fortified with fairness and be handed down so that he may have eternity for his faithful service and have his reward from God."[35]

The social pressure to conform to the revolutionary party was too strong for some Amish young people. A number left (or just never joined) the church and instead cast their futures with the patriot Committees. Again, Amish family traditions have kept alive stories of sons who went off to battle and were killed in action.[36] The division and heartbreak in some Amish families must have been enormous as the older generation, who had fled the militarism of Europe, watched their children follow the sound of the muster drum.

All of the peace churches suffered during the war through imprisonments, harassment and defecting sons. As a result of the patriot takeover of Pennsylvania, some politically active Quakers withdrew from government for good and a few Mennonites later moved to Canada. The Amish congregations likely lost a good many members during and after the war.[37] A cause-and-effect relationship is only speculative, but at least one Amish historian believes that the war probably set the church back significantly. On one level the war directly drained members and potential members from the fellowship. On a deeper level, the conflict challenged Amish identity: how American was this church? Was freedom in the New World really the freedom to reject what had been preserved through European martyrdom?

Precarious Position

As the Amish completed their first century as a distinct people, their existence was little surer than it had been in 1693. In America the Amish were barely maintaining themselves after more than a half century of settlement. The challenges of frontier living, revivalist faith, and new wealth had each taken their tolls. Patriotic war brought Amish church growth to a near standstill. Genealogical studies show that in no Amish immigrant family did all of the children join their parents' church. In fact, probably less than forty percent of the first generations continued in the Amish tradition.

Entire families were lost. Amish surnames such as Reichenbach, Schenck, and Schowalter drop out of the Amish story after the first few generations. Although about 500 Amish had come to Pennsylvania in the eighteenth century and most had large families, by 1800 there were likely still fewer than one thousand Amish in America.[38] Numerically, the American wing of the church was not strong on its hundredth birthday.

Several decades earlier, an Amish immigrant had written to friends in Europe advising them to come to America, because "in this country is a very good living."[39] The Amish had, in fact, survived and prospered in colonial Pennsylvania, despite the odds. But American "good living" had also been a problem for the Amish. At times living in America had meant becoming American, with all its revivalistic and patriotic trappings. Nevertheless, the Amish persisted, and more and more left Europe to join in the "good living" in America.

A Time of Testing: The Amish in Europe, 1790-1860

"The few who still remain . . . exiles wandering through the land."
    —*from the Ausbund*

In the early years of the nineteenth century, the Amish community around the Palatinate village of Kircheimbolanden met for Sunday services in a second floor room of a former Roman Catholic monastery known as the Münsterhof. The so-called "Emperor's Road" between Paris and Berlin ran several hundred yards north of this place of worship. In 1813 the French Emperor Napoleon I and his beleaguered, defeated army used the Emperor's Road as they retreated from their disastrous attack on Russia. Family tradition holds that sons of the Amish Virkler family marched into Russia as part of Napoleon's army. They

The Münsterhof monastery, near Kircheimbolanden, Germany. During the early 1800s the local Amish congregation met for worship on the building's second floor.

returned as well. As they struggled back to France, perhaps these Amish boys passed the old Münsterhof cloister and its surrounding Amish tenant farms.

How did it happen that Amish men had become a part of the French military? Both the Virklers and the Amish congregation at the Münsterhof suffered during the first half of the nineteenth century. The forces of war, politics and popular culture battered the Amish church. At least one of the Virklers, Rudolph, eventually left for America and its promise of freedom of conscience. And within about fifty years the Münsterhof congregation had itself died out.[1] These were not easy years for the European Amish.

Toleration—And Civic Duty

Until the early 1800s, Amish, Mennonites and other minority ethnic and religious groups often experienced persecution and harassment throughout Europe. Yet here and there, a tolerant noble or an aristocrat in need of good tenant farmers would offer a safe haven for unwanted peoples. Always the Mennonites and Amish received such limited freedom as an exceptional *gift*, never as a civil *right*. Tolerance and liberty of conscience were dispensed at the goodwill of the landlord and might be revoked at any time.

After 1789, the coming of the French Revolution profoundly changed western European politics and thought. Besides overthrowing the French king and the powerful noble elite, the Revolution also ultimately introduced influential and novel ways of thinking about how people and governments relate. One of the major tenets of the Revolution was its new view of citizen- ship—a view which was exported to other countries especially after 1800. Following the French Revolution, "citizenship" would no longer be determined by ancestry or state church membership; rather, the state would offer citizenship on equal terms to everyone living within its borders. Ideally the government would not deny rights to the Amish simply because they were members of a minority religious group. The French Revolutionary idea of equal citizenship opened the door for the eventual social acceptance of the Amish. While the Amish were potentially freed from further persecution, they were also potentially freed to be swallowed up by larger society and culture.[2]

The French revolutionary government did make one *un*equal

"Expert in All Lines of Agricultural Industry"

Writing in 1819, a French journalist offered this description of the Alsatian Amish:

"The entire number of souls may be twelve or fifteen hundred. . . . I do not think that there is a single family living in any of the towns. They are small farmers being found especially as tenants on the estates of noblemen. Through their industry, intelligence, and experience as farmers they have become expert in all lines of agricultural industry. This circumstance as well as their reliability and punctuality in meeting all their financial obligations have made them much sought after by noblemen as farmers on their estates. . . .

"To their credit be it said that, unlike many others, they pay their debts, not in worthless assignats [government-issued land bonds], but in good coin. They do not use tobacco, nor play cards. To music [other than their hymns] they are strangers. They do not go to [sue at] law. They take care of their poor and come to the rescue of their members who have financial reverses for which they were not responsible personally. On the whole they are rather illiterate, but honest, temperate, industrious and of good moral character."

Excerpted from C. Henry Smith and Cornelius Krahn, *Smith's Story of the Mennonites*, fifth ed. (Newton, Kans.: Faith and Life Press, 1981), p. 213.

distinction between Amish and non-Amish citizens: the Amish (and Mennonites) were exempt from military involvement. A document signed by the Revolution's famous and powerful leader Maximilien Robespierre directed all local French officials "to exercise the same kindness and gentleness towards them [the Amish and Mennonites] as is their character, and to prevent their being persecuted."[3] But Paris did expect some type of extra tax or public-works construction from the nonresistants. Before such details were ever fully worked out, however, the revolutionary government was *itself* overthrown by one of its own military heroes.

Napoleon Bonaparte's rise to power in 1799 and his crowning as emperor in 1804 changed the lives of nearly all western

Europeans. Not only was the next decade filled with the destruction of Napoleon's many wars, but also the new emperor decided to push the French Revolution's idea of citizenship to its logical conclusion. All citizens would thereafter receive the same civic rights *and the same civic responsibilities*—regardless of religious affiliation. For the Amish, that decision meant that they were now not only full citizens, but also no longer exempt from military service or other civil duties.[4] Napoleon would treat the Amish and their neighbors "equally"—including requiring equal military service from both. Napoleon's military and political tactics had moved beyond what small, professional armies could accomplish; he needed a large fighting force which he could only raise

An Alsatian Amish couple, early nineteenth century.

through universal conscription. Eventually Napoleon came to directly or indirectly control nearly every area of Europe in which the Amish lived, so virtually all the Amish had to face this newly-assigned citizenship duty.

The Amish response to the situation was mixed. Some members were so glad for an end to their second-class citizenship that they willingly agreed to surrender their baptismal vows. Or, Amishmen might purchase the services of a substitute to muster in their place. Others tried to escape Napoleon's military draft by hiding or fleeing. And some did not know what to do and so went along with state demands—but under strong resistance and protest (such seems to have been the case of the Virklers, above). According to one observer, some Alsatian Amish also reluctantly agreed to wear the tricolor cockade—symbol of the French republic—after wearing such "was made a duty."[5]

Little information exists to fully document the Amish response to universal military conscription, but the reaction of fellow Mennonites along the Rhine may give some clues. In 1803 and 1805 Mennonites met in general conference to discuss the growing problems of living in Napoleon's Europe. The Mennonite leaders at the meeting rejected military participation and civil office holding. Soldiers were not to receive communion, the church said. The conferees also set aside a day of prayer and fasting for the trouble caused by the war. While upholding traditional Mennonite (and Amish) doctrines, the conference's tone was so defensive that one may surmise that members were in fact rejecting traditional nonresistance and peace teaching.[5] The situation could have been the same among the Amish, considering Amish family lore which preserves the memory of militarily-involved sons.

In June 1808 a group of Amish leaders met and discussed the problem of universal military conscription. A half year later, in January 1809, representatives of the Amish congregations in the French Lorraine actually sent two French-speaking church leaders to beg the Emperor to recognize conscientious objection to war.[7] Amish ministers Christian Engel (c.1765-1838) and Christian Guengerich (1740-1825) served as the Paris delegates. The two were not able to meet with the proper government official until spring, and even then their request went unanswered. In 1811 another gathering of church leaders decided to once again petition the national government for exemption from the military.

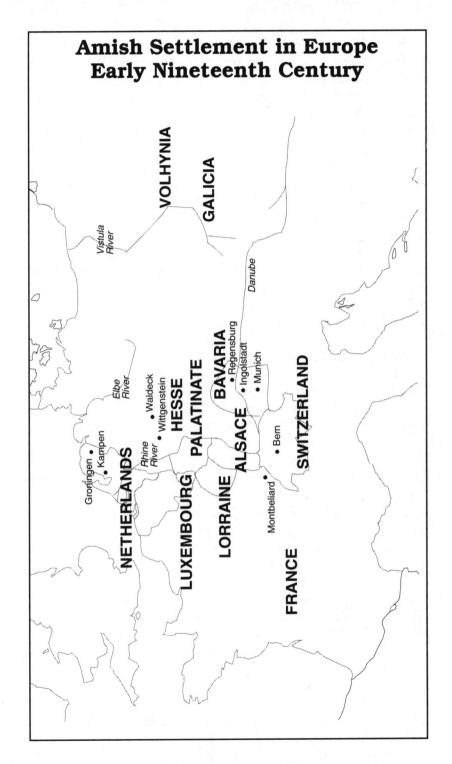

Amish Settlement in Europe
Early Nineteenth Century

VOLHYNIA

GALICIA

Vistula River

Danube

Elbe River

Waldeck

Wittgenstein

HESSE

BAVARIA

Regensburg

Ingolstadt

Munich

PALATINATE

ALSACE

SWITZERLAND

Groningen

Kampen

Rhine River

NETHERLANDS

LUXEMBOURG

LORRAINE

Bern

Montbeliard

FRANCE

Early in 1812, Engel, along with Hans Lugbüll (1760-1835), Joseph Hirschy and Hans Graber (1761-1814) were in Paris, but they received no satisfaction from state officials. After two meetings with the Minister of Religion, the Amishmen returned home, their request denied.[8]

Not only men of conscriptable age, but also Amish women and children suffered through the seemingly endless Napoleonic campaigns. Joseph and Barbara Rupp Roth and their family lived in the Alsace where Joseph was a successful miller. In 1802 the Roths had to leave their home and hide in the woods for more than a week as the battle lines neared their home and soldiers dealt heavy damage to their mill. Twelve years later, Napoleon's forces were again in the area and stopped at the mill to demand money from Roth. Finding nothing, the troops beat Roth, completely ruined the milling machinery, and broke all of the building's precious glass windows. Both of the Roth parents soon died, leaving five orphaned sons to live with relatives.[9]

Faith and Farming

The troubled times did not bury the European Amish church; tradition and a strong sense of peoplehood supported many through the adversity. During the first half of the nineteenth century, the Amish continued many of the traditions which gave a richness to their church life. Singing from the *Ausbund* during worship services kept alive and fresh the memory of faithful martyrs. Simplicity in dress and household furnishings gave concrete expression to biblical teachings on humility, modesty and stewardship. The excommunication and social shunning of unrepentant members not only witnessed to the integrity and seriousness of the Christian life, but also encouraged daily discipleship. Holding a literal footwashing service as a part of communion (after the pattern of Jesus and the disciples in John 13) reminded members of their role as servants. Footwashing still marked Amish communion practices as different from the Mennonites well into the 1800s.

The Amish still maintained their own body of doctrinal and devotional literature, but much of it was shared with the Mennonites. The Amish and Mennonites seemed to have more and more in common. In 1780 an Amish elder and a Mennonite minister cooperated in publishing the Anabaptist history book *Martyrs Mirror*. The prayer book *Die Ernsthafte Christenpflicht*

An early nineteenth century drawing of a French Amish farmer.

(Devoted Christian's Prayer Book) became very popular in both Mennonite and Amish homes and worship services.[10] *Christliches Glaubens-Bekentnus* (an edition of the *Dordrecht Confession* with a collection of prayers and songs), published by a Dutch Mennonite elder in 1664, was widely read among both fellowships.[11] Another Mennonite-written book, *Die Wandlende Seel* (*The Wandering Soul*, which recounted biblical history as its narrator traveled through time and conversed with biblical characters), was well loved in Amish circles.[12] And common in the homes of both Amish and Mennonite families were a Swiss-German dialect translation of the Bible first printed in parts in 1524/29 by Christopher Froschauer, and a collection of the Psalms put in rhymed German verse by Reformed church pastor Ambrosias Lobwasser. In addition, many European Amish con-

gregations began using a Mennonite catechism commonly known among the Amish as the "Waldeck Catechism."[13]

In some places, the cooperation between smaller Amish congregations and nearby larger Mennonite ones was so thorough that the Amish were actually absorbed into the surrounding Mennonite community. Of the Amish congregations in the Netherlands, for example, the group at Kampen merged with the neighboring Mennonite church in 1822; the Groningen Amish did the same in 1824.[14] By the mid-nineteenth century in Eastern Europe, the Volhynian Amish community had also gradually lost its Amish identity and became indistinguishable from the nearby Mennonites.[15] Meanwhile the Amish in Bavaria had begun using their old *Ausbund*s less and less often, and in 1843 produced a new songbook to replace the old Anabaptist hymnal.[16]

While some Amish were losing their historic faith identity, other Amish gained a new reputation as superior farmers. Already in the eighteenth century, some landlords had sought Amish and Mennonite tenant farmers. Even before the French Revolution, the Amish had adopted crop rotation and fertilization with manure and gypsum as ways of naturally replenishing depleted soils. In the wake of the Revolution and their increased social acceptance as "citizens," Amish families received more recognition for their work in agriculture. Around Montbeliard, France, the Amish Graber family successfully developed a new breed of cattle. Other Amish families drained marshes and increased their pasture lands. By the early nineteenth century, in fact, the term "Anabaptist" became nearly synonymous with good farming[17] (see "Expert in All Lines of Agricultural Industry," p. 78).

In 1812 a new French farming almanac appeared under the title *L'Anabaptiste ou Le Cultivateur Par Experience (The Anabaptist, or The Experienced Farmer)*. The almanac's publisher issued the booklet with the cooperation of French Amishman Jacques Klopfenstein (1763-1843), a successful farmer widely known for his agricultural expertise and financial generosity. By connecting the almanac to the name of this influential Amish farmer, the publisher hoped to increase the booklet's circulation and popular appeal. Issued until 1845, the almanac offered suggestions for new and innovative farming methods. The association with Klopfenstein was natural, since the Amishman had, in fact, received national recognition from Napoleon's Imperial Society of

L'ANABAPTISTE
OU LE CULTIVATEUR
PAR EXPERIENCE. 1812.
N.º 1.   2.ᵐᵉ Tirage.

The cover of one of the Klopfenstein almanacs showing an Amish farmer.

Agriculture for his progressive farming methods.

But Jacques Klopfenstein also symbolized how politically assimilated some in his church had become under the strong pressure and influence of surrounding Napoleonic culture. Each year for more than a decade, local politicians appointed the successful farmer and almanac sponsor to the town council. Perhaps not surprisingly then, the Klopfenstein farming almanac also included articles in support of the French emperor and his military program. The cover of one of the early issues included a farming landscape in which the sun in the sky was replaced with the imperial coat of arms![18]

Leaving the Church or Leaving the Continent

During the first half of the 1800s, some of Jacques's extended Klopfenstein family immigrated to America, but most remained in French territory and eventually joined the state church. These two forces which pulled at the Klopfensteins—political and religious acculturation, and immigration to North America—tugged at most European Amish, especially from about 1815 until 1860. The final fall of Napoleon in 1815 did not end the influence of his politics and thought. The years of upheaval and war had ruined some of the tolerant nobles (and their estates) who had earlier granted the Amish privileges and freedoms in exchange for their farming skills. Moreover, the small political states which rose from the ashes of the French Empire had all been brought up on the revolutionary ideals of universal citizenship, and the need for standing armies maintained through universal conscription.

The Amish in western Europe felt a great deal of pressure to blend with their larger, surrounding society. The new citizenship offered tempting social mobility. Meanwhile military service requirements were throwing young men into a foreign environment, away from fellow church members and influences. And while the state churches had lost some of their political power and influence, the official denominations still offered a measure of social status to their members. Genealogical records of the Amish in the Waldeck and Wittgenstein communities in Hesse, Germany, show that people of non-Amish backgrounds did join the Amish congregations there during the early nineteenth century. But the same records indicate that the reverse was equally as true—prosperous Amish families married into and requested membership with the official state churches of that region.[19]

Other signs of acculturation were more subtle. Many congregations survived nominally as "Amish," but internal shifts in attitudes and social adaptations portended coming acculturation. In the 1840s the Ixheim congregation, in Germany's Saarland, constructed a meetinghouse.[20] A physical church building signaled an important change in Amish self-perception—ultimately it was a shift away from an Amish understanding of "church" as the *people* of God, to a more Protestant idea of "church" as the *property* on which preaching and the sacraments are found. And apparently by about 1830 some of the Amish in Hesse were playing pianos in their homes.[21] The use of musical instruments marked another way in which those Amish were adopting popular cultural practices into their own communities.

Resisting the cultural melting pot, some Amish families migrated within Europe in order to find farms and strengthen the church. In 1843 Daniel and Elise Beller Oesch and their eleven children found a rental property in Luxembourg and began the first Amish community in the grand duchy when they moved there the next year. Eventually joined by other families, the Oeschs' congregation was able to retain a number of its distinctive Amish traditions.[22] For many other Amish, remaining faithful disciples required leaving Europe completely. The choice for many seemed to be between leaving the church and leaving the Continent.

The Second Great Amish Emigration from Europe

Emigration from Europe had slowed during the years of Napoleon's many campaigns and Great Britain's "War of 1812" with the United States. After about 1815, however, as sea travel became more regular and safe, immigration to North America increased. Between 1820 and 1860, more than five million Europeans left for Canada or the United States; some twenty-seven percent of all those who settled in America were German-speaking.[23] Most German emigrants were tired of seemingly endless wars and heavy taxes. Others were looking for adventure or a chance to become rich.

All of these motives surely influenced some Amish decisions to leave their homes and venture across the Atlantic. A good many Swiss Amish and Mennonites left their Jura Mountain farms after crop failures and famines in 1816 and 1819 ruined them financially. North America, some thought, might just be the promised land for which they hoped. Amish families already in America might lure their relatives in Europe with images of America's golden opportunities. As one letter from a settler in Bureau County, Illinois, reported to those in the Old Country, "Cattle you can have as many as you want [in Illinois]. . . . On one small piece of land you make a great deal of hay. You can live a great del more comfortable herr than in Germany. The land is much more productive."[24]

Amish Immigration from Europe to North America

c. 1736-1770: About 500 persons. Settled in eastern Pennsylvania. In the years which followed, a few of the immigrants themselves and many of their descendents moved westward.

1804-1810: Several families. Most eventually settled in the Midwest.

1817-1860: About 3,000 persons. Almost all settled directly in Ohio, Illinois, Indiana, Ontario, New York and Iowa. Some settled first in Pennsylvania for a few years and then moved north or west. A few remained in Pennsylvania permanently.

1860-1900: As many as fifty families. Virtually all settled in established Midwestern Amish communities.

Some Amish had purposes other than economic, too. Many Amish families dearly wanted to find a place in which they and their children could follow what they saw as the clear teachings of Christ. Citizenship in Europe meant participation in both the military and an increasingly secular culture.

It seemed that some Mennonites had already surrendered biblical faith for social acceptance. At a general congress of German states held in 1848-49, two Mennonites appeared as elected delegates. If their political participation was not enough, one of the Mennonites spoke out *against* conscientious objection to military involvement and in *favor* of the universal defense of what he called "the welfare of the Fatherland."[25] Would the Amish eventually find themselves speaking such things in similar gatherings? Many decided not to wait to find out; they would leave for North America.

Amish families such as Andreas and Elizabeth Eiman Ropp chose to emigrate when their sons reached draft age.[26] Others, like Daniel and Elizabeth Bauman Bender would send only their son; at age fifteen Wilhelm Bender sailed alone from Europe to avoid conscription.[27] Not all Amish completely avoided the European military, though. Joseph Wuerkler was actually drafted, but in 1829 he escaped the French army and fled to America.[28] At times, nearly an entire Amish congregation in Bavaria or Hesse left together as one large group.[29] Several Amish communities in those regions were so weakened by mass emigration to America that they eventually disbanded. Did those who tried to carry on the Amish tradition in Europe see themselves in the old *Ausbund* hymn which spoke of the faithful "few who still remain . . . exiles wandering through the land."[30] Or did that verse apply to the emigrants as well?

A few Amish had emigrated during the first decades of the nineteenth century.[31] However, most sailed after 1818. Most Amish who chose to leave Europe did so by 1860 (although even until 1900 a few continued to pack their bags). Probably about three thousand Amish adults left Europe between 1817 and 1860. This sizable nineteenth century emigration greatly weakened the remaining Amish church in Europe. Likely fewer than 2,000 members were left in the Continent.[32]

Although the number of emigrants was much larger than it had been in the 1700s, the trials of a nineteenth century trip

Most of the Old Order Amish who live around Milverton, Ontario, are descendants of Amish families who left Europe during the decades after 1820.

were much the same as they had been a hundred years earlier. Often Atlantic crossings lasted two to four months.[33] Those who left European shores hoped and prayed to safely reach America.

But to what America were these Amish going? Change had affected both sides of the Atlantic since the first Amish had sailed for Penn's Woods. While Napoleon had been raising armies in Europe, he was also selling more than 830,000 square miles (2.15 million square kilometers) of "Louisiana Purchase" to the new United States. Opportunities for settlement in America now stretched far beyond eastern Pennsylvania. The former "Thirteen Colonies" had become an aggressive, expansive nation. Canada was also changing. An expanding population called for limited self-rule from Britain, and a mild nationalism swept through the provinces when they held their own against the Americans in the War of 1812. Would the early nineteenth-century immigrant Amish feel any more at home in North America than they had in Europe? Could those who remained in Europe resist being swallowed up by secular culture?

An Ocean Voyage

During the summer of 1833 Daniel P. Guengerich (1813-1889) sailed from Europe to America with his mother, stepfather, brothers and sister. On May 9, the family left their Waldeck home and traveled overland to the Weser River. From May 13-20, the group sailed northward to the city of Bremen. On June 1, the ocean-going vessel on which they had boarded passage set off from Bremen. The trip lasted until August 11. Excerpts from Guengerich's writings:

"On June 5th toward noon we had a strong west wind right against us causing the ship to lie sometimes on its left side, so we could hardly walk on the deck without slipping. . . .

"On this day [24th] a passenger, who had been sick already when he came on the ship, died. . . .

"On the 28th we had the same west wind yet. The night was so stormy that we could not lie still in bed, being thrown one upon the other as the ship tilted to the side. Several tied themselves down in order to remain lying in one bed which is so low that one can hardly sit upright without bumping himself. . . .

"On the 4th [of July] we had west winds so that we made no progress at all. On the 5th we had storm in the forenoon, and the seasickness recurred with many. In the afternoon we had west wind again. . . .

"On the 13th, 14th, 15th, and 16th we always had bad wind. The captain says we have made only half of the way. It made us sad to hear that, for we have already sailed over six weeks. On the 17th we made some headway but it was slow. The 18th was very hot and quiet, one could only see that the ship moved a little, and in the night it was so hot that many went on deck and slept there. . . .

"The 25th . . . we had rain in the morning at 4 o'clock but not much, otherwise there was a strong west wind and a clear sky. We also saw flying fishes, but they were not any larger than herring. In the afternoon at 6 o'clock there was a thunder storm with thunder and lightning. . . .

"On the 10th [of August] we saw 8 to 12 ships. . . . One also sees many large fish daily. . . . In the evening between 8 and 9 o'clock the pilot came [on board to guide the ship into harbor], then there was great joy on the ship among the people."

From Daniel P. Guengerich, *An Account of the Voyage from Germany to America* (Kalona, Ia.: Jacob F. Swartzendruber, n.d.) Swartzendruber was a great-grandson of Guengerich.

— 6 —

Prosperity and Promise in North America, 1800-1865

> "We had everything in abundance."
> —*Amish Bishop David Beiler*

Another Century

In 1800 the future of the Amish church in America was unsure. The American Revolution and the influence of revivalist preachers had drawn many Amish youth away from their parents' church during the 1700s. Scattered and few in number, the American Amish had little but spiritual commitment on their side as they faced another century.

By 1800 the old Amish communities in Berks County, Pennsylvania, had mostly disappeared as their members moved to better soils in Lancaster County or farther west in the state. The Lebanon County Amish settlement lost so many members to other church groups that it, too, was practically extinct before the nineteenth century began. Even the Chester County Amish—who seemed to be a healthy group in 1800—had virtually all moved away by 1830. And in central and northeastern Lancaster County, where two Amish congregations persisted, membership remained small until about 1840.[1]

Troubled church life in the east probably caused some Amish families to move westward in the hopes of establishing stronger congregations. Yet even in Somerset County, of three original Amish communities, only one ultimately survived. The freedom of the frontier and the influence of revivalists took their tolls there as well.

If some Amish moved west to preserve a more traditional church and family lifestyle, others had different ideas. Amishman Joseph Schantz (1749-1813) moved to the border of Somerset and Cambria Counties and took up farming. In the fall of 1800, Schantz (often anglicized as "Johns") took the novel step of chartering a town on part of his property. Schantz ("Johns") laid out lots—including space for public schools and church buildings—and proceeded to sell to interested non-Amish parties. Even when he then moved to another farm some miles away, the civic-minded Amishman remained a local public figure. Although he had chosen the American Indian designation "Conemaugh" for his planned town, the new residents officially changed its name to "Johnstown" twenty-one years after the Amishman's death.[2] Such was the worldly civic activity of one Amishman who left the east.

But by that time Somerset County was itself becoming "the east" as white settlers pushed relentlessly westward into the Ohio River Valley. The Amish were among them. In 1809 the family of Amish Preacher Jacob Miller (1754-1835) moved from Somerset to Tuscarawas County, Ohio. The Millers' nephew, Amishman Jonas Stutzman (1788-1871), traveled with the family but settled nearby in Holmes County (see "'White' Jonas Stutzman," p. 100). Four years later, other Amish from Somerset and Mifflin Counties, Pennsylvania, relocated to Wayne County, Ohio.[3] Meanwhile, Amish settlers moved to Juniata and Centre Counties, Pennsylvania, in 1806 and 1813.[4]

New Arrivals

Hardly had the Amish already in America begun migrating westward, than hundreds of European Amish immigrants began arriving on the North American shore. Eventually totaling some three thousand adults, the nineteenth-century Amish arrivals were fleeing the economic and military consequences of life in post-Napoleonic Europe.

The first ripple of what would become a wave of nineteenth century Amish immigrants was the Christian Augspurger (1782-1848) family of Hesse which scouted out Ohio lands in 1817. Returning to Europe, the Augspurgers rallied more families to join them, and in 1819 returned to Ohio's Butler County and founded an Amish community made up of direct European Amish immigrants.[4] The nineteenth-century arrivals settled as groups not only in Butler County, but also in places like Stark County, Ohio (1823), Waterloo County, Ontario (1824), Lewis County, New York (1831), Fulton County, Ohio (1834), and Allen and Adams Counties, Indiana (1850 and 1852). Other immigrants joined already established Amish communities such as

Elizabeth Zug (1786-1855) lived in Lancaster County, Pennsylvania, near the town of Eden.

those in Lancaster and Somerset Counties, Pennsylvania, or helped American Amish form new settlements in places as far west as Iowa (after 1840). In Wayne County, Ohio, the new immigrants moved close to the original Amish settlers, but remained on the edges of the already established community.[6]

Many of the Amish who came to North America after 1817 arrived in the ports of New York, Philadelphia or Baltimore.

Others, heading directly for the midwest, sailed from Europe to New Orleans. From there they would take paddlewheel steamboats up the Mississippi to the Ohio or Illinois rivers. Another boat (or travel by foot) awaited them there. Through the years a few Amish stayed on in New Orleans and established a small congregation near the city. Some of the members, such as the Christian Oswald or Bishop Joseph Maurer (c.1815-1867) families, remained in Louisiana only a short time before continuing on to Illinois. But others never left. From the time of his 1846 arrival from the Alsace until his death, Preacher Christopher Maurer (1813-1872) served this southern Amish group. In order to maintain some connection with the larger American Amish church, Bishop Peter Naffziger (1787-1885) twice walked from Ohio to New Orleans to minister to the small city congregation and bring news from fellow believers in the north. (The Amish dubbed Naffziger "the apostle" because of his extensive ministry of travel.) The Louisiana group seems to have dissolved in the latter 1800s.[7]

During the 1820s a larger and more permanent Amish community took shape in Ontario. The nineteenth century Amish immigrants to Canada were not the first members of their church in the Dominion, however. By 1789 the family of Christian and Barbara Yoder Troyer[8] had moved from Bedford County, Pennsylvania to Norfolk County, Ontario.[9] Lack of a larger church community, the defection of family members to other denominations and possibly harassment from the Canadian government during the War of 1812 all induced the Amish Troyers to move to Holmes County, Ohio, about 1815.[10]

A new Ontario Amish settlement began during the next decade. In 1822, Christian Nafziger (1776-1836) arrived in New Orleans to look for land for his eager-to-immigrate Palatinate Amish congregation. Nafziger traveled on foot from Louisiana to Lancaster, Pennsylvania, where fellow Amish informed him of good, cheap land in Canada. Arriving in Ontario, he negotiated the purchase of a large tract in Waterloo County and returned to Europe to share the news of his good fortune. On his return trip, Nafziger's ship stopped in England, where according to family lore, the Amishman had a private audience with King George IV who officially certified the Canadian land deal. Beginning in 1824, a number of European Amish families immigrated to Waterloo County, Ontario. By 1837 Amish families were plowing farms in Perth County, Ontario, as well. The group was also

David Mast: Farming Entrepreneur

James L. Morris (1810-1849) was a storekeeper and civic leader in Morgantown, Pennsylvania. His colorful diaries reported the activities of his many neighbors, including members of the Conestoga Amish community. A series of Morris' diary entries point to the agricultural experimentation of Amish Deacon David Mast (1798-1869). As a means of replenishing soils poor in phosphorus and potassium, Mast's use of ground bone later became rather widespread in southeastern Pennsylvania.

September 12, 1845: "This David Mast is one of the most enterprising men of our neighborhood and as an agriculturalist he has scarcely his equal. To a knowledge of the various theories he adds an extensive practice and is not too timid to indulge in experiments."

October 15, 1845: "David Mast purposes manuring the Watts farm (which is very poor) with bone dust. He has offered $5.00 per ton for all the bones that can be collected and wants 30 or more tons. This is the first attempt in this neighborhood to use bone manure."

June 10, 1846: "David Mast whom I mentioned last winter as having erected a bone mill, strewed or sowed a quantity of bone dust upon poor forest land on which he sowed oats. A small patch of land was left unstrewn and the difference is remarkable. On the land on which the bone dust was applied, the oats is [sic] equal to any in the good valley land, while on the other it is merely 'forest oats.'"

Morris diary quoted in Grant M. Stoltzfus, "History of the First Amish Mennonite Communities in America," *The Mennonite Quarterly Review* 28 (October 1954): 256. Original Morris diary housed at the Historical Society of Berks County (Pennsylvania).

joined by other settlers from Pennsylvania, with members of both groups coming to the aid of the other when needed.[11]

Helping One Another

Amish immigrants of the nineteenth century were the beneficiaries of their church's serious commitment to Christian mutual aid. Church members were to help other members, no matter what the cost; no one would starve or be homeless on the North American frontier. Even as "an old man [of] nearly eighty years," Amishman Christian Ropp (1812-1896) well remembered the welcome which the Chester County, Pennsylvania, Zook family had offered the tired Ropps after they arrived in Philadelphia in 1826.[12] Individual Amish persons without money enough to immigrate also received the aid of their fellow church members. Amishman Peter Kinsinger paid the passage fare for young Wilhelm Bender. Once in America, Bishop Benedict Miller (1781-1835) of Somerset County, bought Bender's services and brought the boy to the Somerset community, where Bender and Miller's daughter Catherine later married.[13]

Another recipient of her church's generosity was Jacobina Schwartzentruber Nafzinger (1793-1869). Widowed during her 1827 Atlantic crossing, Nafzinger, her six young children and her two brothers landed in Baltimore but made their way to Philadelphia. When Chester County Amishman Christian Zook[14] heard of the family and its dire situation, he went to Philadelphia himself and picked them up. The Nafzingers then lived with the Zooks for three months until the Nafzingers settled in Lancaster County where other Amish families helped to take care of, and support, Jacobina's children.[15]

Amish mutual aid practices did not end with their own people. In 1817 immigrant Hans Nussbaum was among a group of Mennonite families arriving in Pennsylvania with few resources.[16] On October 9, Nussbaum's ship anchored near Philadelphia. Already a week later the group was staying in the homes of Chester County Amish families. Next, the party traveled to Lancaster County where they were the guests of that area's Amish for another week. The following seven days the immigrants lived with Mifflin County church members, who in turn guided them to fellow Amish in Somerset County. In each case, according to Nussbaum, the "very kind treatment" of the hosts included giving the immigrants "much to eat, and" charging them "nothing." Finally arriving at their Ohio destination, the Nussbaum party received the practical advice of already-settled Amish families who directed them towards the best available land.[17]

Quite a number of Amish families also took care of non-Amish orphans or children whose households could not afford to take care of them. Both Leah Lewis's and James Morrell's families apprenticed them to Mifflin County Amish couples who were to

Bishop Isaac Schmucker spent most of his adult life in northern Indiana as leader of that area's progressive Amish congregations.

train and take care of the two children. In 1827, just before completing their required years of service, Lewis (1805-1886) and Morrell (1807-1880) married and joined the Amish church. They later moved to Elkhart County, Indiana, where a sizable Amish community gathered, beginning in 1841.[18]

The most famous orphan raised in an Amish home was

Rosanna McGonegal (1837-1895). An orphaned Irish baby from a immigrant Roman Catholic family, Rosanna grew up in the home of Christian and Elizabeth Yoder Kauffman in Centre and Juniata Counties, Pennsylvania. Rosanna chose to be baptized into the Amish church and married Christian Z. Yoder (1837-1915). One of Rosanna's sons, Joseph W. Yoder, wrote his mother's life story in *Rosanna of the Amish.* Still in print, the book has been enormously popular over the years with both children and adults.[19]

East and West, North and South: Migration Continues

The Amish of Canada and the United States were a very mobile people during the first half of the nineteenth century. Amish families moved often in search of more or cheaper land. New immigrants from Europe settled as groups in the Midwest and Ontario, although individual immigrant families might be found in the old Lancaster County settlement or in a new community such as Hickory County, Missouri (after 1855). Families might move three times in as many decades. Some Amish communities were rather homogeneous, to be sure. The Amish of Logan and Champaign Counties, Ohio, for instance, had nearly all their family roots in Mifflin County, Pennsylvania.[20] But even in Logan-Champaign one might find a family or two from elsewhere.

The travels of Bishop Isaac Schmucker (1810-1893) illustrate Amish mobility. Schmucker was born in Lancaster County in 1810. He moved with his parents to Mifflin County, Pennsylvania, and later lived with his wife Sarah Troyer (1811-1886) in Wayne and Knox Counties, Ohio. In 1841, Schmucker led one of the first groups of Amish settlers to what became the large Amish community in northern Indiana's Elkhart and Lagrange Counties. Ten years later he was living in central Illinois, but a year later ill health in the family caused the Schmuckers to return to Indiana.[21]

The forces of migration which took families north and west might also bring them back south and east. For three years after their 1829 arrival in America, the Christian Ebersol, Sr. (1788-1862) family lived in Lancaster County, Pennsylvania, before resettling more permanently in Waterloo County, Ontario. After moving to Ontario, one of the older Ebersol boys decided to return to Lancaster. He married Elizabeth Stoltzfus (whose family had not left eastern Pennsylvania since their own 1766 arrival) and

"White" Jonas Stutzman
(1788-1871)

In 1809 Jonas Stutzman became the first Amish settler to live in Holmes County, Ohio. Nearly two hundred years later, he remains the most unusual of that community's members—best known because he wore only white clothes for much of his life.

Stutzman moved with relatives from Somerset County, Pennsylvania, to eastern Ohio. They settled in Tuscarawas, County; he, across the border in Holmes. Three years later he married Magdalena Gerber (1794-d. by 1840), and after her death, was married to a woman named Catherine. Jonas had at least eight children.

In 1850 Stutzman published a thirty-page book of his writings entitled *First, Second, and Third Appeals to All Men to Prepare for the Approaching Kingdom of God Upon Earth*. The collection is the first known booklet of original material published by an American Amish person. Of the three "Appeals" printed in the book, the first was dated July 19, 1849, and the second and third both dated November 22, 1849.

Highly unusual were the book's contents. In its pages, Stutzman announced that he had received revelations from God warning all people to repent since the return of Christ and the end of time were both near at hand. Church leaders were to stop observing communion in their congregations, but instead begin to earnestly repent and purify themselves for the coming Kingdom of God.

Using a numerology derived from the apocalyptic passages of the biblical book of Daniel, Stutzman predicted Christ's second coming to be 1853. More than simply human predictions, Stutzman believed that his "Appeals" were divine revelations. "God has deemed me worthy, his humble servant, to reveal unto me clearly and distinctly that the time of the fulfillment of his plan with mankind is at hand. . . . He revealed this unto me not for my sake only, but that I proclaim it before all men, so that every one may prepare himself," Stutzman noted

So sure of Christ's imminent return was Stutzman, that he

uilt a chair for Jesus to sit in when he arrived. It was nine inches larger than a standard-size chair.

"White" Jonas's entire booklet appeared in English. One Amish historian is sure that Stutzman used English because he "was appealing to a wider audience than [German-speaking] Amish and Mennonites." Stutzman also included his own address in the book, and urged all who were waiting for the predicted return of the Lord to write to him.

Another of "White" Jonas's visions affected his choice in clothing and gave him his famous nickname. "According to what I have seen in the spirit," he wrote, "there are three colors for the children of God: the fallow [beige], gray, and white—the colors of eagles and sheep." For the rest of his life Jonas Stutzman wore only white clothes. Some said that he was also obsessed with cleanliness. Even after his predicted date of Christ's return passed without incident, he continued to wear white until he died.

Although the Amish rejected Jonas Stutzman's teachings, he remained a member in good standing of his church all his life. Most of his children joined the Old Order Amish Church. Says one Amish historian, "His peculiar views and dress were not seen as a threat to anyone, for he never had any followers." Stutzman's peculiar life and beliefs grew out of his unusual personality, not out of a spirit of rebellion.

For more information, see David Luthy, "'White' Jonas Stutzman" *Family Life* (February 1980): 19-21. In Stutzman's published *Appeals* his name is spelled Stutzmann.

remained in her community. Nevertheless, the Ontario and Pennsylvania Ebersols kept up family contacts through the years, traveling to visit one another by horseback and railroad.[22]

A few younger Amishmen probably moved in search of adventure. One Andrew Baechler (1828-1911) traveled extensively for about fifteen years during which time he worked in the gold mines of California, Idaho, British Columbia, Montana and even across the Pacific in Australia. In 1867 Baechler finally settled among fellow Amish in central Illinois.[23] Others, like Bishop Schmucker, may have pulled up stakes in part to escape conflict and church difficulties in their home communities.[24] Some reasons for migrating were more personal and preferential.

the Andreas and Elizabeth Eiman Ropp family left Ontario, Canada."[25] The Ropps had come from the French Alsace and later ended up in Butler County, Ohio, because "it was far too cold" in central Illinois.

The quest for farmland seems to have been the most common reason for moving. The vast majority of Amish spent their lives farming. And even an Amish blacksmith and locksmith like Preacher Christian Beck (1798-1882) of Fulton County, Ohio, or a school teacher like Amishman Christian Erismann (1835-1905) of central Illinois, needed to remain in their people's rural communities. Cheap land in the West lured many settlers. After her husband died, Magdalena Augspurger (1819-1898) and her children moved from Butler County, Ohio, to Davis County, Iowa, where they homesteaded in the small Amish community in that area. In 1854 Augspurger purchased 160 acres of government land for a fraction of the price it would have cost her to expand her holdings in Ohio.[26] Earlier, in 1846, another Butler County farmer, Bishop Joseph Goldsmith (1796-1876), had also moved to Iowa in search of cheaper land, but he had little choice. Goldsmith's financial difficulties had forced him to sell his Ohio property and relocate on more affordable farmland in Iowa's Lee County.[27]

Inexpensive land enticed many settlers, even if dishonest land agents sometimes cheated the Amish out of money and property, as happened to the Daniel and Susanna Nafsinger Raber family in Hickory County, Missouri. The Rabers paid for two hundred acres of land which turned out to be not for sale.[28] Nevertheless migrations continued in large numbers, at time depleting eastern settlements. Only a small cemetery remained in Knox County, Ohio, after the entire Amish community in that place scattered in search of more affordable land. Some moved to other places in Ohio, others went on to Illinois and Iowa.[29]

While most Amish searched for what was considered good farmland, other families settled on soil deemed useless. Fulton County, in Ohio's northwestern corner, contained the so-called "Black Swamp," an area avoided by most white pioneers. In 1834 a sizable group of European Amish immigrants arrived in the swamp—so wild a place that it took the Amish eleven days to travel their last twenty miles. Clearing and draining the land, the Amish developed some of the richest and most productive fields in the state.[30]

Many of the Amish who did migrate westward were young families with small children. A study of a number of the original Elkhart County, Indiana, Amish settlers revealed that the average age of male family heads was 33, and of females only 28, when those settlers arrived in northern Indiana. With the exception of one rather well-off family, the Amish settlers averaged about as much wealth per person as their non-Amish neighbors.[31] Here, as other places, ambitious farm couples with large families, moderate financial means and good land founded lasting communities.

Immigrant Challenges

The nineteenth century Amish immigration to North America greatly changed not only the size, but also the geographic center of the church. By 1851, for example, the area with the largest Amish population was not the old Lancaster County settlement with its (by then) four Amish congregations, but rather central Illinois with eight Amish congregations.[32] The Amish had settled in the American Midwest in great numbers.

But the changes were more than numeric and geographic. During the first sixty years of the nineteenth century the Amish in America struggled to decide how they were to relate to the American society in which they found themselves. Were they still the separate people they had been in Europe? How much change could the church accept and still be true to the standards of Christ? Now that they were living in a democracy, were they responsible to participate in government and politics? These and many other questions taunted the Amish.

Some traditionalists, like Lancaster County Bishop David Beiler (1786-1871), saw the Amish immigrants of the 1800s as bringing progressive new ideas into the American church. These "many foreign immigrants with strange manners and customs" corrupted the church, in Beiler's opinion. Beiler longed for the good old days when "Christian simplicity was practiced much more, and much more submission was shown toward the ministers. . . ."[33] Clothing, household furniture, carriages and even family meals had become so fancy—so wasteful—during Beiler's lifetime that it hurt him to even think about it. The Amish church was becoming more worldly, he thought, as its members patterned their lifestyle after their neighbors and fashionable society, rather than on the simple teaching of Scripture. Now Amis'

In the 1850s the so-called "Swiss" Amish settled in Allen (shown here) and Adams Counties, Indiana. The Swiss Amish have remained quite conservative—for example, members drive only open buggies.

youth clamored for months of education each year. Beiler thought that they should be satisfied with knowing how to read and write—anything more would surely lead to a competitive spirit and pride.

Beiler was partly right. Immigrants after 1817 were very often more progressive-minded than their American-born cousins. A group of Hessian Amish arriving in Butler County, Ohio (1832), some of whom later moved to McLean County, Illinois (1837), were especially known for their liberal attitudes. The Hessian men wore buttons on their coats, and their families even had pianos in their homes, while their leaders seemed to be quite flexible with matters of doctrine and belief.[34]

Like all stereotypes, the label "liberal immigrant" was only *mostly* true. Isaac Schmucker, for example, was born into a Lancaster County family which had lived in Pennsylvania since before the American Revolution. Yet Schmucker spent most of his adult life in Elkhart-Lagrange Counties, Indiana, as the leader of progressive Amish congregations in that area. Meanwhile, Bishop Christian Ropp, immigrant of 1826, remained a leading conservative voice throughout his life in Illinois. The so-called "Swiss Amish" who immigrated to America in the 1850s and settled in Allen and Adams Counties, Indiana, were also a very traditional, though late arriving, group.[35]

Struggles of the Amish Church

Unorganized and with little clear direction in 1800, the Amish church struggled to gain and maintain spiritual authority in the first half of the nineteenth century. In the Conestoga Amish community on the Lancaster-Berks Counties' border, the strong leadership of Bishop Jacob Mast (1738-1808) consolidated the congregation and strengthened the group as it entered the new century. Deeply respected for his own personal spirituality and piety, Mast was also self-educated, owning some eighteen books at the time of his death—a notable home library for the time.[36]

Strong leadership became the key to many other congregations' health and survival. Often Amish communities consisted of large extended and interrelated families. In such situations, kinship ties and parental decisions often carried as much or more weight than did church teaching. Within several decades, however, the Amish were able to ordain resident leaders in every sizable Amish community and begin holding regular bi-weekly Sunday worship services. Church teaching and discipline took on greater importance as a result (see "Amish Church Structure and Leadership," p. 110).

The church also strengthened its authority by holding parents more accountable for the actions of their children. As an Anabaptist church, the Amish practiced adult (believers') baptism. Persons made the voluntary choice to become Christians and join the church as adults. Since young children and teens were not members of the church they were not, strictly speaking, fully accountable to their parents' fellowship.

During the early 1800s, however, church leaders took steps to discipline members who tolerated their children's deviant social behavior. No one was to be forced to become a Christian, but neither were parents to encourage their rebellious children in sin. So in 1837, the Somerset County church decided that it would no longer allow parents to dress their children in fancy, worldly clothing (as some parents had been doing). Neither would parents be allowed to turn a blind eye to youthful courting practices. Some courting teens, the church leaders said, "take the liberty to sleep or lie together without any fear or shame." If such

Native Americans, Native Canadians and the Amish

The westward migration and Midwestern immigration of Amish families was part of the larger story of European settlement in North America. As such, it is also the story of the disinheritance of the continent's Native Peoples. In some cases the Amish moved onto land from which the Indians had been expelled only a few months before. In Elkhart and Lagrange Counties, Indiana, for example, U.S. troops forced the last Natives to leave in 1840, and the first Amish arrived in 1841. In one case, central Illinois Amishman John Engel (1801-1888) assisted with the army's job of Native removal. Engel served as a teamster during the bloody Black Hawk War of 1832 in which the Sauk tribe was virtually exterminated. Engel's experience was highly unusual among the Amish.

Historian Russell Krabill has noted that no documentation exists to show "how the Amish felt about taking over the land which had been taken from the native peoples." Krabill has suggested that perhaps the Amish, like other white settlers, "were so busy carving out their homes in the wilderness that they did not give it much thought."

After 1840 in Lee County, Iowa, however, the small Amish community which began there came to an end when its settlers discovered that they were living on land reserved for Indian peoples. The Amish moved away. Yet even while living there, the Natives and Amish got along rather well, judging from Amish family tradition. One Lee County Amish woman often served pumpkin butter to visiting Indians. Her hospitality earned her a gift of bear claws from the local chief.

In Ontario, Native Canadians got along so well with one of the Amish Schwartzentruber families that the Indians often took young Michael Schwartzentruber (1827-1912) along on hunting trips and showed him how to bow hunt. And in the early days of the Wayne County, Ohio, Amish community, both Natives and Amish farmers seem to have lived peaceably, side-by-side, along the Sugar Creek.

While documentation is slim, nearly all the stories which

have come down to the late twentieth century concerning Native-Amish relationships are ones of friendship and goodwill.

Steven R. Estes, *Living Stones: A History of the Metamora Mennonite Church* (Metamora, Ill.: Metamora Mennonite Church, 1984), pp. 30-32; Orland Gingerich, *The Amish of Canada* (Waterloo, Ont.: Conrad Press, 1972), p. 33; Russell Krabill, "The Coming of the Amish Mennonites to Elkhart County, Indiana," *Mennonite Historical Bulletin* 52 (January 1991): 3, 4; David Luthy, *The Amish in America: Settlements That Failed, 1840-1960* (Aylmer, Ont. and Lagrange, Ind.: Pathway Publishers, 1986), pp. 115, 116, 227, 263, 328, 356, 380, 381, 472.

happened "with the knowledge of the parents," the Amish concluded that the "parents shall not go unpunished." Parental authority would have to yield to church standards; increasingly the bishops and preachers, not the fathers and mothers, had the final word.[37]

Those Somerset County decisions grew out of a regional meeting of Amish church leaders, held in 1837. Other conferences of Amish leadership gathered in 1809 (held somewhere in eastern Pennsylvania), 1826 (Pennsylvania), 1827 (eastern Ohio), 1830 (Somerset County, Pennsylvania), 1831 (eastern Ohio) and 1849 (Ohio).[38] The result of these meetings was a general strengthening of church life and commitment. Leaders resolved to teach and practice personal humility, excommunication of unrepentant members and the social shunning of the banned. Expensive furniture, fancy porcelain and decorative dishes all had the single purpose of showing off one's wealth, the meetings' participants decided. Thus, the church forbade members to own them. By reaffirming their rejection of such items, the Amish renewed their commitment to faithful simplicity and meekness.

More than just issues of lifestyle, the meetings also gave attention to some very important doctrinal issues. For example: Would Mennonites (who had also, of course, been baptized as adults) need to be baptized again if they chose to join the Amish? After extended debate the Amish decided that, yes, former Mennonites would have to accept adult baptism again.[39] Would members who left the Amish church be excommunicated and shunned if they then joined other churches? Again, most Amish said yes.

In the 1850s, a third divisive issue among the Amish involved so-called "stream baptism." The Amish traditionally held baptismal services, like worship services, in private homes. But some Amish came to believe that because Jesus was baptized *in* the Jordan River, candidates should also kneel *in* a stream or river while the baptizing bishop poured water on their heads. Long discussion and debate finally ended when the church decided to compromise and allow both methods. No bishop would be compelled to use a method with which he was uncomfortable.[40] (A few Amish—mostly in Mifflin County, Pennsylvania—practiced stream baptism until about 1910.)

Innovation and Involvement

Behind all the discussion, issues and debate in the Amish church, there were a number of very real changes taking place. A sizable portion of Amish were accepting innovations in church life and practice. Signaling a shift in their understanding of "the church," some Amish began constructing church buildings (often called "meetinghouses"). While these structures were quite plain and simple, they symbolized a rather significant

Partridge Creek (Metamora), Illinois, Amish meetinghouse, built in 1854 and replaced by another buiding in 1889.

change. No longer would "the church" be simply the people, meeting from place to place in private homes. No longer would the congregation remain at the host family's house after services for a whole-group meal and afternoon fellowship. The church was now *a place*—to go to and to leave at selected times during the week. In 1853 the Amish around Rock Creek near Danvers, Illinois, erected the first permanent Amish meetinghouse.[41] The neighboring Partridge (Metamora) Illinois, Amish community had a structure the following year. In 1855 the Logan-Champaign Counties, Ohio, Amish built the first of several meetinghouses, and the Haw Patch (Topeka), Indiana, Amish gathered in a church building beginning in 1856. In the years which followed, more change-minded Amish congregations also put up meetinghouses.

The Logan County Amish also became the first Amish to sponsor a regular Sunday school program. During the early 1800s, Sunday schools had become widespread among American Protestants.[42] Many of these Protestant Sunday schools were "union schools," that is, they were community-sponsored programs supported by several local denominations. An innovative form of Christian education, Sunday schools would increase biblical knowledge and foster disciplined Bible study, supporters claimed. But, opponents warned, Sunday schools also systematized and compartmentalized religious education by separating children from parents and using uniform materials written by unknown, inter-denominational authors. Awarding high marks or even prizes to those who performed well in Sunday school promoted the worldly ideals of competition, pride and earned status.[43] None of these aspects of Sunday school made the idea popular with conservative Amish.

In the 1850s, some Amish children and youth from Logan and Champaign Counties attended union Sunday schools held in their area. In June 1863 Bishop Jacob Kenagy and Preacher David Plank opened the first permanent Sunday school among the Amish at their own meetinghouse. (Since 1840 some Ontario Mennonites and Pennsylvania Amish had operated Sunday schools occasionally, but none of these experiments had lasted.) Plank had earlier visited a local union school, from which he drew his ideas and inspiration. The new school was not without some opposition. Several of the Amish claimed that Sunday school, held in the afternoons during those early years, would prohibit community fellowship and family visiting on Sundays. Others

Amish Church Structure and Leadership

As organized in North America, the Amish church was "congregational," that is, each congregation was independent of every other congregation. While the individual congregations helped, supported and communicated with one another quite extensively, they nonetheless had no *formal* national or regional organization. Before 1862, Amish church leaders' conferences, while important, were irregular and never included all Amish communities. Church hierarchy did not extend beyond the local congregation itself. Each congregation had its own leadership. The Amish church recognized four church offices:

1. *Völliger Diener* (Full Servant), or Bishop.

The bishop provided spiritual leadership for the congregation. Along with the preachers, a bishop took his regular turn in preaching Sunday morning sermons. More importantly, the bishop was authorized to perform baptisms, marriages and ordinations. Also, the holders of this office pronounced excommunication if and when the congregation expelled an unrepentant member. With the counsel of the congregation, bishops could also restore excommunicated persons to full church membership. In Europe this church office was known as *Aeltester* (Elder). The term "bishop" is a more recent English designation.

2. *Diener zum Buch* (Servant of the Book/Bible), or Preacher.

The preacher was to assist the bishop in preaching and teaching. Sometimes preachers were simply called "ministers."

3. *Völliger Armendiener* (Full Servant of the Poor), or Full Deacon.

The full deacon performed all the duties of a deacon (listed below), plus a number of additional ones. The full deacon assisted with baptisms, and in some places took a regular turn in preaching. Full deacons also served as guardians of doctrinal orthodoxy. They listened to the sermons of the bishops and preachers and corrected speakers later (in private) if sermons included false teaching. More common in Europe, the office of full deacon was rarely used in most of North American Amish history and is used today in only two Amish communities (Camden, Michigan and South Whitley, Indiana).

4. *Armendiener* (Servant of the Poor), or Deacon.

The deacon was to look after the physical welfare of the congregation. The deacon received donated funds from members which he kept in an "alms fund" and distributed to other needy ones in the church. During a Sunday morning church service he also read the assigned chapters from the Bible for that day. In addition, deacons assisted bishops in performing baptisms, administering communion and in dealing with matters of church discipline.

In many European Amish communities, church members elected leaders by a simple plurality of votes. Preachers and deacons were chosen from among the male members of the congregation. Bishops were then chosen from among the preachers, and full deacons from among the deacons. Leaders received no formal training and no pay.

In America it became common to chose church leaders not by simple vote, but by "lot." After the congregation had voted for persons to fill a particular position, all those who had received (usually) two or more votes would draw lots. Each candidate would choose a book from a row of specially prepared Bibles or hymnbooks, one of which included a slip of paper. Whoever drew the book which contained the paper lot was considered chosen of God and ordained. (The Lewis County, New York, Amish continued to use the process of simple election, instead of the lot, well into the nineteenth century.)

The church considered ordination a life calling. If a man moved, his ordination moved with him. Thus, some midwestern Amish congregations might end up with four or more bishops, if bishops from several areas migrated to the same place. Under normal circumstances, though, each congregation had only one bishop, two preachers and one deacon.

An Amish congregation held worship services every other Sunday. (The "in-between" Sundays were spent attending other Amish congregations which *were* having church, or visiting family and friends.) Services included singing, two prayers and Bible reading as well as a short "opening sermon," and a longer "main sermon." In addition, each ordained man present offered a response, or "testimony," to the biblical correctness of the sermons.

Twice yearly, before the spring and autumn communion services, each congregation had a council meeting. During council, members were to be reconciled with anyone in the group with whom they had a disagreement. Communion would only take place if and when *all* members who wished to participate were at peace with one another. Also, the congregation worked through any lingering or new questions regarding appropriate lifestyle and daily Christian conduct. All members in full agreement with the church's decisions could then commune together on Sunday. Council meetings greatly strengthened congregational unity and accountability.

When a congregation grew so large that it could no longer comfortably meet in its members' homes, it would divide into two smaller groups. Congregations always divided geographically, and eventually congregations even came to be called "districts" since members living in a given area made up a given congregation. In much of the literature on Amish church life, the term "district" is used in the same way that the term "congregation" would be used by Protestant denominations.

For a great deal more information, see Paton Yoder, *Tradition and Transition: Amish Mennonites and Old Order Amish, 1800-1900* (Scottdale, Pa. and Waterloo, Ont.: Herald Press, 1991), chps. 3-6; and Stephen E. Scott, *The Amish Wedding and Other Special Occasions of the Old Order Communities* (Intercourse, Pa.: Good Books, 1988).

were unsure of the doctrinal content of the school's materials. Still, the Logan County Sunday school continued; it had the support of its progressive-minded members.[44]

The nearby Champaign County Amish congregation, under the leadership of Preacher John Warye (1824-1903), soon established a Sunday school as well. An even more progressive group than the Logan County congregation, the Champaign County Amish also permitted members to drive more expensive closed carriages instead of the more common open buggies used by the Amish in those days. But even progressives drew the line at some point. When two young Pennsylvania Amishmen visited a Sunday service in Champaign County and began to show off their harmonic skills during a congregational song, "[Preacher] Warye rose to his feet, struck the pulpit desk with his fist, and commanded the congregation to stop and after his stern rebuke, 'Net Bass singa' [No bass singing!], he permitted the congregation to proceed."[45] Worshipers were to think about what—not how—they were singing.

For conservative Amish who could see the very real changes which the adoption of meetinghouses and Sunday schools portended, there seemed cause for worry. How far could the Amish go in organizing their church along secular models and still remain faithful? Since the Amish began they had been a church of earnest believers whose principles had guided their lives even when nonconformity to larger society was extremely unpopular. Conservatives correctly sensed that adopting styles and patterns from surrounding culture—be they new, more fashionable clothing trends or abstract, bureaucratic Christian education programs—weakened the church, since they did not grow naturally from an Amish understanding of faithful discipleship. Biblical teachings on humility, modesty, simplicity and faith did not easily fit with the aggressive American notion that whatever was bigger, newer and more expensive was always better.

Despite the growing rift between the more conservative and the relatively progressive Amish, the North American church remained united, with traditionalists and change-minded congregations generally recognizing one another and fellowshipping together. One exception was a small Mifflin County, Pennsylvania, Amish group under the leadership of Bishops Samuel B. King (1798-1876) and "Long Christian" Zook (1776-1851). After 1849, the King group broke all fellowship with the larger Amish church (except for a small Amish community in Lawrence County, Pennsylvania, with which they maintained contact). The exact disagreement between King's congregation and other Amish is no longer clear; however, the King group (later known as the "Byler Amish") represented a more conservative and traditional Amish lifestyle.[46]

Conservatives noticed that progressives did not stop with innovations in church life; change-minded Amish folks also seemed to be becoming more involved in the secular goings-on of larger American society. Increased business contacts among enterprising Amish in some cases blurred the line between the church and the world. Mississippi River steamboat owner and operator Henry Detweiler (1825-1903) managed to balance his social and business life with his Amish church's lifestyle expectations—for a time. Eventually, though, Henry and his wife Magdalena Bachman (1826-1888) were excommunicated from the Amish church because of their poor church attendance. They proved unable to fulfill their duties in both their church and their work.[47] And in other Amish communities, such as Wayne County, Ohio, running after the world's fads and fashions had even led some Amish to vainly pose and pay for photographs of themselves.

Amish involvement in larger society also included contact with those of other beliefs. After 1850, Waterloo County, Ontario, Bishop Peter Litwiller (1809-1878) served as his congregation's religious leader, while his neighbor, Father Eugene Funcken, was the spiritual overseer of the region's Roman Catholic population. Litwiller and Funcken became good friends, and were "known to frequently engage in religious discussion."[48] The priest even tolled his own church's bells for the older Amishman's funeral and wrote an account of Litwiller's life for the local newspaper.

The Amish did not actively recruit new members by means of verbal evangelism, but they nonetheless offered their religious views when asked. In 1843 when Preacher George Jutzi of Stark County, Ohio, went to Canton on business, he heard that an itinerant evangelist had just been through town and had caused quite a stir. With charts, tables and unique numerology, the evangelist had predicted the specific date on which Christ was to return. Jutzi met a local non-Amish couple who confessed confusion over this new teaching on the Second Coming and asked Jutzi's opinion. The Amish minister then spent about an hour talking with the two, refuting the teaching of the evangelist and carefully explaining the certain, but unpredictable future return of the Lord.[49]

Some contacts with other church groups proved detrimental to the Amish. A newly formed Swiss evangelical church, which came to be called the Apostolic Christian Church, drew converts from several Amish settlements.[50] In some areas, in fact, the new church became known as the "New Amish" after scores of former Amish church members joined them (see "The Apostolic Christian Church," p. 116). The Lewis County, New York, Amish community was especially hard hit. After 1847 the Amish church there lost not only a majority of its members, but also four preachers and a bishop, to the "New Amish." A few families chose to remain Amish, and with the resolute leadership of

Bishop Michael Zehr (1790-1880), maintained their own church tradition in the face of strong opposition.[51] "New Amish" congregations also sprang up in Woodford County, Illinois; Wayne and Fulton Counties, Ohio; Davis County, Iowa, and elsewhere. In each case many Amish joined them.

Innovations in church life, involvements in worldly business and ecumenical discussions pulled some of the Amish towards mainstream American national life. Engagements in government and politics marked yet another step in that direction. Though conservatives like David Beiler might warn and protest against too much accommodation with "the world," there was no doubt that many Amish were identifying more and more with larger American culture—including its system of political power and authority.

Democrats, Whigs, Republicans and Amish

Politics became something of an American national pastime during the second quarter of the nineteenth century. Beginning with the 1828 election of the "People's President," Andrew Jackson, more Americans took an active interest in politics. Political parties, organized on a local grass-roots level after about 1830, served as a popular channel for civic-minded Americans to involve themselves in their home communities. Tree stump speeches, torchlight parades and bonfire rallies became standard campaign fare as family, friends and neighbors debated the merits of electoral candidates. Democracy was popular.

Would the Amish involve themselves in this increasingly popular phase of the American experience? Several factors discouraged their participation. First, the entire political process was really directed towards English-speaking America. The Amish were bilingual (German dialect and English), to be sure, yet they were less in tune with the trends and tempo of larger American society, growing as it did out of an English-speaking culture. In this respect the Amish were no different from other ethnic immigrant groups which also tended to live on the edges of the American political scene during the period.

Moreover, important Amish beliefs tended to discourage involvement in politics. The sharp Anabaptist separation between church and state, along with a lingering Amish suspicion that governments were probably agents of persecution and harassment, made the Amish wary of entanglements with Caesar. The

1837 Amish ministers' meeting held in Somerset County, Pennsylvania, had emphatically declared that public office-holding, jury service and voting were all taboo. The very boastful and haughty nature of electoral politics smacked of pride—if not outright untruth.[52]

Yet despite these discouraging influences, some Amish did take an active part in local government. While it is impossible to know exactly how many Amish became involved in local politics, it is clear that enough did take part to greatly concern conservative Amish leaders across the country.[53]

One civic-minded Amishman was Christian Ebersol, Jr. (1814-1890). An immigrant of 1829, Ebersol lived most of his adult life in Lancaster County, Pennsylvania, where he remained a rather traditional and conservative member of his church. But Ebersol was also active in community affairs. He served as his township's first road supervisor, and later as one of its public school directors. Since his township had for a time seriously considered not supporting any schools at all, Ebersol's early involvement in school plans shows him to have had more confidence in public education than even many of his non-Amish neighbors.[54]

The Apostolic Christian Church

Sometimes associated with the Amish in America, the Apostolic Christian Church has its own rich, unique history. The church traces its beginnings to 1832, when Samuel Heinrich Froehlich (1803-1857), a Swiss Reformed Church theology student, questioned his church's doctrines and found himself excommunicated.

Froehlich traveled extensively through Switzerland and met with a multitude of disaffected churches, including a number of Mennonite congregations. Two Mennonite ministers who felt that the spiritual life of their own people was intolerably low joined Froehlich in gathering believers at Langau. Froehlich and his followers espoused the typical Mennonite teachings on adult baptism (but by immersion rather than pouring) and nonresistance to violence. Additionally they practiced excommunication and social shunning as a form of church discipline. Important for Froehlich and his group was a strong sense of inner Christian repentance, conversion and sanctification.

Persecuted and harassed, a number of the group left for America by the 1840s. The first members of the Froehlich church (which eventually came to be known as the Apostolic Christian Church) settled in Wayne County, Ohio, and Lewis County, New York—two communities with Amish populations. Especially in New York state, quite a few Amish persons left their church and united with the Froehlich group. Locally the new church was often nicknamed the "New Amish," both because many of its members were formerly Amish and because a number of the group's key doctrines seemed to mirror Amish practice.

Later, Apostolic Christian Church members established congregations in other Amish communities. The Amish who joined the Apostolic Christian Church seem to have been attracted by the group's warm piety, deep sense of a new birth, holy living and teaching on sanctification.

Today the Apostolic Christian Church, along with four smaller related groups, have a United States membership of about 16,000. Typical Amish and Mennonite surnames are still found in some Apostolic Christian congregations.

For more information, see Perry A. Klopfenstein, *Marching to Zion: A History of the Apostolic Christian Church of America, 1847-1982* (Fort Scott, Kans.: Sekan Printing Company, 1984).

Not only Ebersol—a product of nineteenth century Amish immigration—but also the descendants of the earlier eighteenth century Amish settlers became involved in civic activities. In Mifflin County, Pennsylvania, quite a number of Amish church members held local posts. Already in 1797 Abraham Yoder (c.1772-1813) served as a township road supervisor. The next year Christian Lantz (b. c.1751) and Christian Zook (1750-1805) were named public overseers of the poor. Historian S. Duane Kauffman has discovered about three dozen Amishmen who filled local government offices in Mifflin County through the 1840s.[55] While the Amish generally avoided law enforcement offices which required the use of violence, a number served as township supervisors, overseers of the poor, school directors, assessors,

Amish widow Maria von Gunden (1804-1892) immigrated from Europe to McLean County, Illinois, in 1859.

auditors, tax collectors and in one case, county commissioner.

Most notable was Mifflin County's Shem Zook (1798-1880), who not only served multiple terms in at least five different township and county offices, but also took an interest in political party machinery. Zook was one of several Mifflin County Amishmen who were active in both the Anti-Masonic and later, the Whig political parties. Both the "Anti-s" and the Whigs represented the conservative business interests of the day. Local lore preserves the folk legend that the Pennsylvania Railroad, so impressed with Zook's political savvy, asked the Amishman to run for governor after Zook successfully negotiated an important land deal for their track right-of-way.[56]

The McLean County, Illinois, Amish were also caught up in popular politics in the 1840s and '50s. Members held posts as township, road and school supervisors, and one Joseph W. Zook (1837-1915) served as justice of the peace. Most of the Amish who were active in Illinois politics supported the conservative Whig party, but the Hessian Amish were well-known supporters of the Democrats. After the Republican Party formed in 1854, it drew heavy McLean Amish support.[57]

Maverick Illinois Amish school teacher Joseph Joder (1797-1887) was an ardent Republican and abolitionist. Come election day, every "freedom-loving citizen," Joder wrote, was to "come forward to the ballot box and silently decide in favor of freedom." Among Joder's many non-Amish associates was a young lawyer named Abraham Lincoln. A number of Illinois Amish seem to have had casual contact with Honest Abe while he practiced law in the state. During the financial panic of 1857, when Amish Preacher Christian Farni (1800-1882) of McLean County became entangled in a fraudulent European-based investment scheme, it was Lincoln who offered Farni legal opinions and advice.[58]

Ironically, it was Lincoln's very election to the presidency which marked the limits of Amish political participation. With Lincoln in the White House the American Civil War seemed inevitable. How much farther could Amish participation in politics go? Until 1861 many Amish could be active in both their church and their state without noticing the underlying tension between the two. But when the state assumed the authority to decide life and death on the battlefield (much as it had earlier assumed the authority to authorize human slavery) the idolatrous claims of Washington, D.C., could no longer be ignored. Having identified with the American nation through their political participation, would civic-minded Amish now fulfill *all* their duties as citizens?

Uncivil War

The April 1861 shooting between Charleston, South Carolina, and Fort Sumter marked the beginning of the violent and bitter struggle between North and South. Nearly all the Amish lived in what was considered northern territory, and many had sympathies for the ruling northern party, the Republicans. Moreover, the Amish had never been friends of slavery (although virtually none had taken an active part in the abolitionist movement, either). How would they now respond to a divided nation which had exhausted compromise and demanded that its citizens choose sides?

Some Amish families ended up as fractured as the country. In Woodford County, Illinois, for example, two sons of Amish Bishop Johannes and Barbara Gerber Gingerich chose different paths. While Peter Gingerich (1826-1866) refused military induction, in 1862 his older brother Christian (1823-1895) enlisted in the Union army. For men such as Christian, the Union cause was so clearly justified that religious duty seem to all but *require* joining in the fray. But for Peter and others, killing could never be justified—even as a means to a greater good.[59]

Christian was not alone among his people in marching with the Yankees. Some Amish had become so accustomed to military service in Europe that they may not have even seen the American war as a matter of conscience. Amishman J. Emile Strubhar (1844-1915), in fact, joined the Northern army so as to more quickly become a U.S. citizen after the hostilities would cease. Already at home in the American social and political milieu, Valentine Nafziger, of Hessian Amish background, served in the military both during and after the war, and then joined a national veterans' organization.[60]

It is probably impossible to know how many Amish men joined the regular fighting forces of the Union army. Most seem to have used the legal means available to avoid such service.[61] State, and later federal, draft laws offered at least two ways in which men could free themselves of their military obligations—either by hiring substitutes to muster in their place, or by paying a fee (usually $300).

Paying the commutation fee was "the most well-defined and consistent response of the Amish church to the draft laws of the war period," according to historian Paton Yoder.[62] In some cases, young Amishmen hired substitutes to fill their draft calls. Yet not all Amish leaders approved of the practice of using substitutes. While admitting that substitution was widespread in his own congregation, an Amish bishop in Iowa harshly criticized the practice as hypocritical[63] (see "Jacob Schwarzendruber Speaks Out During the Civil War," p. 122). And years after the war was over, John S. Stoltzfus (1828-1902) of Lancaster County, Pennsylvania, still kept as a tragic reminder the uniform which his draft substitute had worn before dying in battle.[64]

Even for those not liable for the draft, community pressure to join in the war's spirit was a challenge. In Wayne County, Ohio, public coercion to contribute money to a so-called "Voluntary Fund" for the war was intense. While Wayne County's nonresistant Mennonites contributed heavily, the Amish there were much less willing to give and better resisted the community's pressure.[65]

For other Amish the war's deepest impressions came not so much from the conscription of man and money, as from the stark realities of the war itself. The war left many deep memories which eventually became often-repeated family tales. After stealing a wagon load of wheat from a Hickory County, Missouri, farmer, Southern troops forced teenage Christian Raber of the area's local Amish community, to haul the grain some thirty or forty miles in Raber's father's wagon. A frightening experience, it was not Raber's last run-in with troops. During the war's later years, an intoxicated Union soldier stopped the wagon which young Raber and a friend were driving. Not satisfied with the answers which the Amish boys gave his questions, the soldier shot and killed Raber's traveling companion. "Very shaken," Raber drove the twelve miles home with his friend's body. The soldier was later acquitted of wrongdoing and given an honorable discharge.[66]

Soldiers also forced Amishman Christian Petersheim (1826-1897) of Aurora, West Virginia, to haul supplies for weeks—meanwhile his family did not know whether he was dead or alive.[67] And the Amish of Davis County, Iowa, never forgot the fall 1864 morning when Southern sympathizers from nearby Missouri rode through their community—stealing and looting from barns and homes. Such was war, even among neighbors.[68]

"Who Is There That Has Not Deserved it?"

The American Civil War was the bloodiest, most costly conflict in United States history. Beyond the physical and financial toll, some contemporaries saw in the war a great moral purpose. On March 4, 1865, at his second inauguration, Abraham Lincoln reflected on the meaning of the war and concluded that perhaps God was teaching America a lesson through all the death and destruction. In the form of war, the sin of tolerating slavery had visited its curse upon the Union, the president suggested.

Three months and two days later, Amish Bishop Jacob Schwarzendruber (1800-1868) of Johnson County, Iowa, expressed somewhat similar thoughts in a letter to fellow Amish church leaders. Schwarzendruber saw God using the war to test the faithfulness of the church. "The war in this country is a permission or a sending of God to punish the people because of their sins," the bishop wrote, unknowingly repeating the president's idea. "And who is there that has not deserved it"?

Bishop Jacob Schwarzendruber Speaks Out During the Civil War

During the American Civil War, several state and federal conscription laws allowed a draftee to hire a substitute to serve in the draftee's place. Apparently a number of Amish young men bought substitutes and used this legal loophole to avoid military induction. Not all Amish were comfortable with the ethics of such an arrangement. Amish Bishop Jacob Schwarzendruber of Johnson County, Iowa, expressed his strong opposition to the practice in a letter composed in the late spring of 1865, after the war's conclusion:

"Concerning the draft, or buying volunteer substitutes or paying volunteers to send them out to fight, I hold that it is wrong according to God's Word and the teaching of Jesus and the apostles. . . .

"Are we then still nonresistant according to the teachings of Jesus and the apostles who have proclaimed to us the perfect will of the Father? . . . 'Whoso sheddeth man's blood, by man shall his blood be shed,' for God made man in his image [Genesis 9:6]. So we do not want to go ourselves or to pay others that they would go. How is this right before the eyes of God? . . . The Saviour's teaching is not as we have done, that we should be permitted to buy substitutes or help pay for people and let them go to kill others.

"Are we then still nonresistant? Jesus says* in Luke chapter

3 verse 14 to the soldier, 'Do violence or injustice to no man.' Dare I then pay someone to do injustice? Matthew 5:7, 'Blessed are the merciful for they shall obtain mercy,' and this is before the righteous judge, and how unmerciful things go in war with those who have never harmed us, and are also created after the image of God. Do we do right then voluntarily to support the war with money and to vote for those who want to make war? All vengeance is forbidden to the follower of Jesus.
. . . Jesus says 'Love your enemies, bless them that persecute you, do good to them that hate you, pray for those who despitefully use you and persecute you, then we shall be the children of the heavenly Father.' . . . [In Acts 7:60] Stephen prayed for those who stoned him, and what do we do? We send people to fight. Are we then still nonresistant? . . .

*The quotation is from John the Baptist. Schwarzendruber used a loose citation which viewed all of the New Testament in harmony with and reflecting the teachings of Jesus.
Excerpted from Harold S. Bender, ed. and trans., "An Amish Bishop's Conference Epistle of 1865" *The Mennonite Quarterly Review* 20 (July 1946): 222-29.

The lesson for the Amish was far too clear to Schwarzendruber. His church had gradually become more worldly and progressive, too much involved in an American culture which included injustice and war. As a result the Amish were now in part responsible for the nation's tragic calamity. "Our people should all keep themselves apart from all party matters in political things," he warned, "where brother votes against brother and father against son." Entangled in the war machinery, the Amish church had "departed from the example of Jesus and the martyrs," he feared.[69] Conservatives like Schwarzendruber believed that the tragedy of the Civil War demanded the remorse, repentance and reform of the Amish church.

Half a continent to the east, in Lancaster County, Pennsylvania, seventy-six-year-old Bishop David Beiler had already seen God's judgment in the war's events. "Perhaps with war and strife and bloodshed," Beiler thought, Providence was teaching the Amish church to live more simply and obediently. The first half of the nineteenth century had been a time of material and social prosperity among the Amish, Beiler was sure. But, he wondered, in having "everything in abundance according to natural things," had some Amish "become forgetful of the great goodness of God?" Looking back over some sixty years of American Amish history, he saw a struggle within his church which reminded him of the schism between the American North and South. Just as two different sections of the nation had years before chosen divergent political paths, so also, two groups within the Amish church—the conservatives and the progressives—had chosen incompatible ways of living and participating in American society.[70] The nation had divided. Could the church hope for more?

Beiler's observations were to the point. The Amish in North America, both the descendants of the eighteenth century immigrants and the new arrivals of the 1800s, had prospered abundantly. Their prosperity stemmed in a large part from their own beliefs and practices: simplicity, community, mutual aid. But American prosperity had also led them to a fork in the road, with one path leading toward greater integration into North American society and the other pointing toward some type of separatism. For many of the Amish the choice became especially acute in the 1860s, the same decade in which the United States painfully struggled to remain united. The Amish church also struggled—and ultimately divided.

— 7 —
Years of Division, 1850-1878

> "In many places patience has grown cold."
> — *Open letter from a group of Amish ministers, 1861*

Decades of Dissension

As the Amish church approached mid-century it seemed to be on a collision course with North American culture. While many Amish had immigrated to the New World to escape the pressure and influence of European culture, once in America the Amish— like all other minority groups—had to decide how much they would allow their new homeland to shape them. Since the mid-1700s some Amish had been adapting quickly to American ideals and ways of doing things, while others tried to maintain their values in the face of their host society.

At times these new North American ideas caused a considerable amount of tension with Amish faith understanding. Individual freedom of choice, for example, was a very important American cultural tenet, but one which clashed with the historic Amish concern for community authority and group commitment.[1] Bold faith in human progress, achievement and education drove Americans to conquer a continent, produce secular self-government and place a profound hope in the abilities of improved technology. For the Amish, on the other hand, commitment to the church kept migration for the most part in family groups; separation from the world entailed less-than-full participation in politics; and simplicity and modesty cautioned against always striving for the bigger, the better and the newer.

Yet some Amish strongly felt the pull of the larger culture. The push for change and the pull of tradition troubled many Amish congregations. After 1850 the tension within some Amish church districts split the groups in two.

The third quarter of the nineteenth century was a time of unparalleled disagreement, dissension and schism among the Amish. While the Amish church was still nominally united in the 1850s, twenty-five years later the controversies had caused severe divisions. The events of those years remarkably influenced the later history of the Amish; the results of the decisions and divisions of the 1850s, '60s and '70s are still obvious more than a century later. Those Amish who resisted the forces of American progressivism and modernization were able to maintain a distinctive, viable way of life. Those who chose the way of social accommodation and adaption eventually became indistinguishable from larger American society.[2]

Background of the Controversy

While this period of time is very important for understanding Amish history, it is often confusing and difficult to describe. One reason for the vagueness associated with the internal Amish division is that no single division took place. The division which eventually touched virtually all Amish communities worked its way out in different places and at different times. "Sorting out" might be a better way to describe the divisive process. For while the Amish in northern Indiana broke into tradition-minded and change-minded factions by 1860, the Ontario Amish did not divide until the 1880s, and the church in Iowa split only in the 1890s. The division among the Amish was more of a *process* than a single schism.

Also important for understanding the debate within the Amish church after midcentury was the Amish idea of church order, or *Ordnung*.[3] The *Ordnung* embodied the teachings and practices of the church, defined members' lifestyle and conduct, and served to unify the highly congregational Amish church. Without a hierarchy or systematic, scholarly theology, it was the common order of life and practice which held the Amish church together. The Amish *Ordnung* included such general principles as "modesty" and "simplicity," and such specific applications as wearing certain plain clothes and avoiding costly, showy household furniture. The *Ordnung* was generally not a written code or rule book, but rather a tradition of order and life which evolved slowly over time and did allow for gradual, thought-through changes. (Occasionally a regional ministers' meeting or a local congregation published a brief, written *Ordnung*, but these documents were never all-inclusive and usually summed only important or controversial points.)

During the mid-nineteenth century, the purpose of church order became unclear. For some Amish, church order was something with which to tamper only very carefully and cautiously. For other Amish, the *Ordnung* was a more dynamic principle which guided change and certainly did not prohibit innovation. The conservatives saw a very direct connection between faith and practice. For them the *Ordnung* gave physical expression to biblical teachings and virtues. For the progressives, those teachings and virtues could be expressed in a number of different ways in an ever changing world; the Amish *Ordnung* merely embodied biblical ideals which in turn guided selective change. Different views on order and change necessarily led to a division in the Amish church.[4] With a common *Ordnung* as the church's only organizational glue, disagreement on the purpose and use of *Ordnung* naturally led to unavoidable fracture in the Amish church.

Clouds of Controversy Gather

After about 1850 several undeniable problems surfaced in various Amish communities. Northern Indiana, eastern Ohio and central Pennsylvania were the hotbeds of discontent during that decade and ripples of their dissension at times disturbed the shores of other more peaceful Amish communities. In no case were these early controversies by themselves enough to split the entire church, but each one signaled the growing tension which would eventually divide the whole fellowship. As precursors for the coming schism, these difficulties were significant.

Already in the late 1840s trouble surfaced in Northern Indiana. The first Amish settlers had arrived in Elkhart and Lagrange Counties in 1841, from Ohio and Pennsylvania. Soon it became clear that most of those Amish with roots in Ohio (most of whom settled in Elkhart County) were less conservative and tradition-minded than many of those from Pennsylvania (who by-and-large ended up in Lagrange). When the Elkhart-Lagrange church grew too large to comfortably meet in its members' homes, it separated into two church districts—one in each county—and the two factions became even more distinct.[5]

Under the progressive leadership of Bishops Isaac Schmucker and Jonas D.Troyer (1811-1897), the Elkhart County Amish had

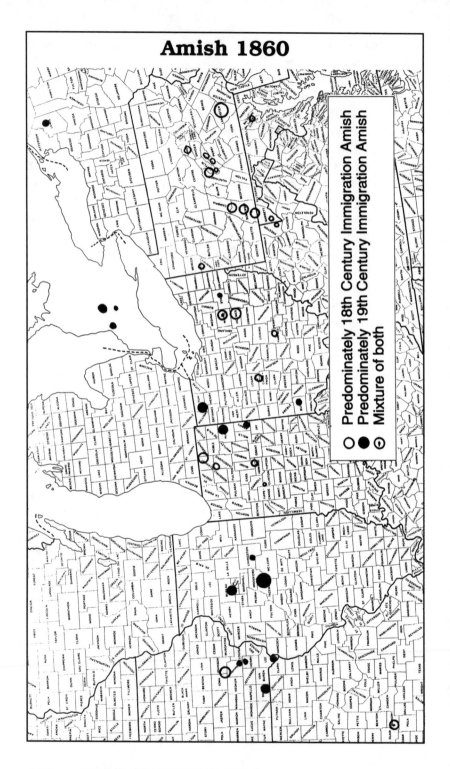

Amish 1860

Predominately 18th Century Immigration Amish
Predominately 19th Century Immigration Amish
Mixture of both

tolerated expensive, fancy clothing, more formal and extended education, and the holding of government offices. All such innovations were prime examples of the struggle to fit into a host society. How better to become accepted fellow citizens than to dress and work like one's neighbors and become involved in public life? To the more tradition-minded Lagrange Amish, such innovations smacked of compromise and an undermining of the Christian values of simplicity, humility and community decision-making. As conservative Lagrange County Amishman John "Hansi" E. Borntreger (1837-1930) interpreted the events of the late 1840s, "Most of the church members were in harmony with their [conservative] ministers, but several preachers . . . and part of the church . . . had much to say in opposition, causing the faithful ones much concern and grief."[6] Borntreger believed that the liberals had drifted from their biblical foundation and had simply "started a new church according to their own opinions."[7]

The deep difference of opinion in northern Indiana was not yet a schism. Both groups still recognized one another and hoped that the other would see its way to reconciliation. Even Borntreger himself occasionally attended the worship services of his more progressive Amish neighbors. Yet, in retrospect, the seeds of division had been planted and were growing. The different perspectives obvious in each Amish group could hardly be covered over or expected to go away. To the change-minded Amish, selective innovation was a means of making the church relevant and appealing in a new and constantly changing world. For the Amish opposed to such adaptation, the Elkhart County innovations represented a lack of commitment and faith. Was not the church to be different from "the world" in both faith and life?

Controversies in Pennsylvania and Ohio mirrored in some ways the Indiana conflict. In the two eastern states the disagreement began over the proper mode of baptism. Some argued for baptism in a stream while others held to a traditional type of baptism performed in the context of an indoor church service. While the Amish on both sides of the issue eventually compromised and recognized both modes of baptism as equally legitimate, the division in those communities persisted—largely because the baptism dispute had always been a symbolic issue anyway. On a deeper level those who championed stream baptism also tended toward a more progressive, innovative church life, while those who favored baptism among fellow church

Bishop Joseph Stuckey of Danvers, Illinois.

members in a home were more cautious about having the church try to catch up with and adapt to its surrounding culture. For example, Mifflin County stream-baptism advocate Shem Zook was also involved in politics, writing and publishing, and big business contacts with major railroad companies. Similarly, the Wayne County proponent of stream-baptism was Bishop Jacob D. Yoder (c.1821-1878), who engaged in shady business deals, raced mules, traded in horses and held to a heretical interpretation of the biblical story of Adam and Eve. (According to contemporaries, Yoder taught that the sin of the first humans was not disobedience to God's command, but only lying.[8])

Clearly, conservatives thought that they had something to worry about when change-minded Amish began to introduce new things. Even a new form of baptism (which the conservatives never rejected categorically) appeared to be merely the first step toward wholesale involvement in society and, in the case of Bishop Yoder, even heresy. Tampering with the *Ordnung* which regulated baptism unsettled other beliefs and practices. The stiff resistance to change on the part of some Amish grew out of a realization that humans cannot easily make selective changes; choosing to adapt in one area of life often leads to unforseen and undesirable changes in another.

Even though the Indiana, Ohio and Pennsylvania controversies of the 1850s did not result in out-right breaks of fellowship between conservatives and progressives, the tension between the two groups grew. While the change-minded and tradition-minded Amish recognized one another as Amish, they also recognized that they could not much longer overlook the growing gap which separated them. As Lancaster County's David Beiler observed in 1862, "The split appears to be becoming almost irreparable."[9] It was during this time of uncertainty and confusion that conservatives proposed an innovative idea.

Diener-Versammlungen

Two conservative Amish bishops proposed that the Amish hold a national gathering of Amish church leaders—a *Diener-Versammlung* (ministers' meeting). The ministers' meeting would address the specific problems irritating particular communities, as well as set a national course for a return to unity of belief and practice among North American Amish. The meeting would hopefully set the direction and tone of future church activity and slow the pace of damaging change. Working together—in the best tradition of Amish community—the church could set out a clear, united witness to a Christian life of humility, dedication, service and peace. In short, a *Diener-Versammlung* could reassert the importance of practical *Ordnung*.

Already in 1851 David Beiler had written to a fellow bishop in Holmes County, Ohio, that Beiler had "often thought that a church-wide ministers' meeting" would be very helpful. Such a meeting could serve as a forum for discussion, but more importantly as a setting in which the whole church, together, could "take the Word of God as the plumbline" and come to unity.[10] In the past, regional ministers' meetings in Europe and America had proved to be gatherings which strengthened church life and commitment. At times they had even produced written guidelines outlining agreed-upon principles and practices. Presumably Beiler thought that a national meeting of the same type would reunify the Amish around traditional values. Dissension and division might dry up if church leaders from around the United States and Canada met together to re-affirm Amish distinctives. Similarly, Holmes County Bishop Frederick Hege (1794-1863) had also suggested that a general ministers' conference could settle local problems, such as those that grew up in his part of eastern Ohio. Like Beiler, Hege was a tradition-minded man.[11]

A national Amish leaders' meeting was a novel solution to the problems facing the church at mid-century. While the Amish had used local or regional group conferences to address issues in the past, no meeting had ever been national in scope. Nor had a meeting ever set out to address the general question of church direction and future; past gatherings had looked at specific problems only. But although the idea was originally that of Amish conservatives, it fell to a moderately-progressive Amish deacon to call the first ministers' conference. Deacon John Stoltzfus (1805-1887) served the Amish church in eastern Lancaster County Pennsylvania. While he never broke with the conservative church while he lived there, John and his wife Catherine Holly Stoltzfus later moved to Tennessee where Deacon "Tennessee" John allied himself with the change-minded Amish. On March 8, 1861, Stoltzfus issued an "Open Letter to Amish Church Leaders" in which he suggested that a national conference of Amish leaders meet and "put together and achieve [an agreement] suitable to the peace and forbearance of the Gospel."[12]

Another document, perhaps representing a formal response to Stoltzfus on the part of other leaders, recorded the feelings of fellow ordained men. "It is now the case," the second letter stated, "that in many places patience has grown cold, so much so that neglect and division have crept in."[13] This second letter

The *Diener-Versammlungen*

The Amish *Diener-Versammlungen* (ministers' meetings) met annually from 1862 until 1878 (except 1877). The chart shows the location, moderator and registered attendance of each meeting. In addition to the registered bishops, preachers and deacons who participated in the ministers' meetings, up to fifteen hundred interested Amish laymen and -women attended some of the proceedings. Full Deacon (later Bishop) Samuel Yoder (1824-1884) of Mifflin County, Pennsylvania, was the only leader who attended every gathering.

The *Diener-Versammlung* was always held in either May or June. Except for the 1864 meeting, all were held around Pentecost. Bishop Abner Yoder (1814-1883) of Somerset County, Pennsylvania (later moved to Johnson County, Iowa), was the only moderator who eventually sided with the Old Order Amish; all of the other moderators chose the Amish Mennonite path.

	Location	Moderator	Registered Attendance
1862	Wayne Co., Ohio	Jonathan Yoder	72
1863	Mifflin Co., Pennsylvania	Abner Yoder	42
1864	Elkhart Co., Indiana	John K. Yoder	71
1865	Wayne Co., Ohio	unknown	89
1866	McLean Co., Illinois	Samuel Yoder	75
1867	Logan Co., Ohio	Elias Riehl	42
1868	Mifflin Co., Pennsylvania	John K. Yoder	34
1869	Holmes Co., Ohio	Samuel Yoder	27
1870	Fulton Co., Ohio	John P. King	40
1871	Livingston Co., Illinois	Samuel Yoder	56
1872	Lagrange Co., Indiana	John P. King	56
1873	Wayne Co., Ohio	Samuel Yoder	41
1874	Washington Co., Iowa	John K. Yoder	28
1875	Tazewell Co., Illinois	John P. King	38
1876	Fulton Co., Ohio	Samuel Yoder	30
1877	not held		
1878	Woodford Co., Illinois	John K. Yoder	43

suggested meeting in Holmes County, Ohio, later that same year. For unknown reasons the gatherings did not take place for another nine months and then in a different county. These early letters implied that such a national ministers' meeting should become an annual event, and for nearly seventeen years it was.

The first all-church Amish ministers' meeting convened in Wayne County, Ohio, on June 9-12, 1862.[14] Seventy-two leaders registered and participated in the proceedings. More than half were from Ohio, but leaders from five other states were also present. Many lay members attended the sessions (in 1862 more than 400, according to Deacon Stoltzfus), but did not participate in the discussions or vote. The large number of persons prohibited the meeting from being held in a house, so the group met in the barn of Amishman Samuel Schrock (1820-1893). Many attendees arrived by train, taking advantage of the good network of rails in the northern United States.

From the start, the ministers' conferences tended to favor the change-minded Amish agenda. Both the first year's moderator, Bishop Jonathan Yoder (1795-1869) from McLean County, Illinois, and the assistant moderator, Bishop John Esh (1807-1879) of Juniata County, Pennsylvania, were well-known Amish progressives. The remarkable layman Shem Zook of Mifflin County, Pennsylvania, served as the first recording secretary. As for the allegiance of the rest of the registrants, not only did progressive leaders attend in greater numbers (about fifty of the seventy-two could be considered change-minded), but conservative Holmes County Bishop Levi Miller (1799-1884) charged that not all the tradition-minded church districts had been informed of the meeting and had thus been left out.[15] Miller's charge was only partly true; conservative David Beiler and other Lancaster County bishops and ministers, for instance, stayed away from the meeting on purpose. Although Beiler had originally suggested the ministers' meeting, he soon sensed that it might just become a vehicle for bringing *more* change into the church rather than creating a unified front against it.

The proceedings of the *Diener-Versammlung* were rather informal. Sessions opened with sermons—these being the highlight for many participants who otherwise had little opportunity to hear bishops or preachers from other states. Issues or problems brought to the conference received floor discussion and debate. Special committees took up important questions and drew up

Amishman Christian Sutter's barn (built 1868), near Hopedale, Illinois. The 1875 Diener-Versammlung *met in the barn.*

written responses which they then presented to the larger group. The first two annual meetings used an informal consensus method to approve or reject committee findings, but by 1864 the ministers' meeting was using a system of majority vote.[16] One major limitation of the conference was the inability of the group to carry out its decisions. Because the Amish retained their independent congregational authority at a very local level, congregations which disagreed with a particular ministers' meeting decision could simply ignore it.[17]

The first meetings were somewhat successful in restoring unity to the badly strained Amish communities in Indiana, Ohio and central Pennsylvania. The local difficulties appeared to find resolution, or so attenders thought at the time. Although the change-minded and traditional Amish within those communities eventually went their separate ways, immediately after 1862 some Amish were optimistic that the annual meetings might bring harmony. Said the 1863 proceedings, "there is hope for healing."[18] On the practical question of defining the roles of the deacon and full deacon (hotly debated in Logan and Champaign Counties, Ohio, and Mifflin County, Pennsylvania), the first few ministers' meetings were also helpful in establishing guidelines.[19] Moreover, the annual gathering *was* united in its feeling toward and response to the liberal Hessian Amish of Butler County, Ohio. So long as the Hessians insisted on using worldly musical instruments, other Amish—traditionalists and progressives alike—would not fellowship with them nor assist them in ordaining new leadership.[20] Neither would ministers' conference participants approve of joining a state militia, holding membership in secret societies or posing for photographs (picture-taking was a sure sign of vanity and pride, and might even be a form of graven images prohibited by the Ten Commandments).[21]

Despite the hard line which the annual meetings took with the Hessians and a few other expressions of popular culture, many conservatives were deeply disappointed with the tone and outcome of conference discussions and committee reports. On the question of social shunning, long a New Testament doctrine taught by the Amish, some ministers' meeting resolutions and committee reports at times seemed to waffle.[22] The conferences also refused to forbid political participation.[23] Moreover, the suggested way of bringing peace to most disagreements tended to be asking conservatives to be more tolerant of changes.

"It seems to me that each was allowed to have his own opinion," David Beiler concluded after hearing reports of the conferences. Perceptively, Beiler saw that the so-called peace achieved by the ministers' conferences was really "a conciliatory spirit without coming to the point which was and is the real reason for the differing views." The annual meetings addressed a few symptoms without ever dealing with the deep underlying disagreements between the conservative and change-minded points of view. "If we wish to destroy a weed," Beiler said, drawing on agricultural imagery, "we must pull it up by the roots; otherwise it will just keep growing." Certainly "if the causes of offense are not put away, then, according to my opinion, no real unity can be restored."[24] The growing tension between the two halves of the Amish church was building, not lessening, in the wake of the national Amish ministers' meetings.

1865

Originally designed to bring unity and harmony to the church, the Amish ministers' conferences seemed to simply point up the great gulf which separated the church's members. With the change-minded group in control of the national forum, many conservatives felt ignored by the *Diener-Versammlungen* which they had begun attending in good faith. In 1864 a group of tradition-minded Amish leaders met in Lancaster County to try their hand at solving the tension in their state's Mifflin County Amish community. That gathering fared no better than the national conference, but it did demonstrate that the conservatives were interested in working as a group to address the divisions in their church; they were not simply ignoring the problems at hand.[25]

Quite disturbing to conservatives was that year's national meeting. The gathering went ahead and "settled" the disagreement between northern Indiana conservatives and progressives before all the tradition-minded leaders from Ohio had even arrived.[26] The conservatives felt betrayed.

The following year, tradition-minded Amish leaders made one final, bold attempt to put their views before the larger Amish church for response. The 1865 ministers' meeting met again in Wayne County, Ohio—home to a sizable progressive Amish community. Just to the south in Holmes County, most of the Amish were more tradition-minded. Thirty-four conservative Amish leaders gathered in Holmes County several days before the official *Diener-Versammlung*. The conservatives represented Amish from Ohio, Indiana, Ontario and western Pennsylvania. The gathering drew up a statement much in the tradition of the *Ordnung* statements which had come from regional ministers' gatherings in the decades past. The Holmes County statement served as a type of "manifesto" of the conservative Amish position. The conservatives took a firm stand against that which was "destructive to . . . salvation and contrary to God's Word." Many popular and widely accepted social practices which were tempting the Amish church, in truth "serve to express pomp and pride," they said. Worse still, they "lead away from God."[27]

As a result Christians should, in the thought of the conservatives, separate themselves from worldly carnivals, the pride and wasted expense of "speckled, striped, flowered, clothing," from "unnecessary, gorgeous, household furnishings," and "pompous carriages." Activities which tore away at the fabric of church community or stymied the practice of mutual aid—such as commercial property insurance or operating large-scale businesses "according to the ways of the world"—were taboo for the tradition-minded group. The conservative Amish also addressed church practice, warning against lax church discipline and the

Too Much Money in the Offering?

In order to cover conference expenses, the later Amish Mennonite annual ministers' meetings collected free-will offerings
from attenders. In 1873, the man charged with collecting and
counting the funds was shocked by the huge donation one
member had contributed. Several months later Amish Mennonite leaders ran the following advertisement in the Mennonite
periodical *Herald of Truth* (which many Amish Mennonites
read):

"Notice.—At the collection taken at the Amish Conference,
held this year, near Orrville, [Wayne County] Ohio, a twenty
dollar bill was thrown in. Bro. Jacob King, who received it,
thinks the giver probably made a mistake. If so it will be
returned to the claimant giving satisfactory evidence that he
was the giver."

From *Herald of Truth*, 10 (September 1873): 152.

singing of catchy, popular hymns with spiritually shallow lyrics.

There was no doubting the purpose of the statement; it defined
the terms under which the tradition-minded Amish were willing
to work without compromise. Its authors clearly stated that "all
those who affirm such with us and demonstrate with works and
deeds we are willing to recognize as brothers and sisters and
resume fellowship with them. . . ." Hard-hitting and specific as
the document was, it ended with a marvelous invitation and
spiritual openness. The conservatives desired nothing more
than a spiritual renewal to result from their call for separation
from sin and they recognized that what they called for absolutely
required the enabling grace which God offered to anyone who
would follow. So the statement closed: "And the gate is portrayed
for us as straight and the way as narrow, but is not therefore ever
closed, but stands open for all repentant souls, and as the Savior
says in Luke 14:33, 'Whoever does not forsake all that he has
cannot be my disciple.'"

With their clearly stated position in hand, nearly all of the
thirty-four signatories headed north to the 1865 annual meeting
in Wayne County. The conference was the best ever attended,

with eighty-nine leaders registered. Also unique to this assembly was the number of tradition-minded Amish who attended—about forty percent of total registrants. Never before had so many conservatives been present. The printed proceedings of the 1865 meeting are the least clear of any of the conferences' recordings, so it is somewhat difficult to determine an exact order of events. Apparently the ministers' meeting took up the conservatives' paper near the end of its business session and did little with it.[28] While no formal statement on the part of the Holmes County conferees survives, it appears that they were bitterly disappointed by the outcome of the national conference. Only a very few conservative Amish leaders ever attended an annual meeting again. Ignored out of their church, the traditionalists withdrew from the activities of the Amish majority. (It is impossible to say how many Amish sided with the conservatives, but later estimates put the number at about a third of the Amish congregations.)

The year 1865 became a symbolic point of separation between change-minded and tradition-minded Amish. In some communities, it took quite some time until the Amish "sorted out" into one of the two camps. For example, the Amish in Ontario and some parts of Iowa remained largely single, united groups until the 1880s and '90s. Only then did the split between the conservatives and change-minded Amish become large enough to actually divide the two. In 1877 the Lancaster County, Pennsylvania, Amish community experienced division, but most of the members sided with the conservatives. In central Illinois nearly the opposite situation transpired: all the Amish congregations there chose the course of change.

Because the conservatives had defined their concerns in terms of the traditional understanding of Ordnung (the "old order"), others eventually labeled them the "Old Order Amish."[29] Meanwhile the change-minded group eventually had closer and closer relations with the Mennonites, many of whom felt a close affinity for the tolerant, change-minded attitude of the Amish progressives. The Amish majority received the designation "Amish Mennonite." After the 1865 ministers' meeting, the terms "Old Order Amish" and "Amish Mennonite" designate the two major paths which members of the Amish church chose. Strictly speaking, these titles were not labels as such by that date, but the division between the two groups was undeniable after the

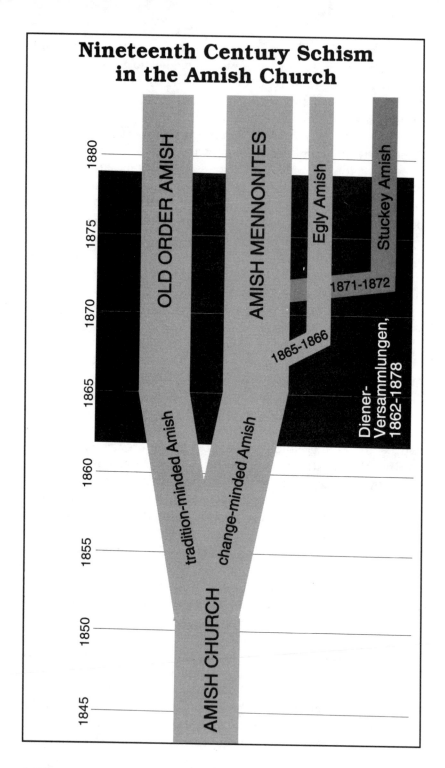

Nineteenth Century Schism in the Amish Church

OLD ORDER AMISH

AMISH MENNONITES

Egly Amish

Stuckey Amish

1871-1872

1865-1866

tradition-minded Amish

change-minded Amish

Diener-Versammlungen, 1862-1878

AMISH CHURCH

1845 1850 1855 1860 1865 1870 1875 1880

Wayne County ministers' conference. The change-minded group (Amish Mennonite) and the conservatives (Old Order Amish) were clearly going their separate ways.

Later Ministers' Meetings

Twelve more national meetings followed the 1865 gathering. Except for 1877, the meetings continued annually. During those later years attendance varied from a high of seventy-five to a low of twenty-seven. The meetings continued to draw large crowds of lay members, often to hear the preaching of visiting ministers. After 1865, however, the nature of the conferences changed in a small, but important way.

The ministers' meetings had begun as mass consultations which had set out to bring unity and sense of purpose to the Amish church. Having only partial participation after 1865, the meetings took on a more formal, deliberative—almost legislative—flavor. More rules of order came into place and references to past proceedings became more common.[30] In 1867, for example, the conference "decided that all rulings of former meetings are in force at the present" (unless proved otherwise by Scripture). Moreover, "no minister who is a participant in the assembly shall have the right to make any changes afterward."[31] The Amish Mennonites chose to address issues on a case-by-case basis, but they did so in a more formal way. The Old Order Amish, in contrast, had outlined a good number of out-right prohibitions and rules in 1865, but handled the specific application of that *Ordnung* in the more informal and personal setting of individual congregations. The Amish Mennonites were again adapting (in a very limited way) values and methods from larger American society. A measure of tolerance and a method of formal structure marked their decision-making process. While the Amish Mennonites never gave up church discipline entirely nor established elaborate denominational bureaucracy, they had moved a bit farther in that direction than did the Old Order Amish who maintained a more tradition-guided, but informally managed, church life.

Despite their adaptation (to some degree) of North American methods of organization and decision-making, the Amish Mennonites found themselves rejecting other aspects of American national life. The Civil War had left a number of new questions with which the Amish had to wrestle. Could nonresistant Christians contribute toward the building of war monuments and memorials? The 1867 *Diener-Versammlung* said no.[32] The next year, the Amish Mennonite gathering responded to inquiries for church membership from a veteran who was receiving a government pension. The ministers' meeting decided that the applicant could become a church member if he broke all ties with the military—including his pension. The church was to cover his living expenses if he was disabled.[33] And what of Grange membership? The Grange was a popular midwestern farmers' union formed to fight for rural rights as well as organize social fun and recreation in farm communities. The Amish Mennonites rejected Grange membership.[34]

The ministers' conferences continued to address issues peculiar to the Amish church as well, such as the type and manner of church discipline, modesty in dress and the extent to which members could grow wealthy by patenting inventions.[35] Modera-

Excerpts from the Proceedings of the Amish *Diener-Versammlungen*

1863: "Should likenesses [photographs] be permitted?" [Answer:] "It was decided almost unanimously that they [the delegates] want to repell this thing [photography]."

1866: "May a person who, for the sake of worldly income, produces intoxicating beverages . . . be considered a useful member of the congregation?" [Answer:] "It was looked upon as improper and it would throw a bad light on the church. We would be much better off to avoid it and stay away from such drinking places and avoid the bad results which follow. For at such places chains, nets, and snares are set up in order to catch innocent souls."

1867: May church members contribute toward the building of Civil War monuments "which cost thousands of dollars, and benefit neither the dead nor the living"? [Answer:] "There are always poor and needy among us whom we can help and in that way make better use of that which we have."

1868: "We declare service in the army to be unevangelical. . . . [It] must be forsaken with true penitance and sorrow, and also by leaving off and renouncing everything connected with it . . . including pensions. If there is need, it is the duty of the church to support the poor, rather than" the government.

1870: On frequenting "fairs" and "shows": "It was witnessed clearly, and with power that, according to God's Word, to frequent such places . . . would give an evil appearance and that, according to the words of Jesus, one cannot let his light shine . . . if he takes part in and supports them. . . . In fact, these [amusements] might be compared to the fair or vanity fair in the City of Vanity, described by John Bunyan [in his book *Pilgrim's Progress*]. . . . All were therefore admonished to avoid all such evil appearance. . . ."

1875: "According to God's Word is it right for a brother to . . . borrow money on low interest and then loan it out again with high interest?" [Answer:] "We consider it to be unjust. . . ."

Exerpted from the "Proceedings" of the *Diener-Versammlungen*, 1862-1878, as translated by Paton Yoder, Goshen, Indiana, and held by Steven R. Estes, Hopedale, Illinois. (A refined, annotated translation of the "Proceedings" will be a forthcoming publication of Yoder and Estes.)

tion served as a guide in answering such queries. Yet, despite the fact that Old Order spokesmen were no longer presenting alternative answers to ministers' meeting issues, at times unity was still out of reach. Even after 1865, things did not always run smoothly for the change-minded Amish Mennonites.

Division Among the Amish Mennonites

It soon became clear that the problems and struggles facing the Amish had not resulted only from the presence of conservative, tradition-minded Amish. Indeed, nearly as soon as the Old Order Amish left the ministers' meetings, the change-minded Amish Mennonites who remained a part of the annual gatherings began to disagree among themselves as to what type of changes they should accept. Division followed division for the Amish Mennonites after the conservatives opted out of the national forum. With the voices of tradition absent, the change-minded leaders were free to press each other on just how much change they each had in mind.

The first major division among the Amish Mennonites occurred in 1865 and involved the thought and practice of a reform-minded Amish bishop named Henry Egly (1824-1890), a European-born Amish immigrant living in Adams County, Indiana.[36] Sometime in the 1840s Egly experienced a powerful spiritual awakening while suffering a lengthy illness. The force of Egly's personal conversion convinced him that his was an experience God wanted all Christians to have. After his 1854 ordination as a preacher (he had been a deacon since 1850), Egly stressed the importance of each individual having an inner, experiential encounter with God as a prerequisite for forgiveness and salvation. Only those persons who had such an experience could really be considered Christian and be baptized, Egly said. The spiritual life and temper of some Amish congregations was appalling, he felt. It seemed to Egly that a few Amish were relying on their church membership for salvation, rather than on a personal conversion. Was not baptism without true conversion the same as infant baptism which the Anabaptists had rejected long ago?

To some Amish, Egly's teaching seemed to be the just another version of Protestant revivalism which stressed emotionalism and ignored the biblical injunctions for obedience. And if overstated, some Amish feared, Egly's emphasis on a conversion "experience" would weaken similarly important teachings on discipleship. Salvation by grace through faith was a foundational doctrine for the Amish, but they feared that an inordinate preoccupation with the *process of becoming* a Christian naturally detracted from balanced teaching on what *being* a Christian meant. Did not the New Testament speak more about living the Christian life than it did about the exact method one followed to get there? While other Amish persons did not reject Egly's personal testimony nor deny that he may have had a very close encounter with God while ill, they did resist his teaching that everyone should come to faith in the same way that he did.

About half of Egly's congregation agreed with and supported him, to the chagrin of the rest of the group. In January 1858 the congregation called on three Amish leaders from Holmes County, Ohio, to address the controversy. But instead of disciplining Egly as some in the congregation had hoped would happen, the Ohio delegation ordained Egly a bishop![37] The problem then only became worse, since Egly, as a bishop, was now in charge of baptisms and refused to baptize those whom he felt had not experienced a proper, personal and inner conversion. Since his definition of conversion was a bit different from that of some who came to him for baptism, the candidates whom he refused resented his not taking their claims of Christian faith seriously. But, Egly argued, baptism without proper conversion was no baptism at all, and he even offered to re-baptize those who later experienced encounters with God's grace.

In the spring of 1865 the situation reached a breaking point. Egly refused to discipline church members whom he claimed were not really church members because they had never been properly baptized. He also would not shun persons whom he felt were improperly excommunicated. Egly's ideas were also catching on in Ohio, Illinois and other parts of Indiana, as some Amish saw Egly as a true reformer. While the ministers' meeting of 1865 tried to address Egly's concerns, the gathered ministers seemed to be getting tired of Egly's name-calling and complaining about what he saw as weaknesses in the larger Amish fellowship.[38]

That fall Egly's own congregation could not come to unity under his leadership and could therefore not celebrate communion together. The situation degenerated into a stubborn stalemate on both sides and the church split.[39] The next year in 1866, Egly traveled around the Midwest meeting with Amish persons who were sympathetic toward him. They formed a loose unity popularly known as the "Egly Amish." Egly continued to stay abreast of what was happening in the Amish Mennonite world, but he never attended another annual ministers' conference. The rest of the Amish Mennonites showed little interest in winning the Egly Amish back; both sides seemed to have quietly agreed to separate.[40]

The "Egly division" was complex. Egly had come to America from Europe in the nineteenth century, yet he was not simply a "liberal immigrant." Much of what Egly stressed was very traditionally Amish. Egly's followers maintained very conservative dress standards and for many years worshiped in the German language. But Egly also mixed parts of American evangelicalism into his Amish church. As a church leader he exercised considerable personal authority over his congregation, down-played discipline and corporate decision-making, and demanded individual experiential conversion of a particular type—all common traits among evangelicals of that day. Additionally, Egly was influenced by the social reform movements of the latter 1800s and preached vigorously against any use of alcohol or tobacco (substances for which the Amish had traditionally taught only temperance). Egly's mixture of Amish traditions, American evangelicalism and popular reformism blended to form a unique spirituality which was inviting to a number of Amish Mennonites searching for a very personal and individual faith. That some Amish Mennonites were attracted to Egly's brand of Christianity shows that the change-minded Amish were not as unified as one might have imagined. All were influenced by the popular winds of culture blowing through North America, but different breezes caught the attention of different Amish Mennonites. For some, change had meant meetinghouses and greater choice of attire. For others, change primarily involved re-orienting one's religious world to include emphases from American evangelicalism and social reform. New winds kicked up, too, and the American virtues of tolerance and broad-mindedness split the Amish Mennonite ministers' meetings again.

Joseph Stuckey

In 1872 a second division transpired within Amish Mennonite ranks. Again doctrinal differences sparked the schism, but concerns for appropriate Christian lifestyle and church practice also gathered about this new controversy. The person around whom the division swirled was Bishop Joseph Stuckey (1826-1902) of McLean County, Illinois.[41] In 1860 Stuckey became a minister and his ordination as bishop came only four years later.

Stuckey was somewhat typical of the many progressive Amish church leaders in central Illinois. While the Old Order Amish would have considered Stuckey a wholly liberal-minded leader, he was at times cautious about changes in the church. Stuckey rejected portrait photography and also opposed Sunday schools, believing that they were a new and unnecessary innovation (he soon changed his mind and backed Sunday schools, however).[42]

Yet Stuckey was definitely a change-minded man. Dress standards in Stuckey's Rock Creek (later named North Danvers) congregation were lax compared with those of other Amish communities. Taking their grooming cues from store windows instead of from church teaching on simplicity, some of the Rock Creek Amish men wore buttons on their coats, styled their hair and sported neckties. The changes did not stop with attire. The Rock Creek Amish also used the old Reformation-era *Ausbund* hymnal less and less often. And one Amish family donated an organ to accompany the singing of a local community Sunday school to which many of the families sent their children.[43]

Especially grating to the more conservative leaders was Stuckey's practice of allowing excommunicated Amish church members to join the more tolerant congregations under his oversight. The McLean County bishop seemed to be undercutting church discipline by accepting as members those persons who had been excommunicated by other, more conservative, Amish congregations. Traditionally, Amish leaders had acknowledged and respected the discipline of other Amish groups, even if the other group's discipline was more strict. Stuckey's action seemed to open the door to a "consumer" church membership, whereby persons not liking what they found in their home congregation could simply shop around and find a group more suitable to them.[44]

The issue which caused the break between Stuckey and his fellow Amish Mennonites was one of doctrine and discipline. One member of Stuckey's congregation was Joseph Joder, a school teacher and poet. Joder had studied Latin, Greek and Hebrew, dabbled in Republican Party politics, and otherwise stood-out as a rather remarkable nineteenth century Amishman.[45] One of the peculiar features of Joder's personal theology was his belief in universalism. Universalism is the belief that God will save all people, even the most evil, in his great love for humanity. There is no place for hell or any eternal punishment in the universalist scheme of thought—heaven is the destination of all humankind. Throughout the history of the church various Christian groups have taught universalism, but in almost every case the larger church has considered universalism to be heresy.

In the mid-nineteenth century, however, universalism was an increasingly popular Christian doctrine in America. Universalist circuit riders spread the teaching throughout the midwestern United States and founded a number of Universalist churches. By 1850 there were large Universalist congregations in the Illinois cities of Peoria and Champaign. Perhaps Joder learned of the doctrine through these churches, or perhaps he came to his universalist beliefs through his own private Bible study. Before the Stuckey controversy, universalism had made a small impact on the Illinois Amish church when Preacher Daniel Holly (1816-1887) left his ministry in a Putnam County Amish congregation to join the Universalists. Nearby, in the late 1850s, Amish

Amish school teacher Joseph Joder, McLean County, Illinois. Joder's universalist views caused quite a stir among the Amish Mennonites.

lay member Moses Ropp (1828-1891) found himself excommunicated for his universalist views.[46]

Joder's case, however, became the celebrated confrontation between the Amish church and universalism. Joder had written a number of poems which readers could have taken as defenses of universalism, but these he had written in English and so they attracted little attention among the Amish. In 1869, Joder wrote twenty-six stanzas of verse under the title "*Die Frohe Botschaft*" ("Glad Tidings"). This new poem was both in German and more explicitly universalist—and it did not escape the notice of other Amish church leaders[47] (see "Joseph Joder's Controversial Poem," p. 150).

Copies of the poem showed up at the ministers' meeting of 1872. Since, for the past few years, Stuckey had been under suspicion—and even investigation by committees from the *Diener-Versammlungen*—on account of his lax church discipline,[48] the group gathered in 1872 decided that the presence of universalism in Stuckey's congregation called for serious and direct attention. Later that year three Amish Mennonite leaders visited Stuckey and asked him why he had tolerated Joseph Joder as a member of the church when Joder's heretical views were so widely and obviously known. Stuckey revealed that he had not excommunicated Joder, nor was he yet ready to do so. One of Stuckey's statements could have been interpreted to mean that Stuckey agreed with Joder (although Stuckey later denied this). Thereupon the other Amish Mennonite leaders, unofficially representing all Amish Mennonites, withdrew fellowship from Joseph Stuckey, his congregation and several other Illinois Amish congregations which supported him.[49]

Stuckey could have pointed out to his visitors that in the congregationally-structured Amish church, he, as a leader, could not single-handedly excommunicate anyone without the support of the congregation—and the congregation wanted to exercise more patience with Joder. Eventually, in 1873, Stuckey and his church did refuse to allow Joder to join them in observing communion, but only after they found Joder incorrigible.[50] Joseph Stuckey represented a patient, open-minded approach to church organization and administration. Tolerance was important for Stuckey and the Amish who looked to him for leadership.

Several of the questions Stuckey had posed at the annual ministers' conferences which he had earlier attended seem to indicate that he was unsure whether strict discipline really would bring people to repentance. Only God could turn unbelief and disobedience around, he seemed to have said in 1867. The church might have to be patient and loving and wait for God to work, instead of jumping to excommunication and shunning.

Rather than bringing erring members back to the church, tough discipline just might drive some people further away.[51]

Stuckey was not alone in his more relaxed approach to church administration and discipline. Several other Illinois Amish congregations allied themselves more closely with Stuckey and became known as the "Stuckey Amish." Also, several relatively liberal Amish congregations remained independent of both the larger Amish Mennonite fellowship (represented by the *Diener-Versammlungen*) and the "Stuckey Amish." These more liberal congregations included two in Iowa under the leadership of recent European immigrants Bishop Benjamin Eicher (1832-1893) and Preacher Philip Roulet (1828-1904), and two Butler County, Ohio, congregations. Stuckey maintained some contact with these liberals, but they preferred to remain largely independent.

The more tolerant "Stuckey Amish" represented the limits of the change-minded Amish Mennonites. While rejecting the Old Order option, neither were the Amish Mennonites willing to go

Joseph Joder's Controversial Poem

Amish school teacher and poet Joseph Joder caused quite a sensation with his poem "*Die Frohe Botschaft*" ("Glad Tidings"). Written in German in 1869, the lines of verse drew harsh criticism from many quarters of the Amish church. Opponents of Joder claimed that the poem advocated *universalism* (the belief that God will save *all* humanity; there is no such thing as hell or punishment for the wicked).

The poem was on the whole an affirmation of the Christian doctrine of salvation by God's grace through faith alone. Interspersed with traditional orthodoxy were several stanzas which supported a universalist perspective. Controversial portions of the poem included these lines:

Stanza two: "Such teachings/As we frequently hear/Of eternal torment in hell/Cannot possibly be the truth;/They deny God's goodness/And make His spirit harsh."

Stanza fifteen: "It is not at all reasonable [to believe]/That in the future the torment of hell/Should last forever./Only insanity can so delude us/As to believe or hear/What God's word does not teach."

Stanza sixteen: "It [the idea of eternal punishment for the wicked] is pure fable,/A heathen suggestion;/Lack of understanding honors only/The darkness in the corner;/Sectarian presumption/Builds up hatred and quarreling."

Stanza twenty-six: "Love flows forth from God/And works its way into the whole of creation,/Makes everything like unto itself,/Until the whole earth/Shall become one universe,/A Heavenly Kingdom of Peace."

When Joder's bishop, Joseph Stuckey, did not discipline Joder quickly enough for his universalist beliefs, other Amish Mennonite congregations censured Stuckey.

Translated by Jennie A. Whitten and published in Steven R. Estes, *A Goodly Heritage: A History of the North Danvers Mennonite Church* (Danvers, Ill.: North Danvers Mennonite Church, 1982), pp. 296-300.

so far in the direction of tolerance as had Joseph Stuckey. Most Amish Mennonites also rejected the way of Henry Egly and his particular type of spirituality. The majority of the Amish Mennonites took a moderate course between the Old Orders on one hand, and the evangelicals and liberals on the other.

The Future of the Amish Mennonites

In 1878 in Woodford County, Illinois, the last of the annual Amish Mennonite ministers' meetings convened. Since about 1870 the meetings had given more and more time to sermons and less and less time to church business and controversy settlement. For the Amish Mennonites who remained a part of the annual meetings, fewer problems and controversies from the 1850s and 1860s remained. The one issue which gradually did become important, though, focused on the future of the annual meetings. What was the purpose of the *Diener-Versammlungen* now that permanent division, instead of unity, had resulted from them? Should the ministers' meetings be discontinued? Should the meetings go on, but become a kind of legislative, deliberative body to "govern" the Amish Mennonites? At the final 1878 gathering, a committee appointed to discover ways of strengthening the ministers' gatherings reported on a plan to fully organize the Amish Mennonite church.[52]

Under the committee's provisions, congregations would operate autonomously. If congregations became involved in situations which they could not peacefully handle, they would need to bring the matter to a regional meeting of Amish Mennonite leaders. Should that group not be able to successfully address

Bishop Benjamin Eicher, leader of the progressive Amish Mennonites of Washington County, Iowa.

the local problem, the matter would come before the annual meeting for all of North America. The decision of the national conference would then be final for those originally involved. Such a formal, rational bureaucratic approach to church government was foreign to the Amish tradition of local congregational authority. The three-tiered system of appeal and review was more in line with the practices of the denominationally-oriented Protestants. The committee's proposal was a radical departure from traditional Amish congregationalism.

But before the Amish Mennonites could test the committee's idea of a highly structured, denominational Amish church, the annual *Diener-Versammlungen* mysteriously came to an end; after 1878 no one called another such gathering. The Amish Mennonites never tried the committee's recommendations for re-structuring their church as a national denomination. Historian Paton Yoder has suggested that perhaps the demise of the annual meetings stemmed from a personal falling-out between ministers' conference advocates Bishop John K. Yoder (1824-1906) of Wayne County, Ohio, and Full Deacon John P. King (1827-1887) of Ohio's Logan County.[53] Without the united leadership of Yoder and King, the Amish Mennonites lacked the drive and vision to sustain the yearly conference schedule.[54] But perhaps, too, the meetings ended because they no longer served a purpose. After all, the conferences were originally supposed to settle local disturbances and unify the church. The church had found unity—or rather *unities*—by dividing into several factions each of which sought renewal through different means. As the ministers' meetings ended, the Amish church lay shattered and confused, perhaps more broken than either conservatives or progressives could have imagined seventeen years earlier when all sides had gathered to find common ground.[55]

The results of the great division were not all apparent in 1878. It took more than another decade to fully sort out which Amish congregations would choose the path of selective change and which would maintain a more tradition-oriented approach. All groups shared a common desire for church renewal. That renewal did take place (in very different ways) amid the confusion of the 1860s and 70s. The Old Order Amish looked for spiritual renewal through group commitment and discipleship guided by a common *Ordnung*. The Egly churches sought new life through individual, personal spirituality, while the Stuckey people found new Christian strength and love through a measure of tolerance and broadmindedness. The turbulent years of the *Diener-Versammlungen* produced a number of Amish churches, each fairly united within itself—but not with each other. In the decades which followed, the gap between the groups only widened as the Old Order Amish continued to maintain a distinctive life and faith while their progressive Amish Mennonite cousins abandoned their historic identity.

The Merging of Two Peoples: Amish Mennonite Union With the Mennonites in North America and Europe, 1870-1937

"We are willing to join hand in hand."
— *Mennonites and Amish Mennonites in Antrim County, Michigan, 1886*

The Amish Mennonites in the Late Nineteenth Century

"On Sunday Sept. 17th, we met at the house of Joel Detweiler, and organized a German Sabbath-school under the auspices of the Omish [sic] Mennonite Church. . . . By the grace of God we hope to derive such spiritual blessings therefrom, as will enable us to grow in grace. . . ."[1]

This news from Tennessee came from a new Amish Mennonite settlement. In 1871 under the leadership of Deacon "Tennessee" John Stoltzfus, the new Knox County congregation established itself in the upper South. Almost immediately the group established a Sunday school program and announced its beginning in the Mennonite-published English language periodical *Herald of Truth*. That an Amish Sunday school news item appeared in a Mennonite magazine was illustrative. It pointed up both the continued interest in and advocation of progressive ideas and programs such as Sunday schools by the Amish Mennonites, as well as the growing connection between that group and the Mennonites.[2] Within a few years, Mifflin County Amish Mennonite layman Jonathan K. Hartzler (1838-1906) was supplying children's stories for the Mennonite paper, and Amish Mennonite obituaries found listing on its back pages. Most North American Amish Mennonites would eventually give up their distinct identity and merge with the Mennonites who published the *Herald*.

Three generations of Amish Mennonite/Mennonite women, from Wayne County, Ohio: Mary Conrad Smiley (1825-1912), Elizabeth Smiley Ramseyer (1853-1928), and Clara Ramseyer Miller (1885-1918), holding her son Lloyd (b.1907). Notice the progressive change in dress styles.

The Sunday school article portended changes to come.

The number of Amish identifying with the Amish Mennonite wing of the church grew significantly after 1865. Most of the increase in membership came as more Amish congregations chose the Amish Mennonite path after the annual ministers' meetings discontinued. Until the 1880s in some areas—notably Ontario, parts of Pennsylvania, and Iowa—many Amish congregations did not decide whether they would affiliate with the Old Order Amish or Amish Mennonites. Also, some change-minded members in conservative Old Order fellowships left their congregations for more progressive neighboring Amish Mennonite churches. Despite the possibility of being excommunicated and shunned should they leave their Old Order home congregations, some did switch to the Amish Mennonite camp.

However, banning and shunning did not always follow a change of affiliation. In the late nineteenth century there seems to have been a measure of acceptance and mutual recognition on the part of both the Old Order Amish and their progressive cousins. Until about 1896, for example, in eastern Pennsylvania's Conestoga Amish community, shunning was not always practiced against those who left the Old Order group for the more liberal church. Joining the Amish Mennonites was a frowned-upon, but tolerated, "release valve" for those Amish who would not bend to Old Order discipline, yet wanted to remain a part of family and broader Amish community affairs.[3]

Some people chose the Amish Mennonite church for other familial reasons. John Lais (1849-1894) was a Roman Catholic immigrant from Germany who found himself working as a hired hand on an Indiana Amish farm. Attracted to the faith and life of the Amish, Lais wanted to join the Old Order church, but his wife Susannah Plank Lais (1860-1936), did not. Susannah was herself of Amish background and she had been disenchanted by what she perceived to be Old Order legalism. The Laises compromised and joined the Amish Mennonites. John and Susannah ended up living in northwestern Oregon's Amish Mennonite community.[4]

The Amish Mennonite churches were spread across the continent by century's end. Not only did the older Amish communities in Pennsylvania, Ohio, Ontario and Indiana include some progressive Amish Mennonites, but almost all of Illinois and large numbers of the Iowa Amish were of the change-minded stripe. Then too, many younger Amish settlements in Arkansas, Colorado, Kansas, Missouri, Nebraska, Oklahoma, Oregon and Tennessee joined Amish Mennonite ranks. The church was growing.

The church was also changing. Of course a group as scattered as the Amish Mennonites exhibited a good deal of variety from one congregation to another, but several trends were noticeable. Members were becoming generally more acculturated into American life. Less traditional clothing styles, the use of English instead of German in family conversations, and the taking up of popular American pastimes were several measures of Amish Mennonite movement toward fuller ownership of the rights and privileges of their surrounding culture.

Mahala Yoder (1850-1879), an Amish Mennonite woman in her twenties, kept a diary for several years, observing life around her in McLean County, Illinois.[5] While her family affiliated with the quite progressive Joseph Stuckey congregation, some of Yoder's comments reflect attitudes common to many other Amish Mennonites. To Mahala, her first-generation Amish Mennonite parents still seemed too conservative. Her father bought "the very plainest wooden" chairs for their home when Mahala had hoped for fancy new cane-bottoms. And her step-mother gave "the girls so little liberty to visit their friends," Mahala felt sad for her sisters. Nevertheless the Yoder household was raising a very different second generation of Amish Mennonites.

The luxuries of an industrial society were becoming more common for the Yoder young folks. For her twenty-first birthday Mahala received carpeting for her bedroom. Her room looked so much better, she thought. It needed "only a table and pictures" to be complete. Her sister Mary went to town some weeks later—and with the full knowledge of their step-mother—chose new spring hats. "She got white straw hats," Mahala observed, "trimmed with blue ribbons and a pretty red rose."

Recreation, too, was changing. The Yoder family now played what Mahala called "a new game"—the card "game of Authors." And they read *Scribner's* magazine. Although she herself was barred from traveling much because of a physical handicap, Mahala's siblings and friends went to town to see "Barnum's [Circus] Show" and an orchestra in Bloomington. Step-sister Magdalena even found a social outlet in political party politics. Around election day, 1876, she spent "all afternoon . . . doing up her white dress and making a cap and sash." The next day she was going to a Republican "mass meeting at Bloomington" as part of a delegation of "twenty-nine girls in uniform to represent the states of the Union."

Mahala was able to go to church, and her comments on its services also reveal changing Amish Mennonite attitudes. Not much longer would congregations be satisfied with preachers who stumbled through traditional sermons or spoke extemporaneously. Mahala strongly approved when a visiting preacher addressed the Stuckey congregation using "pure, rich German . . . which did one's soul good to hear." Proper German or standard English were fine by Mahala, but not the "horrid 'Pennsylvania Dutch'" dialect which she so much detested. Ethnic dialects only detracted from worship. She believed that her "church-going" did her "more good because the sermon was delivered in simple, correct language." In Mahala's way of thinking, "The beautiful goes with the good and true, always, in God's method." Beyond proper sermons, Yoder also received theological insight from reading contemporary novels—one of which she found "as helpful and encouraging and suggestive as so many chapters of the Bible." She wondered why some Amish Mennonites were "ashamed to read a good novel." But her wonderment only betrayed how far removed Mahala's generation was from traditional Amish understandings which viewed secular entertainment as frivolous, wasteful and perhaps even dangerous.

Where Would It End?

Central Illinois was not the only place where Amish Mennonites were becoming more heavily involved in the larger secular world. Near Johnstown, Pennsylvania, Amish Mennonite Isaac Kaufman (1806-1886) involved himself in financing toll roads, Johnstown's First National Bank and various federal bond programs. As an important local financier, Kaufman's portrait hung in the lobby of the Johnstown bank. His heirs received $246,000 from their money-wise Amish Mennonite forbearer.[6] And in eastern Pennsylvania, the Conestoga Amish Mennonite congregation had a bishop, John "Johnny P." Mast (1826-1888), who served as a local bank director and successful miller.[7]

While such commercially financial activity was remarkable even for Amish Mennonites, it illustrates the continued general acceptability of upward mobility among church members. In the early nineteenth century a number of Amish persons had always engaged in big business and politics, or had purchased the latest in household furnishings. But then there had been some resistance to doing so, and even an Old Order reaction against it. Since 1865, among the Amish Mennonites few voices were left to speak a slowing word. In 1889 the Oak Grove Amish Mennonite congregation in Ohio's Wayne County even went so far as to grant seven lay members the privilege of formulating a new, more relaxed church discipline.[8]

In their later years some of the older, first generation Amish Mennonite leaders were alarmed that so much change had come so quickly into their congregations. The rapid pace of innovation among the next generations of Amish Mennonites unnerved old *Diener-Versammlungen* promoters "Tennessee" John Stoltzfus and John P. King.[9] Earlier leaders like Stoltzfus and King had envisioned a church guided by moderate progressive philosophy—not a wholesale selling-out of Amish Mennonite beliefs and practices. Nevertheless, as the nineteenth century's last decades closed, North America's Amish Mennonites were taking more hints from larger society as they organized and operated their churches.

Jacob Goldsmith (1841-1930) and Magdalena Shantz Goldsmith (1853-1936), Amish Mennonites from Henry County, Iowa, in fashionable attire.

Some of the strongest reaction against the increasingly liberal "drift" of the Amish Mennonites came from a number of very unusual Amish Mennonite lay ministers. Known as the "sleeping preachers," these men addressed audiences while in a deep sleep-like trance. Convinced that their unconscious sermons were messages from the Lord, these preachers and their adherents prefered the designation "Spirit preaching" to describe the phemonenon. The Spirit preacher would typically seem to fall asleep early in the evening, only to rise several hours later and begin to preach (in German or English) on the themes of repentance, spiritual renewal or the return to simpler lifestyles.[10]

Two of the best known Spirit preachers were Noah Troyer (1831-1886), Johnson County, Iowa, and John D. Kauffman (1847-1913), Elkhart County, Indiana. Troyer began preaching in 1878 and Kauffman in 1880. Both men claimed to have no knowledge of what happened during their ecstatic state, who listened to them or what they said. Other Amish Mennonites affirmed the Spirit preachers' messages with revelations of their own. Barbara Hochstetler Stutzman (1848-1888), for example, claimed to have received a death-bed revelation which confirmed the Spirit-preaching truth of Kauffman.[11] A member of Elkhart County's Clinton Frame Amish Mennonite Church, Stutzman was herself very disturbed by her congregation's rapid pace of change.[12]

For the true believers, Spirit preaching was nothing other than divine revelation. For the doubters, men like Troyer and Kauffman were either victims of self-induced hypnosis or charlatans. But Spirit preaching was a phenomenon in other groups during the period, too. In nineteenth century Europe and North America, Spirit preaching occurred among various Protestant denominations and among the Native Americans' so-called "Ghost Dancers." The Amish Mennonites were certainly not the only group to experience it.[13]

Most Amish Mennonites eventually discounted the Spirit preachers. In fact local opposition to Kauffman forced him to move to Shelby County, Illinois in 1907. There Kauffman and his followers formed their own congregation, commonly known as the "Sleeping Preacher Amish." The group grew and spread to other parts of the country. It remains active at the end of the twentieth century, although the act of Spirit preaching itself has long since ceased in the group.[14]

Progressives in Institution Building

Institution building occupied the time and energy of many Americans during the late nineteenth century. States organized university systems. Banks and businesses formed dozens of new corporations, trusts and holding companies. Charitable organizations created inner-city shelters and settlement houses. Special interest groups—from the National Geographic Society to the American Federation of Labor—formed during this period. Churches were not immune from the spirit of the age, forming national denominational offices, publications, schools and programs at a rate until then unparalleled in American history.

The Amish Mennonites were institution builders as well—even cooperating at times with fellow Mennonites who were also hard at work creating their own institutional world. The cooperation and association of Amish Mennonites with fellow Mennonites occurred at even the level of family magazine subscriptions. More and more Amish Mennonites were getting their news from Mennonite church magazines. In fact so many Amish Mennonites read the Mennonite periodical *Herald of Truth* (and its German language companion *Herold der Wahrheit*) that for a time its editor listed the paper as the "Organ of 14 Mennonite and Amish Conferences"[15] (even though it never really held any such official status).

The Amish Mennonite "conferences" to which the *Herald's* masthead referred were real Amish Mennonite creations, however. Organizing as a denomination was one of the major Amish Mennonite tasks of the 1880s and 1890s. Absorbing the pulse and feel of larger society, the Amish Mennonites were quick to adopt structures and programs which clearly marked their divergence from the style and tenor of the Old Order Amish. The demise of the *Diener-Versammlungen* had not brought Amish Mennonite conversation or connectedness to an end. So while the years after 1878 did not see a direct continuance of the national ministers' meetings, within a decade new gatherings had taken their place.

Perhaps taking their cues from the regionally-organized Mennonites who reported their church activities in the *Herald*, the Amish Mennonites also decided to hold conferences on a regional, rather than national, level. Three groups of Amish Mennonites were soon meeting on a frequent, but irregular, basis: Indiana-Michigan Amish Mennonites, Ohio Amish Mennonites,

Division and Merger Among the Amish Mennonites and Old Order Amish, 1880-1950

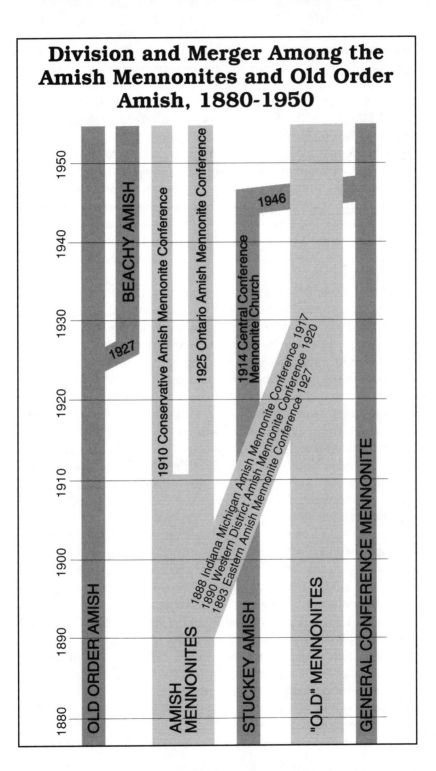

OLD ORDER AMISH

BEACHY AMISH

1927

1910 Conservative Amish Mennonite Conference

1925 Ontario Amish Mennonite Conference

1914 Central Conference Mennonite Church

1946

1888 Indiana Michigan Amish Mennonite Conference 1917
1890 Western District Amish Mennonite Conference 1927
1893 Eastern Amish Mennonite Conference 1920

AMISH MENNONITES

STUCKEY AMISH

"OLD" MENNONITES

GENERAL CONFERENCE MENNONITE

and Amish Mennonites living in some nine states west of Indiana. In 1888 the Indiana-Michigan group formed itself into a fully-constituted church body known as the Indiana-Michigan Amish Mennonite Conference. Two years later the Western District Amish Mennonite Conference formed.[16] Its membership included Amish Mennonite congregations in Illinois, Iowa, Missouri, Arkansas, Kansas, Oklahoma, Nebraska, Colorado and Oregon. Taking on a few congregations in Pennsylvania, the Ohio Amish Mennonites established the Eastern Amish Mennonite Conference in 1893. Oak Grove, Ohio, Bishop John K. Yoder, so active in the workings of the earlier *Diener-Versammlungen*, played a role in the new Eastern Amish Mennonite organization and provided some continuity between the old ministers' meetings and the new Conference.

Each of these new groups met regularly, had elected moderators and secretaries, and acted as an autonomous, self-governing group. But often leaders from one of the other Amish Mennonite conferences (or even from one of the Mennonite conferences) would attend a regional meeting, demonstrating the loyalty and companionship which the conferences felt for one another. By creating formal conference structures, the Amish Mennonites were one step closer to being indistinguishable from the Mennonites. Earlier, the Amish Mennonites had emphasized the congregational autonomy which was a part of their Amish heritage. Now, by adopting the Mennonite model of regional conference authority and structure, the progressive Amish built another bridge of connection with the Mennonites and further distanced themselves from their own past.

Another field in which the Amish Mennonites left their Amish heritage behind and joined in American institution-building was higher education. While not all Amish Mennonites immediately supported efforts toward formal, advanced education, a surprising number did. Schooling beyond the elementary level was uncommon for all Americans before 1900 (in 1900 only 6.3 percent of all seventeen-year-old Americans graduated from high school[17]), but especially for the Amish, who often down-played the value of worldly knowledge, study beyond grade school was generally uncommon. (Most Amish had, however, supported their local public elementary schools and some Amish served as teachers or directors.)

By the turn of the century, a number of signs pointed toward an Amish Mennonite interest in formal education. When able, more Amish Mennonite youth enrolled in high schools, teachers' colleges ("normal schools") or other universities. Wayne County's sizable Oak Grove Amish Mennonite congregation was well known for its young people's attendance at Ohio's Ada Normal School (now Ohio Northern University) and The College of Wooster.[18] Significantly, Amish Mennonite leaders were at the forefront of one of the first Mennonite secondary schools in America. The Elkhart (Indiana) Institute, a private high school which opened in 1894, had a board of directors made up of four Amish Mennonites and nine Mennonites. While some of the western Amish Mennonites were as yet unsure about the school, by 1899 the Indiana-Michigan Amish Mennonite Conference recommended attendance at Elkhart for its youth who aspired to go on in their studies.[19] One of the Institute's instructors, C. Henry Smith (1875-1948), was himself an Amish Mennonite student who had pursued higher education[20] (see "C. Henry Smith, Ph.D.," p. 185).

Common Cause

The Amish Mennonites were working with the Mennonites in ever more areas of common interest. Both groups often cooperated in Sunday school leaders' gatherings in which they shared ideas and materials. Occasionally, Mennonite and Amish Mennonite ministers preached during one another's Sunday services. At times churches from both groups would invite preaching "teams" made up of one Mennonite and one Amish Mennonite to hold a series of what were known as "protracted meetings" (revival meetings held several nights in a row). Mennonite Bishop John F. Funk (1835-1930) and Amish Mennonite Bishop Daniel J. Johns (1850-1942) were one of the first such teams. Amish Mennonite Bishops Jonathan P. Smucker (1834-1903)[21] and Jonathan Kurtz (1848-1930) also frequently participated in such arrangements, as did Mennonite John S. Coffman (1848-1899).

Such teamwork was not without its hitches. Visiting preachers were supposed to encourage teens and young adults to join their families' local congregations. In 1890 in the Logan County, Ohio, Amish Mennonite community, several youth responded to Johns's and Funk's invitation to follow Christ and join the church. However, the young men and women reported that they wished to join a *Mennonite* congregation—not the Amish Mennonite church of their parents. After much embarrassed deliberation, the visiting preachers suggested that local Amish Mennonite leaders allow the young people to form a separate officially Mennonite fellowship—Bethel Mennonite Church.[22]

The controversy in Logan County pointed up the fact that "Amish Mennonite" and "Mennonite" were still not completely interchangeable designations in the final years of the nineteenth century. In many places the Amish Mennonites still dressed more conservatively, their men wore beards, and many were still committed in principle to shunning (although the actual practice of shunning by the Amish Mennonites quickly and quietly fell into disuse[23]). Many times the Mennonites were perceived to be the more progressive group. Especially for those young people interested in institution building, the larger resources—human and material—of the Mennonites were appealing. Mission interests among the Mennonites also ran strong (by 1899 they would have medical missionaries in India) and so those Amish Mennonites interested in international outreach felt a close kinship with the Mennonites.

For several decades, a few Amish Mennonites and Mennonites had been suggesting the merger of their two groups. Already in the 1860s the traveling Illinois Amish Mennonite school teacher Christian Erismann had begun referring to his Amish people simply as "Mennonites." Even at the 1866 *Diener-Versammlung* there had been talk of the Amish Mennonites joining the Mennonites, but nothing concrete resulted. In 1874 the Indiana Mennonite Conference invited any "Amish [Mennonite] brethren who are of one mind with us" to participate in Mennonite communion services.[24] Three years before, a Mennonite leader had written of his "Omish [sic] brethren," adding, "Now there may be some who think that we are out of place by calling the Omish, brethren." However, in his opinion his church "should not be too ready to censure [the Amish Mennonites]." In fact, "if there was more visiting done [between Amish Mennonites and Mennonites], there would be more union of thought," he was sure.[25]

Some "union of thought" did develop on the local level as a few Mennonite and Amish Mennonite congregations quietly merged. In 1886 the *Herald of Truth* reported on a congregation in northern Michigan's Antrim County in which both Mennonite and Amish Mennonite persons had managed their own merger and formed a joint congregation. They were "willing to join hand in

The family of Amish Mennonites Samuel J. (1842-1924) and Barbara Yoder (1842-1923) Miller (front row) of McPherson County, Kansas. Of the couple's ten children, five joined Mennonite churches, four chose the Church of the Brethren and one did not affiliate with any group. (Two sons-in-law are also pictured.)

hand, and be united as one body in the Lord," the paper reported. Their Amish and Mennonite distinctions did not seem to matter.[26]

Sometimes the local union of Amish Mennonites and Mennonites was the result of the decline of one or another of the groups. "Tennessee" John Stoltzfus's Knox County, Tennessee, community languished and nearly died after the old leader's passing. The appearance of a Mennonite minister and several Virginia Mennonite families revived the group's health and changed its character—the whole group simply became Mennonite. After 1900 when a few Ontario Amish families moved west into Saskatchewan and Alberta they joined existing local Mennonite congregations rather than establishing new Amish Mennonite ones.[27] For a variety of reasons a number of congregations were growing closer together.

Amish Mennonite and "Old" Mennonite Unity

Through both an increase in formal joint ventures and a growing sense of common spirit, many Amish Mennonites and Mennonites began to think and talk seriously about formal union of the two groups. For the most part, the Amish Mennonites considered uniting with Mennonites who were known as "old" Mennonites.[28] Not to be confused with "Old Order," the designation "old" described the Mennonite group which was the largest and oldest in North America. Most of its members were of Swiss and south German decent—the very people with whom the Amish had originally divided in Europe. Over the years, for various reasons, both conservatives and progressives had split from the "old" Mennonites, so that by 1900 the "old" Mennonites represented a rather middle-of-the-road Mennonite church. They were organized into about a dozen regional conferences, each of which was fairly autonomous. Such a regional organization allowed the "old" Mennonites in different areas to work at unity with the Amish Mennonites at their own local pace and with their own regional timing.

After 1898 the regional conferences of the "old" Mennonites met in biannual North American gatherings. From the beginning, Amish Mennonite leaders attended these continent-wide "old" Mennonite meetings. The contact and working relationship established between the two churches at the national level paved the way for the eventual uniting of the two groups in the first quarter of the twentieth century.[29]

In 1917 the Indiana-Michigan Amish Mennonite Conference formally and officially merged with the Indiana Mennonite Conference. The new group's name, Indiana-Michigan Mennonite Conference, did not acknowledge the Amish heritage of half of its members. But that designation seems not to have been the result of Mennonites trying to squash Amish Mennonite identity. Rather it appears that it was the new conference's former Amish Mennonite members who were most ready to forget their past.

For example, Noah Long, trustee of the Clinton Frame Amish Mennonite Church, Elkhart County, Indiana, removed the word "Amish" from the meetinghouse sign only a day or two after his conference voted to merge with the Mennonites.[30] Long's congregation wasted no time in letting passers-by know that Clinton Frame was no longer Amish.

The Western District Amish Mennonite Conference was the next to dissolve itself into a new Mennonite family. In 1920 the Western District Amish Mennonites and the "old" Mennonites living west of Indiana re-shuffled their organizations and formed five new regional Mennonite conferences, each with joint Amish

Mennonite and "old" Mennonite membership. The Amish Mennonites outnumbered the "old" Mennonites 4,400 to 2,800 in these new groups, so there was somewhat less of a drive to surrender Amish identity.[31] Several Amish Mennonite congregations continued to use their historic "Amish" name for a time. For several years after the merger, one of the five new western groups, the Iowa-Nebraska Conference, used neither the word "Amish" nor "Mennonite" in its name in order to not offend either party.[32]

In 1927 the Eastern Amish Mennonite Conference brought Mennonite-Amish merger to Ohio and Pennsylvania. In that year the Amish Mennonites of those two states joined with the Ohio Mennonite Conference. The new group judiciously acknowledged both halves of its merger, using the name Ohio Mennonite and Eastern Amish Mennonite Joint Conference. By mid-century any real Amish Mennonite identity was so far removed from most members that the conference title was simplified to Ohio and Eastern Mennonite Conference.[33]

The Canadian Amish Mennonites represent a final, but different example of unity with the Mennonites. The Ontario Amish Mennonite Conference never merged with the "old" Mennonite conference in its Province. Instead the Ontario Amish Mennonites continued as a separate body, but worked more and more closely with other Mennonites. In 1963 the group dropped the word "Amish" from its name and became known as the Western Ontario Mennonite Conference. The group later did join two other Mennonite bodies to form the Mennonite Conference of Eastern Canada, but by that time the question of Amish identity was hardly an issue.

Thus, in a few short years during the early 1900s, several thousand persons knowingly or unknowingly suffered the loss of their historic Amish faith identity. This was one of the most profound legacies of the merger of the two groups. As historian Paton Yoder, himself a product of an Amish Mennonite home, has lamented, the Amish Mennonites paid the price of lost heritage and "covered their tracks" in the process of so quickly becoming Mennonites. Now Yoder "and all other Mennonites with Amish Mennonite roots, find it necessary to uncover these tracks" in order "to discover—or rediscover—[their] Amish and Amish Mennonite origins."[34]

But the unity of the Amish Mennonite conferences with the

"old" Mennonites was also one of far reaching impact for the Mennonites. The addition of 7,500 to 8,000 Amish Mennonites increased the size of the "old" Mennonites significantly. While the "old" Mennonites had been the largest Mennonite group in 1900, their size had not been much more than the next largest body (the General Conference Mennonite Church). With the absorption of the Amish Mennonites, the "old" Mennonites became by far the largest North American Mennonite group. Had the Amish Mennonites congregations not augmented the "old" Mennonite church in the early 1900s, it is doubtful the "old" Mennonites would have had the human and material resources necessary to engage in the various twentieth century activities which they later did.

The Conservative Amish Mennonites

Some Amish Mennonites were hesitant to so quickly unite with the "old" Mennonites in the first quarter of the twentieth century. They accepted the use of meetinghouses, Sunday schools and organized mission work, but they usually retained German-language worship, conservative clothing standards and other marks of traditional Amish church life. Often they were less sure that the benefits of higher education always outweighed its threats to community, and they wanted to retain more local congregational autonomy. These "conservative" Amish Mennonites were certainly not Old Order, but neither were they completely comfortable with the Amish Mennonite groups—some of whom seemed to put too much emphasis on immediate unity with the Mennonites.

In 1910 representatives of three such Amish Mennonites congregations met in Pigeon, Michigan, and formed a loose fellowship with the name "Conservative Amish Mennonite Conference."[35] Under the leadership of Pigeon's Bishop Solomon J. Swartzendruber (1856-1932), the Conservative Conference grew to include congregations throughout the midwest, Pennsylvania and Maryland. An important center of Conservative Amish Mennonite membership was Lewis County, New York. The sizable Amish community there had never associated too closely with the *Diener-Versammlungen* or other Amish Mennonite groups.

Later, other congregations joined the conference: conservative Amish Mennonites and progressive Old Orders found a middle ground in the Conservative Conference. For a time, some con-

Lunch at a Conservative Amish Mennonite Conference Sunday school meeting, Grantsville, Maryland, in 1912.

gregations in Ontario considered membership in the Conservative Conference, but then decided against it. Interestingly, the Canadian Amish Mennonites were always a bit unsure of taking on the name "Conservative Amish Mennonite Conference" because they thought that the title would seem to connect them with their Dominion's Conservative Party and its politics. Such were the difficulties of international church work: a common, descriptive word in one society held powerful political connotations in another.

The Conservative Amish Mennonite Conference followed the larger Mennonite and Amish Mennonite pattern of church work and institution building, but at a slower pace. Yet organization and programs did develop. A home for orphans opened in 1914, and an official mission board charged with sponsoring domestic and foreign mission activities followed four years later. In 1952 the Conference opened a Bible school near Berlin, Ohio (later moved to Irwin, Ohio, and named Rosedale Bible Institute).

By 1954 the word "Amish" in the Conference name seemed to have little remaining meaning for most members. By a three-fourths majority vote that year, the Conference dropped the term, taking simply the designation Conservative Mennonite Conference. Unofficial connections and official cooperation with the "old" Mennonites grew over the next decades. In 1971 when the "old" Mennonites re-organized themselves as the Mennonite Church (MC), the Conservative Conference loosely affiliated with them. Thus, the Conservative Amish Mennonites eventually did follow a path like that of other Amish Mennonites, but they did so at their own time and on their own terms.

Amish Links to the General Conference Mennonite Church

While the majority of Amish Mennonites who moved toward union with the Mennonites chose to merge or affiliate with the "old" Mennonites, a good number of congregations chose a different road. For the more liberal Stuckey Amish and several independent Amish congregations in Ohio and Iowa, the path of cooperation led to the General Conference Mennonite Church.[36] The General Conference (GC) had organized in 1860 at West Point, Iowa, and represented an attempt among Pennsylvanian and midwestern progressive Mennonites to form a new, more open denomination. The GCs strongly supported higher education, congregational autonomy and mission work at home and abroad. In stressing congregational authority, the General Conference took a position more in line with historic Amish understandings of local church control. (Of course, among the Old Order Amish, congregational autonomy was checked by deference to the established *Ordnung*. GC congregationalism, by contrast, led to relatively more freedom and individualism.)

The General Conference included members of Dutch, Swiss and south German ethnic backgrounds, but remained relatively small until 1874. Then the arrival of several thousand Russian Mennonite immigrants (primarily of Dutch extraction) swelled GC Mennonite ranks. This irenic-spirited, multi-ethnic, progressive Mennonite group attracted the liberal Amish Mennonite congregations. By 1884 the Butler County, Ohio, Amish leader Peter Schrock (1803-1887) was attending the General Conference Mennonites' national meetings. By that time members of his own Augspurger Amish congregation and the neighboring Hessian Amish church were already subscribing to the *Christlicher Bundesbote*, the GC church periodical. Several years later the Butler County Amish adopted the GC hymnal.[37]

In 1892 the Hessian Amish church, now renamed the Apostolic Mennonite Church, relieved its three untrained Amish leaders of their ministerial responsibilities and called Iowa-born

Mennonite Henry J. Krehbiel (1865-1940) as its new minister. Krehbiel had just graduated from Evangelical Theological Seminary (now Eden Theological Seminary) in Saint Louis, Missouri, and was one of the few seminary-trained Mennonite ministers in North America. That same year the Apostolic Mennonite Church formally joined the General Conference Mennonite Church. Five years later the neighboring independent Augspurger Amish Mennonite congregation merged with the Apostolic group.[38]

Two other independent Amish congregations in Washington and Davis Counties, Iowa, also affiliated with the General Conference Mennonites. Under the progressive leadership of Bishop Benjamin Eicher and Preacher Philip Roulet, respectively, these two groups became disenchanted with the Amish Mennonite ministers' meetings of 1862-1878, considering the gatherings too conservative. Eicher did attend the 1874 *Diener-Versammlung* session held in his home county, but appeared only as an outside observer; he did not register as a participating leader. A newspaper reporter covering the gathering described Eicher as "a man of broad and liberal views," one "who has rebelled against the old custom."[39] By then Eicher had already attended GC meetings and had become interested in the idea of world missions. In 1892-1893 his church, under the name Emmanuel Mennonite, joined the General Conference.[40]

Other independent Amish congregations were following suit. The Davis County Amish also had interest in fellowshiping with the GC church. In 1888 Davis County Amish Preacher Roulet had invited a General Conference itinerant evangelist to conduct eight days of special meetings with the independent Amish group. The response of the congregation was so great and the spirit of the two churches so similar that formal unity soon followed.[41] Before the century ended, the GC Mennonites received other congregations of Amish Mennonite background.[42]

The Central Illinois Amish Mennonite Conference

By far the largest movement of Amish to the General Conference Mennonite camp was the collection of Amish congregations which looked for leadership to McLean County, Illinois, Bishop Joseph Stuckey.[43] (So loved was the old bishop that members of his church often called him "Father Stuckey.") Despite his falling-out with Amish Mennonite leaders in 1872 over his leniency with Joseph Joder, Stuckey did not break all of his contacts

The Amish Mennonites Merge with the Mennonites

1865   The Egly Amish division

1872   Joseph Stuckey Amish division

1888   Indiana-Michigan Amish Mennonite Conference forms

1890   Western Amish Mennonite Conference forms, includes Amish Mennonite congregations in Illinois, Iowa, Missouri, Arkansas, Nebraska, Kansas, Oklahoma, Colorado and Oregon

1893   Eastern Amish Mennonite Conference forms, includes congregations in Ohio and Pennsylvania

1908   Egly Amish take the name Defenseless Mennonite Church

1908   Stuckey Amish take the name Central Illinois Mennonite Conference

1910   Conservative Amish Mennonite Conference forms

1914   Central Illinois Mennonite Conference takes the name Central Conference Mennonite Church

1917   Indiana-Michigan Amish Mennonite Conference merges with the Indiana Mennonite Conference to form the Indiana-Michigan Mennonite Conference

1920   Western Amish Mennonite Conference merges with several Mennonite conferences in Illinois, Iowa, Kansas, Missouri, Nebraska and Oregon

1925   Ontario Amish Mennonite Conference forms

1927   Eastern Amish Mennonite Conference merges with the Ohio Mennonite Conference to form the Ohio Mennonite and Eastern Amish Mennonite Joint Conference

1946   Central Conference Mennonite Church affiliates with the General Conference Mennonite Church

1948   Defenseless Mennonite Church takes the name Evangelical Mennonite Church

1954   Conservative Amish Mennonite Conference takes the name Conservative Mennonite Conference

1955   Ohio Mennonite and Eastern Amish Mennonite Joint Conference takes the name Ohio and Eastern Mennonite Conference

1963   Ontario Amish Mennonite Conference takes the name Western Ontario Mennonite Conference

with the Amish Mennonites. While he never attended another ministers' meeting, he did occasionally preach in some of the very congregations whose leaders had expelled him. Most notable was a service held in his own church (by then named North Danvers) in 1889. Visiting from Wayne County, Ohio, Bishop John K. Yoder preached to an audience which included Stuckey and Illinois Amish Mennonite leader Christian Ropp.[44] Just seventeen years before, Ropp had asked Yoder to come and investigate Stuckey's church. That investigation had led to Ropp's and Yoder's breaking fellowship with the North Danvers bishop.

Despite such signs of forgiveness and healed relationships, Stuckey and the several Illinois Amish congregations in fellowship with his never re-joined the larger Amish Mennonite movement represented by Yoder and Ropp. Instead Stuckey found himself drawn more frequently to the goings-on of the General Conference Mennonites.[45] The open stance of the GCs on matters of dress and church organization appealed to Stuckey and his broad-minded friends. While the bishop himself retained his beard and somewhat traditional Amish garb, members of his congregation had quickly adapted their styles and patterns from larger society. Within Stuckey's lifetime female members of his churches stopped wearing their devotional prayer coverings and the dress of male members became largely indistinguishable from their non-Amish neighbors.[46]

After a GC periodical began regular release, Stuckey's articles appeared more frequently in its pages and less often in the "old" Mennonite *Herald of Truth*. Traveling GC preachers often filled Stuckey's pulpit by special invitation. Already in 1890 Stuckey's North Danvers church filed an annual report with the General Conference. Eight years later North Danvers actually hosted a regional GC meeting.[47] But just when Stuckey's loose grouping of churches seemed to be one step from joining the Mennonites, they hesitated and created their own denomination. In 1899 the nine "Stuckey Amish" churches began to hold their own annual gatherings. Stuckey's death in 1902 did not stunt the group's growth. Six years later the Stuckey fellowship had expanded to twelve congregations and organized under a formal constitution as the Central Illinois Conference of Mennonites (changed in 1914 to Central Conference Mennonite Church).[48]

The new Central Conference embarked on an ambitious program of work and witness after its 1908 reorganization. By 1911-1912, a mission board was sending church workers to the Belgian Congo (now Zaire). The missionaries worked in cooperation with the Defenseless Mennonite Church (formerly the Egly Amish, see pp. 176-179).[49] About the same time, the group began city mission work in Chicago and Peoria.[50] Along with the Defenseless Mennonites, the Central Conference also established the Mennonite Hospital in Bloomington, Illinois.[51] Stuckey's spiritual heirs also supported the GC-related college (and later seminary) at Bluffton, Ohio.[52]

The connectedness of the Central Conference (Stuckey Amish) with the General Conference Mennonites continued through the years. In 1946 the one-time Amish congregations of the Central Conference Mennonites officially joined the General Conference Mennonites Church. Eleven years later the Central Conference merged with the GC's Middle Disctrict to form the Central District Conference of the General Conference Mennonite Church. "Father" Stuckey's churches had found a Mennonite home.

The Egly Amish Become the Evangelical Mennonites

Not all the change-minded Amish joined one or another of the existing Mennonite groups. The Egly Amish created their own distinct Mennonite expression.[53] The Egly congregations had always had a unique flavor stemming from their special spirituality, which grew out of Amish practices and American evangelicalism. Under Henry Egly's leadership the loose association of congregations known as the Egly Amish remained rather informal in its organization. Sunday schools gained gradual acceptance as did church buildings.

But in some ways the Egly people remained close to their Amish roots. For example, Egly Amish church buildings often included a kitchen and dining area in which families remained after Sunday services to enjoy a common meal together—continuing in a modified way the old Amish practice of eating a group meal after worship. The Egly church also remained traditionally Amish in its attitude toward attire and worldly fashion. In 1883, the first annual conference of Egly-affiliated churches met and adopted strict standards of nonconformity. Male church members were not to neglect beards and women could not discard prayer coverings. As one historian observed, during "Egly's lifetime his people appear to have learned from revivalism without departing radically from Amish faith and practice."[54]

After Egly died in 1890, the fellowship of churches he had shepherded changed quite rapidly. A series of annual meetings met after 1895, a church periodical *Zion's Call* began publication two years later, and the group took on the more official name "Defenseless Mennonite Church" (dropping the designation "Amish" entirely). In 1896 the church began sponsoring missionaries in the Belgian Congo (now Zaire), and two years later established an orphanage near Flanagan, Illinois.[55] By 1908 the

Barbara Naffziger Springer (c.1840-1921) of Hopedale, Illinois, was a member of an Egly Amish congregation and continued to wear somewhat plain clothes (photograph taken 1917).

The Merging of Two Peoples: 1870-1937 177

C. Michel Richard (1829-1913) and Francoise Conrad Richard (1828-1906), members of the Montbeliard, France, Amish community retained somewhat traditional Amish dress.

church was legally incorporated. The Defenseless Mennonites had constructed church institutions quickly—an indication that they had left behind Egly's Amish informality and taken on more American ways of organized bureaucracy.

If American church structure was a boon to the erstwhile Egly Amish, American doctrinal controversy nearly destroyed the group. Defenseless Mennonite Preacher Joseph E. Ramseyer (1869-1944), along with Henry Egly's son Joseph (1859-1937), introduced new teachings from the larger world of Protestant theology. These new ideas included baptism only by immersion, a deviant view of end-times events and an understanding of salvation whereby the Christian received the Holy Spirit after (rather than as a part of) conversion. The Ontario-born, Amish Mennonite-raised Ramseyer also stressed a highly emotional conversion experience—much more so than had Henry Egly. The doctrinal controversy tore away at the Defenseless Church. In 1896, when Ramseyer refused to modify his stand, and then received a second water baptism from the Christian and Missionary Alliance Church, he was released from Defenseless Mennonite ministry. Joseph Egly and other sympathetic members followed Ramseyer and formed the Missionary Church Association (since 1969, a part of the Missionary Church).[56]

In the wake of the doctrinal controversy, division and emergence of new leadership among the Defenseless Mennonites, the church moved more toward American evangelicalism. Despite expelling influences such as Ramseyer, the Egly churches *were* nevertheless coming more and more under the sway of conservative American Protestantism. By the mid-twentieth century many of the Defenseless churches were aligned with what had come to be called "Fundamentalism." A strict understanding of substitutionary atonement, biblical inerrancy and individual conversion marked the teaching of former Egly Amish churches by the latter 1900s. In 1948 the church changed its name to the Evangelical Mennonite Church (EMC). The loss of the designation "Defenseless" represented more than just a new name: by the last quarter of the twentieth century only a minority of EMC members supported a position of biblical nonresistance to war and violence.[57] One hundred years after Egly's death, caught between identities rooted in Anabaptism and Evangelicalism, the EMC maintained membership in both the Mennonite Central Committee and the National Association of Evangelicals.

The Path of the European Amish

At the same time the North American Amish Mennonites were evolving into or joining one of the American or Canadian Mennonite groups, a similar pattern took shape in Europe. In the Old World, no Old Order Amish group ever developed; all the European Amish took the path of merger with the Mennonites. The European Mennonites (like most of their North American cousins) had always been more a part of the social mainstream than had the Amish. Thus as the European Amish became more acculturated and gave up many of their distinctive dress and worship practices, they naturally came to identify themselves as Mennonites. The distinctive Amish practices of simple apparel, full beards for men and hook-and-eye coats gradually fell into disuse among the spiritual heirs of Jakob Ammann. The one practice which continued to distinguish Amish from Mennonites was the observance of footwashing as a part of communion. The European Mennonites did not hold a literal footwashing service, but the Amish always did.

After 1850 the Amish church in Europe was rather small and never very strong. Heavy emigration to North America had

George Guth (1836-1871) and Magdalena Oesch Guth (1844-1870)
lived near Bitsche in the Lorraine, France, and were members of
the Ixheim Amish congregation. Both died of typhoid fever as a
result of the Franco-Prussian war.

drained the membership and leadership of many congregations.
Although steady emigration ended after 1860, quite a number of
Amish individuals and families continued to leave for North
America throughout the latter nineteenth century (virtually all
joined progressive Amish Mennonite congregations in the mid-
western United States).[58]

However, the drive to leave Europe was lessening as the
European Amish began to assimilate further into their surrounding culture. A young Amishman like Christian M. Nafziger
(1861-1953) might flee German conscription in 1883 and end up
in New York's Lewis County Amish Mennonite settlement, but
many other European members of his church were coming to
terms with military service.[59] Accepting army duty was more and
more common for young Amish (and Mennonite) men. Nor was
the world of politics completely foreign. In the 1880s, fellow
citizens elected Amish Elder Peter Schlabbach to the Prussian
legislature. But within a decade, Schlabbach's Hessian congregation had merged with the Mennonites.[60]

Many fewer Amish were left in Hesse—once a territory with a
high density of the church's members. The few hundred Amish
left there during the second half of the nineteenth century, like
Peter Schlabbach, gradually came to identify themselves with
neighboring Mennonites—or else joined more socially acceptable
Lutheran state churches. Many of the Hessian Amish congregations were quite conscious of their move toward Mennonitism.

At an 1867 Amish ministers' conference held in the Hessian town of Offenthal, seventeen leaders from six Amish congregations met to discuss ways in which they might adapt church doctrine and unite with the Mennonites.[61]

Of the Offenthal Conference's ten-point agreement, four items were especially telling. Regarding footwashing the conferees decided that "It shall be left to each congregation whether it is to be literally carried out" or not. As a symbol of servanthood footwashing might be a fine idea, "But it shall not be the basis of a future division," the leaders decided. On the subject of military participation the conference offered no clear word. "We leave to the careful consideration of each one," the delegates wrote, how "to do justice first to his own conscience and then also to the government." In a world of moral ambiguities and conflicting claims of loyalty, the church would leave such ponderous choices to individual young men. In two other decisions, the Offenthal gathering also approved mixed marriages and rejected social shunning in favor of merely excluding the excommunicated from communion. Most of the Offenthal congregations died out in a decade or two; the few which survived became Mennonite. By 1900 no Amish congregations existed in Hesse.

Likewise, the Bavarian Amish also declined rapidly during the 1800s. By mid-century, two of the territory's three congregations nearly dissolved, due simply to heavy emigration to Illinois and Ontario. A third church, near Regensburg, was still 200 members strong in 1888, but was quickly giving up any distinctive Amish practices. Regensburg member Josef Gingerich (1885-1953) long remembered his turn-of-the-century boyhood when "a considerable number left the [Amish] church."[62] In 1908 Gingerich's congregation both ceased the observance of footwashing and formally joined the German Mennonite Conference.

A sizable number of mostly small Amish congregations also existed, scattered through the French Lorraine, Alsace and Montbeliard regions. They, too, gradually found themselves working more closely with German Mennonites. Especially after 1871, when the Alsace came under German rule and the Lorraine remained French, was the church badly divided both politically and linguistically. The new conscription law of 1872 brought little reaction from the Alsatian Amish. Excommunication occurred less often in the closing decades of the nineteenth century; often the church implemented strict discipline only in cases of mixed marriages.[63]

Convened in 1896, a regional conference of these originally-Amish congregations from the Alsace, the Lorraine and Basel, Switzerland, met to form a more permanent organization. Formally constituted in 1907, the Alsatian Conference considered itself Mennonite despite its historic Amish background. Two other small Amish congregations remaining in Switzerland joined the Swiss Mennonite Conference. The two fellowships—Mennonite and Amish—were quietly reuniting after two centuries of separation; but the reunion was always on Mennonite terms.[64]

Not every vestige of Amish heritage disappeared immediately. Often Mennonite congregations of Amish background continued the Amish practice of footwashing as a part of communion celebration. The Luxembourg Amish-turned-Mennonites, for example, observed footwashing as late as 1941.[65] Still, the connection to an Amish heritage was faint and foggy for most.

The Last European Amish

The few Amish congregations which survived into the twentieth century soon dissolved or merged with other surrounding Mennonite groups. The old Bitscherland Amish congregation in Bitsche, the Alsace, dissolved after its Elder Christian Schantz died in 1902. The members who wanted to remain in an Amish fellowship traveled occasionally to the Palatinate to worship with the Saar or Ixheim Amish.[66] Seven years later another Amish fellowship, Hornbach-Zweibrücken, also ceased meeting after the death of its Elder Christian Stalter. Again, a portion of the membership joined the Ixheim group. Then in 1936 the Saar and Ixheim congregations themselves merged, having a combined membership of 134.[67] Ixheim now represented the sole independent Amish congregation in Europe. The other Amish had either officially or practically affiliated with the Mennonite conferences in the Alsace, the Lorraine or south Germany.

Long one of the most traditional Amish congregations, the Ixheim Amish continued to ordain unsalaried, untrained leaders, and in theory held to the social shunning of excommunicated members. Until 1932, they still practiced a footwashing service as part of their communion observance, and some men wore beards. But Ixheim, too, was considering giving up its independent Amish identity. Serious consideration began after 1929 when a member at Ixheim, Ernst Guth (1903-1986), married Mennonite Susanna Weiss (1903-1984). Weiss's Mennonite Pastor Hugo Scheffler met with

Meetinghouse (built c. 1844) used by the Ixheim Amish until 1937 when the group united with local Mennonites.

Amish Elder Christian Guth to discuss the wedding (since the Ixheim Amish did not approve of mixed marriages). Surprisingly, the conversation resulted in an Amish openness to officially recognizing and cooperating with the Mennonites.

On January 17, 1937, after several years of dialogue, the Ixheim Amish congregation and the nearby Ernstweiler Mennonite congregation united as a single fellowship and took on the name Zweibrücken Mennonite Church. One week later, during a special unity worship service, the two groups sang together, shared a common meal, listened to Mennonite brass instrumentalists and watched a slide show about the previous year's Mennonite World Conference gathering. Amish Elder Guth read a statement of unity and acceptance, and Mennonite Pastor Scheffler officially took over leadership of the new group. The Amish church in Europe lost its distinct identity.[68]

Sociologist John A. Hostetler has said that such a loss of European Amish identity was perhaps inevitable. Being primarily farm renters, the Amish in Europe did not always have the opportunity to live close to one another. They lived on scattered farms and homes often some distance apart. Most of their neighbors were members of other, established churches. The lack of close contact among the Amish kept a strong church solidarity from developing and left them more vulnerable to the influences of culture and the state. The European Amish, like their North American Amish Mennonite cousins, embraced West-

Jakob Schönbeck (1902-1981) of Ingweilerhof, Germany, was one of the last persons baptized into the Ixheim Amish congregation before the group formally merged with the neighboring Mennonites.

ern assumptions about the goodness of technological progress, educational advancement and social mobility. Unable to develop a healthy sense of community and peoplehood, the European Amish lost their reason for being a distinct church.[69]

Within several decades after 1900, the Amish Mennonites on both sides of the Atlantic dropped the word "Amish" as a means of identifying themselves, signalling their own sense of distance from their Amish past. Certainly in giving up the practices of social shunning the Amish Mennonites surrendered one of the key teachings which had set them apart for two centuries. In some quarters the Amish-turned-Mennonite congregations also quickly discontinued the practice of footwashing in conjunction with communion observance, and gave up most of their distinctive dress and appearance customs.

Once-Amish-now-Mennonite persons did continue to stress simple, ethical living as a response to God's gift of grace. A commitment to congregational authority, the church as the body of Christ in the world, and Jesus' teaching of peace and forgiveness also marked erstwhile Amish churches in the twentieth century. However, the Amish Mennonite emphases which such tenets received often expressed themselves through institutions and language which sounded more culturally North American or European than Amish. The carrying on of historic Amish principles, in a way which did not easily adopt society's values and idioms, fell to the Old Order Amish and related churches.

C. Henry Smith, Ph.D., (1875-1948)

One of the best known children of the Amish Mennonite church was C. Henry Smith. An educator, banker and prolific historian, Smith is the first North American Mennonite known to have earned a doctor of philosophy degree.

The son of Amish Mennonite Bishop John and Magdalena Schertz Smith, Henry grew up in the Partridge Creek-Metamora Amish Mennonite Church near Metamora, Illinois. He joined his parents' church at age fifteen and remained a member for about a decade before affiliating with the Mennonites. He was married to Laura Ioder (1880-1973) of Tiskilwa, Illinois.

Smith's educational journey began with high school studies—still rather unusual for Amish Mennonite youth at that time—and the encouragement of his father. Over the years Smith was a student at several colleges and universities, finishing his doctoral studies at the University of Chicago in 1907. By that time he had already taught several years at the Elkhart (Indiana) Institute—a secondary school sponsored by

C. Henry Smith at age seventeen.

a board of Mennonite and Amish Mennonite directors. Smith also taught at the school when it reorganized as Goshen (Indiana) College and came under direct Mennonite church administration. At Goshen, Smith taught history and served as dean.

In 1913 Smith moved to Bluffton, Ohio, and helped establish another Mennonite school, Bluffton College, where he served as professor of history until his death. He encouraged peace studies at both colleges and co-founded the Intercollegiate Peace Oratorical Association. A member of the General Conference Mennonite Church for much of his life, Smith served on its historical and publishing committees.

Smith's ongoing contribution to the Mennonite and Amish churches was his enormous volume of research and writing in Mennonite and Amish history. The author of a dozen books and scores of articles, Smith produced historical narrative and interpretation which is still used today. Smith also helped to organize and edit the 3700-page comprehensive reference work *The Mennonite Encyclopedia* (4 vols., 1955-1959).

In addition to his work in teaching and writing, Smith also organized and directed two national banks, one of which he served as president for many years. He managed both financial institutions so scrupulously that they were able to operate successfully and without restrictions throughout the Great Depression.

Smith was somewhat ambivalent towards his Amish heritage. He prized the Amish tenets of religious liberty and peace. But while acknowledging that "the Amish Mennonites were decidedly religious as well as an industrious people," Smith nevertheless regarded many as too conservative and elitist. The Amish "developed a sense of aloofness . . . that doomed them to . . . spiritual and social isolation," he concluded. While he later wrote that his upbringing left him with "an inferiority complex . . . from which I never recovered," Smith's heritage also inspired him to search out and interpret his people's story. And Smith's church is richer for his work.

See C. Henry Smith, *Mennonite Country Boy: The Early Years of C. Henry Smith* (Newton, Kans.: Faith and Life Press, 1962).

— 9 —

Preservation and Perseverence: The Old Order Amish, 1865-1900

> "We are minded, and promise to strive for simplicity and uniformity in all things."
> — *An Old Order Amish congregation in Iowa, 1891*

Choosing the Old Order

Those conservative Amish who came to be known as the "Old Order Amish" were not a large group during the last decades of the nineteenth century. In the aftermath of the annual ministers' meetings, about two-thirds of the church had chosen the progressive Amish Mennonite path. By the close of the 1800s, those tradition-minded Amish who continued to worship in private homes, maintain traditionally simple clothing patterns and serious church discipline numbered only about 5,000.[1]

Yet despite the trauma of division and the decidedly small size of the conservative group, it did not wither away or disintegrate. The Old Order church proved remarkably healthy for a body which had just undergone a series of wrenching schisms and turbulent unrest.[2] Even while the debates of the *Diener-Versammlungen* were closing the door to compromise and sealing the reality of a fractured Amish church, conservatives who would make up the Old Order fellowship were moving on and establishing new settlements. In 1866 as the progressive Amish Mennonites met for that year's ministers' meeting in McLean County, Illinois, tradition-minded families were also heading for that state. Amish were moving to Moultrie County, Illinois, not to attend that change-minded church gathering, but rather to join a new conservative church district there. During the previous two years, Amish from Somerset County, Pennsylvania, had settled in Moultrie near the small town of Arthur. Before

*A poster advertising land for sale in Michigan noted the presence
of "Colonies of Amish and Mennonites" in the state.*

long, Indiana, Ohio and Iowa families gathered there as well.
Arthur, Illinois, grew into a leading Old Order Amish community.
Founded during the years of Amish controversy and division,
Arthur represented the conservatives' ability to continue and
thrive, even as the majority of their church moved toward broader
social acculturation.[3]

Nor did the great schism among the Amish discourage non-
Amish persons from joining the conservative wing of the church.
Around 1863, for example, Lutheran Jacob Lambright joined the
Old Order church in northern Indiana. Within a decade, the
Bawell, Barkman, Flaud and Whetstone surnames (among oth-
ers) became part of Old Order Amish communities in various

189

Others Who Rejected Modernity or Chose the Way of Tradition

The Old Order Amish were not the only religious group which spurned the progressive spirit of nineteenth century North American life. After 1827 the Primitive Baptists rejected Sunday schools, church bureaucracy, salaried clergy and innovations in traditional Calvinist doctrine.

During the last quarter of the nineteenth century, an influential and wide-ranging Protestant movement known as dispensationalism also stood noticeably opposed to the optimistic tenor of Western culture. Dispensationalists did not hold the common assumption that North American society was improving, but rather felt that the world would become more corrupt as the second coming of Christ neared.

Among the Religious Society of Friends (Quakers) a conservative wing emerged from 1845 to 1904. Known as the Wilburites, these traditional Friends preserved early Quaker worship practices and theology. Members also stressed the importance of wearing plain attire, and maintained traditional Quaker speech patterns.

However, the Old Order groups which emerged from the Amish, Mennonite and Brethren churches rejected most completely both the spirit and practice of North American industrial society in the 1800s. The members of these Anabaptist fellowships chose the way of simple, nonconformed life—often for similar reasons. In 1845 and again from 1871-1901 several groups of Old Order Mennonites formed in Indiana, Ohio, Ontario, Pennsylvania and Virginia. The Mennonites who chose the way of tradition were concerned that their churches were moving too quickly down the path of cultural worldliness and doctrinal compromise. The Old Order Mennonites, for example, rejected Sunday schools and organized church bureaucracy and institutions. In most cases the Old Order Mennonites also retained German-language church services.

In contrast to the Old Order Amish, the Old Order Mennonites met in simple church meetinghouses (rather than members' homes) and did not practice shunning (one small Old Order Mennonite group did practice social avoidance). Old

Order Mennonite men were clean-shaven and wore buttoned coats.

Throughout the twentieth century Old Order Mennonites (like the Old Order Amish) avoided higher formal education, retained traditional clothing patterns, and many continued the use of horse-drawn transportation.

During the 1800s, Old Order groups also formed in other Anabaptist-related churches. Among the German Baptist Brethren ("Dunkers") an Old Order group formed after 1881 and took the name Old German Baptist Brethren (the progressive half of the church became the Church of the Brethren and the Brethren Church). During the first half of the nineteenth century, another related group, the River Brethren, had divided into Old Order River Brethren and (progressive) Brethren in Christ and United Zion camps. In each case, the Old Order churches among the Brethren attempted to preserve the best of their traditions and stave off the negative influences of surrounding secular North American culture. They have continued plain dress and traditional worship patterns, but only a very few drive buggies, and all use English as their first language.

The Old Order Amish, Mennonite and Brethren groups have often found themselves on the same side of controversies with the state regarding matters of compulsory education and welfare laws. Members of various Old Order churches often feel a fraternal bond with one another despite the very real distinctions which exist among them. Many Old Order Mennonites, for example, subscribe and contribute articles to the Old Order Amish magazine *Family Life*. Together the Old Order groups have maintained a remarkably clear and consistent witness to the rest of Western society.

For more information on the beginnings of Old Order groups, see Beulah Stauffer Hostetler, "The Formation of the Old Orders," *The Mennonite Quarterly Review* 66 (January 1992): 5-25; and Theron F. Schlabach, *Peace, Faith, Nation: Mennonites and Amish in Nineteenth-Century America* (Scottdale, Pa. and Kitchener, Ont.: Herald Press, 1988), pp. 201-30.

states as non-Amish persons bearing those family titles joined the tradition-minded Amish church.[4] Clearly, Old Order Amish life and faith appealed to some Americans even as it drove other Amish Mennonites away.

As the Old Order Amish church slowly grew, important new settlements started in Daviess County, Indiana (1868); Reno County, Kansas (1883); and Geauga (1886) and Madison Counties (1896), Ohio. A number of new Old Order church districts also formed in other states, but did not survive. Often troubled church affairs or the economic difficulties of homesteading caused these settlements to dissolve.[5]

While the church spread across North America, Old Order Amish connectedness could have easily fragmented. A few thousand people scattered across a whole continent, the conservatives might have lost all sense of commonality. However, the Old Order Amish remained remarkably close-knit considering their many settlements and relatively small numbers. One way in which Amish persons kept in contact with one another was through reading correspondence newspapers such as *The Belleville* (Pennsylvania) *Times* or *The Sugarcreek* (Ohio) *Budget.* Originally conceived as local, small town papers, journals such as *The Budget* regularly printed news items from Amish communities far and wide. Thus, an Indiana *Budget* subscriber could read news not only of the publisher's Tuscarawas County, Ohio, but also reports from Amish settlements in Iowa, North Dakota, Nebraska, Pennsylvania or elsewhere. Originally *The Budget* was primarily an Amish Mennonite newspaper, but it also functioned within the broader Old Order community as a means of keeping in touch with a growing fellowship[6] (see "*The Budget,*" p. 202).

Old Order Amish communities also remained connected through personal contacts and visiting. Many Amish young people traveled by rail to other Amish settlements. The autograph books of these teens and young adults record the names of friends and acquaintances from across the country.[7] At times young people (most often young men) would take jobs in other Amish settlements for a season or a few years. The youth learned to know other areas and families, and their correspondence with relatives at home offered insights even to those who never traveled. The brothers Isaac and Andrew Ebersol, for example, were among those who left their parents' eastern Pennsylvania farm and lived elsewhere for a time. The Ebersols took jobs with their uncle in Arthur, Illinois. During their time in Arthur, each wrote several letters to their cousin, Sarah E. Lapp (1875-1907), who had remained in Lancaster, Pennsylvania.[8] The boys described life in Illinois, midwestern commodity prices, Moultrie County weather, church affairs and the Arthur young people's social life.

In January 1897 Sarah Lapp received another letter from a traveling Amish youth. This one was from Isaac Zook (1877-1930), a Lancaster boy who had gone to work among the Mifflin County, Pennsylvania, Amish. Zook described Mifflin's "Big Valley" in which he lived, and then told about a minor accident in which he had been involved. He also listed the names of quite a few young Amish couples whose wedding engagements the local bishop had recently "published" (announced to the rest of the church). Zook continued: "If that is the go, I guess I must tell them to have me published while I am here too—" then added, "O excuse me, it takes two Don't it? Well then I'll waite [sic] a while yet I guess. . . ."[9] He did wait and returned to Lancaster. Later that year, Isaac and Sarah married.

Weddings and special occasions were certainly times of celebration among the Old Order Amish. Although most Old Orders avoided extravagance, many exchanged holiday greeting cards. In an extremely rare instance a family might even decorate a tree for the holidays. Two days before Christmas 1888, a young Sallie J. Fisher wrote to her cousin, wishing that the other girl could "see our ever green," because the Old Order Amish Fisher family intended "to make it white with popcorn and candy."[10]

Of course everyday life also included much hard work. One evening, quite tired, Lancaster County teen Bettsy Speicher reported that her family was finally finished with corn husking and making 100 crocks of apple butter, but still had "the whole house left to clean." Speicher also said that her family kept three cows and "a hundred chickens more or less." The animals did provide some little income—selling cream earned the family a few dollars.[11] Several years later, Bettsy's friend Rebecca S. Smucker described her full day of washing and ironing, noting that her mother had been patching clothes, her father caring for the livestock, and her brothers working in the "smith shop" and repairing shoes.[12] Old Order Amish life was like that of other rural Americans—family, fun and strenuous labor combined to challenge the elements of weather and economic unpredictability.

In general, Amish farming practices did not differ significantly from those of their non-Amish neighbors. The Old Order Amish made use of nineteenth-century agricultural inventions such as mechanical hay loaders, grain binders and grain threshing machines. Some observers did note that the Amish often relied more heavily on almanac folklore which many Americans considered

The so-called "Nebraska" Amish of Mifflin County, Pennsylvania, are among the most conservative of all Old Order Amish. The group has retained some clothing patterns from the eighteenth century: men wear white shirts with no suspenders, trousers which tie in the back, and especially wide-brimmed hats. Women's capes and aprons are of a contrasting color from that of their accompanying dresses. Prayer coverings are made of opaque white material. The Nebraska Amish drive very simple buggies with white cloth tops.

outdated and unscientific, yet popular opinion and the national press respected the Amish as accomplished farmers.[13]

Tradition and Change

Although similar in many ways to that of its rural neighbors, Amish life was nevertheless different in that it was so closely guided by a strong sense of church tradition and community. Old Order Amish church districts worked diligently to preserve family and community life. Pride and wastefulness could have no place in the Christian church. The Old Order Amish in the Midwest, for example, continued to drive open carriages throughout the nineteenth century (and even after their switch to closed-top buggies in the early 1900s, their carriages remained simple and functional).[14]

The Amish also maintained traditional grooming styles and patterns. The plain clothing of Old Order Amish men and women physically demonstrated humility and separateness. Men continued the use of hook-and-eye fasteners instead of buttons on their coats, as well as the wearing of untrimmed beards. Amish women wore prayer coverings as a sign of biblical obedience.[15] During the late 1800s, many North American denominations (and especially churches in the Holiness and Adventist traditions) encouraged their members to dress simply and conservatively. But Old Order Amish appearance was noticeably plain, even by the standards of the time. In the opinion of one observer of the Old Order Amish in eastern Pennsylvania, the men wore "remarkably wide brimmed hats," and coats "plainer than those of the plainest Quakers."[16] Community custom, grounded in biblical principle and supported and encouraged by the church, strengthened and formed Old Order Amish life.

Important as tradition and community were, they did not always function as rigid rules of order. A good deal of variation and flexibility seasoned Old Order life. Given particular or peculiar circumstances, Amish church districts permitted individual members a degree of latitude in tampering with community boundaries. Old Order lifestyle prescriptions were flexible enough to handle members' special needs.[17]

Nor were tradition and community stifling forces which smothered creative thinking. Those who took the Old Order path were not uninformed persons who retained conservative values because they knew no better. One important Amish lay leader who

Modern Assumptions and the Old Order World View

Many moderns have difficulty understanding the Old Order way of life and faith. Most of this difficulty results from the very different foundational assumptions which most moderns hold about themselves, their world, their society and their rights. More than simply wearing different clothes, or using different types of technology, Old Order persons actually work with very different assumptions than do Western moderns. It is the Old Order world view which has shaped Old Order life, and it is that Old Order world view which moderns *must* try to understand if they are to make sense of the traditionalists' lifestyle.

Historian Theron Schlabach has suggested that North Americans who want to understand Old Order people need to at least temporarily set aside their own modern assumptions. As Schlabach notes, "To set aside such assumptions momentarily does not mean one must romanticize Old Order groups or finally accept the Old Order outlook and critique of modern life. It is only to step outside the prison of mental habits long enough to understand a different view."

Among the modern "mental habits" which North American observers need to lay aside when trying to understand the Old Order Amish (and Old Order Mennonites) are these: Moderns must *not* assume:

"That ideas expressed and tested in words are brighter and truer than ideas which take their form in personal and community life.

"That people who accept the ideas of the eighteenth century's so-called Age of Reason are the 'enlightened' ones of the world.

"That change is usually good, and usually brings 'progress.' (The Old Order-minded accepted this change or that—a new tool, perhaps, or rail travel. But they were not progressiv*ists*.)

"That the individual is the supreme unit, individual rights the most sacred rights, and human life richest when individuals are most autonomous.

"That the really important human events are those controlled in Washington, New York, Boston, London, Paris, and other centers of power—rather than events around hearths or at barn raisings or in meeting at Weaverland [Pennsylvania, Old Order Mennonite community] or Plain City [Ohio] or Yellow Creek [Indiana, Old Order Mennonite community] or Kalona [Iowa].

"That vigor of programs, institutions, activity (including Protestant-style missions) are a test of a Christian group's validity and faithfulness.

"That large organizations, organizational unity, and denominational and interdenominational tolerance are better measures of Christian success than is close-knit congregational life.

"That people who imbibe some alcohol or use tobacco have deeply compromised their Christianity.

"Similarly, that people are poor Christians if their sons and daughters wait until adulthood to put off youthful rowdiness and become sober-minded Christians.

"That a structure of rules and explicit expectations (some moral, others mainly just practical for group cohesion) is always legalistic and at odds with the Christian idea of grace.

"That *salvation* refers almost entirely to the individual's original transaction and covenant with God at the time of personal conversion.

"That in church history, words such as *reform* or *renewal* apply only to movements which share the progressivist faith and apply new methods and new activities; and that leaders who look to the past, or who think faithfulness may come by strict discipline, are simply reactionary and formalistic."

Freeing themselves from these arbitrary modern assumptions and opinions, observers of Old Order Christians may begin to better understand the way of life these people have chosen.

Quotations from Theron F. Schlabach, *Peace, Faith, Nation: Mennonites and Amish in Nineteenth-Century America* (Scottdale, Pa. and Kitchener, Ont.: Herald Press, 1988), pp. 201, 203.

remained with the Old Order wing of the church for most of his life was the educated and articulate Samuel D. Guengerich (1836-1929).[18] Born in Somerset County, Pennsylvania, Guengerich moved with his family to Ohio and then Iowa. As a young man he taught in local schools and decided to return to Pennsylvania to receive formal training in education. In 1864 he received a teaching certificate from Millersville State Normal School (now Millersville University). He then taught several terms in Somerset County before going back to Iowa.

"A good education and well-cultivated mind may be regarded almost indispensable in many respects," Guengerich wrote at one point in his studies.[19] He cultivated his own mind with visits to such places as Washington, D.C., where in 1889 he saw the Botanical Garden, the Smithsonian Institute, the headquarters of the Federal Fish Commission and the Capitol. At age twenty-eight he had purchased a "telescope and a mikeroscope [sic] and a box of drawing instruments" with which to further explore his world.[20] Always reading and learning, Guengerich also established a private publishing business and issued a German periodical and German youth publication.

Near the end of his life, Guengerich's congregation left the Old Order Amish fellowship and affiliated with the progressive Amish Mennonites, but Guengerich himself seems to have been satisfied with the lifestyle of the Old Order church. He did not view his studies as incompatible with his church membership. Although Guengerich's foray into the classroom was quite unusual, he was accepted by other Old Orders as a student and teacher. His diaries record his regular interaction and full church fellowship with the Old Order Amish of Lancaster County, Pennsylvania, while he studied at the local normal school.

Nor was Guengerich the only trained school teacher among the Old Orders. Isaac Huyard (1865-1940), a Millersville student of a generation after Guengerich, joined the Amish. Huyard came from an English Lutheran family and from 1886 to 1888 attended the Normal School at Millersville. In 1892 he converted to the Old Order Amish faith and remained a committed member the rest of his life. His wife, Mary Zook, had been raised in an Amish home, and Isaac himself had boarded with a Lancaster County Amish family during some of his growing-up years.[21]

In some places, entire Amish communities tested the boundaries of Old Order tradition, but remained within the conservative camp. The Somerset County, Pennsylvania; Kalona, Iowa; and Arthur, Illinois, Old Order settlements, for example, replaced the old Anabaptist hymnal, the *Ausbund*, with a newer collection of songs. First published in 1860, *Eine Unparteiische Lieder-Sammlung* (called "the Baer book" because it was printed by Johann Baer of Lancaster, Pa.) represented an obvious break with tradition, but the book's users did not choose to adopt it as a first step toward giving up their spiritual heritage. Instead, the new songbook strengthened congregational singing where it found a home. Likewise the Daviess County, Indiana, Old Orders switched to the 1892 *Unparteiische Liedersammlung* (called "the Guengerich book," but actually published by Christian J. Swartzendruber). "The Guengerich book" was an even more recent hymn compilation, but also included much of the old *Ausbund* material as well.[22]

Nor were the Old Order Amish completely free from the nineteenth century North American temptations of institution building and reorganization. In the mid-1870s the Lancaster County church created a special mutual aid fund to assist families in the event of fire or storm loss. While the purpose was as old as the church itself, the methods were novel. Instead of church deacons receiving private, anonymous donations of alms for those hurt by the elements of nature, now "Amish Aid Society" directors assessed member families and charged them fixed rates. The whole program was far from bureaucratic and never completely replaced the work of the deacons (who continued to collect money for the needy), but Amish Aid did represent a modest move in the direction of greater church formality and structure.[23]

Perhaps most unusual and innovative were the Somerset County, Pennsylvania, Old Order Amish who built four church meetinghouses. In 1881 they erected two structures in Pennsylvania, and two across the border in Garrett County, Maryland. The appearance of a meetinghouse in an Amish community had always signaled its decided move toward progressive Amish Mennonitism. The Somerset group, however, built physical church structures, *and* remained Old Order Amish.[24] (Such was extremely rare, however; only a very small number of Old Order Amish worship in church buildings.)

Not all communities were so successful in balancing tradition and selective change. In 1891, the Old Order Amish in Johnson County, Iowa, also built meetinghouses with the intent of re-

PUBLIC SALE

The undersigned will offer at public sale about one and one-half miles west and one-fourth mile south of Bertrand

THURSDAY, JAN. 14

at 11 o'clock a. m., the following described property:

HORSES

One mare coming 5 years old, one horse 11 years old, one old mare, one colt coming 1 year old, one mare 6 years old.

CATTLE

Eight milch cows, six coming in early, two later on; eight calves, five of which are steers; one red bull coming 2 years old, mostly Shorthorn.

24   HEAD OF SHOATS   24

FARM IMPLEMENTS

One spring wagon, one J. I. C. riding plow, one walking plow, one Little Dandy riding cultivator, one tongueless cultivator, one 3-section steel harrow, one Farmers' Friend corn planter with checkrower, one walking lister, one 1-horse corn drill, one endgate seeder, one hand corn sheller, 2 wagons, some pump tools, stack of hay and some corn fodder.

HOUSEHOLD GOODS

One cook stove, one heating stove, some chairs, one bureau, one Singer Sewing machine, one clock, two bedsteads and many other articles not mentioned here.

FREE LUNCH AT NOON

TERMS OF SALE

All sums of $10 and under cash, on all sums over $10 a credit of nine months will be given on note with approved security drawing 8 per cent interest from date. Two per cent discount for cash.

C. J. CARLSON,
Auctioneer

Y. B. YODER

Sale bill of Yost B. Yoder (1851-1938) of Gosper County, Nebraska. Yost B. was selling out to move to Pennsylvania and join the "Nebraska" Amish of Mifflin County.

maining conservative. Members even signed a statement which promised, "This church house shall and dare not be a means of granting us more freedom toward worldliness. . . ." In fact, the statement continued, "we are minded, and promise to strive for simplicity and uniformity in all things, and to remain true to the fundamentals of our faith."[25] Such statements summed up Old Order purposes nicely. Yet the two congregations involved proved less than successful; within three decades they had made the move to the progressive Amish Mennonite camp.

The ability to make carefully selected lifestyle changes—yet not be swept away by social acculturation and accommodation— seems to have been an Old Order art. Sensing the times and the implicit dangers of many cultural trends, the Amish reacted in ways which seem today to have had deep sociological insight. But even the Old Order Amish disagreed on how much change was too threatening to Christian community and healthy family life. By 1881, some Mifflin County, Pennsylvania, Old Orders were beginning to feel that their own tradition-minded people were becoming somewhat caught up in material pursuits. New clothing styles, grooming habits and technological innovation had received too much notice even from some conservative families, the concerned group thought. Because the ultra-conservative group was made up only of lay members and a deacon, members wrote to Old Order Amish Bishop Yost H. Yoder (1842-1901) of Gosper County, Nebraska, and asked him to help organize their fellowship. The previous year the bishop had helped to found the Gosper settlement.[26]

Yoder traveled to Pennsylvania to help the new ultra-conservative fellowship get started. His role in the group's beginnings earned them the nickname "Nebraska Amish," despite their Appalachian home. The "Nebraska" (also called "Old School") Amish maintained a very traditional church and family life. The group retained some clothing standards typical of colonial American dress, and adopted remarkably few technological innovations in their farming practices. They became known as the most conservative of all Old Order Amish. After 1904 their numbers increased somewhat. That year Yoder's Gosper County settlement dissolved and several of its families moved to Pennsylvania and joined the group bearing their old state's name.[27]

So within the relatively small Old Order Amish fellowship itself there was a surprising amount of diversity. From the ultra-

The Budget

For more than one hundred years, Amish community news has traveled from place to place on the pages of a weekly newspaper called The Budget. Published in Sugarcreek, Ohio, *The Budget* contains brief reports from Old Order Amish, Beachy Amish, conservative Mennonites and Old Order Mennonite communities throughout North and South America. Correspondents (known as "scribes") in each community keep track of local newsworthy events, including births, deaths, weddings, illnesses, the weather and (in the case of the Old Order Amish) which family hosted church meeting. After writing the week's news into a brief column, the scribe sends the information to Sugarcreek, where editors type-set the material along with that of other scribes, and prepare yet another issue of their very special publication.

First issued in 1890, The Budget was intended to be a bi-weekly local paper for the Sugarcreek community. During its first year, however, the paper included news items from communities as far away as Arkansas. Those who sent news from other states or areas within Ohio generally had relatives living around Sugarcreek and used the paper as a means of staying in contact with them. The paper still included a good amount of local Sugarcreek news and kept its subscription price at fifty cents a year, but in 1891 it became a weekly and took on a more national flavor. By 1899 each issue of *The Budget* contained about thirty letters from correspondents who lived in other areas.

The paper's owner and second editor was Sugarcreek resident John C. Miller (1860-1913). Miller's family was Old Order Amish, but he had joined the progressive Amish Mennonites. Nevertheless, his paper included reports from both groups. By 1900, though, probably less than one third of the correspondents were Old Order Amish; *The Budget* was primarily an Amish Mennonite paper. Some Mennonites read and reported news to the paper as well. The Mennonite school, Goshen (Indiana) College, placed school news, announcements and advertisements in *The Budget*'s pages.

After about 1920 the subscriber list began to change. The

Amish Mennonite merger with the Mennonites made Amish Mennonite readers more eager to purchase officially Mennonite periodicals. Circulation of *The Budget* dropped considerably as many Amish Mennonite and Mennonite readers allowed their subscriptions to expire. Even the Amish Mennonite family which had served as the paper's owners and editors did not retain the business. They sold *The Budget* to Samuel A. Smith (1884-1960), a local Lutheran who was a good friend of the Old Order Amish. Under the editorship of Smith and his son George R. Smith (b. 1907), *The Budget* took on more and more Old Order Amish scribes and readers.

Known as *The Sugarcreek Budget* during its first years, the paper has gone by its shorter name since 1930. The periodical has not forgotten its home community. Since 1946-47 *The Budget* has appeared each week in both a "Local Edition" and a "National Edition." The local run is much like other small-town newspapers and includes news of Sugarcreek's non-Amish community. The "National" offers only the scribes' reports. Often the scribes' correspondence alone fills over twenty pages.

The Budget has served a unique role among the Amish. By providing a forum for the exchange of news and announcements, the paper has helped to link together the Amish community in a much closer and more intimate way than telephones, radios or television ever could have.

Over the years two other papers have offered news from various Amish communities. *The Belleville Times* (published from 1894 to 1973 in Mifflin County, Pennsylvania) and *Die Botschaft* (published since 1975, today in Lancaster County, Pennsylvania) have offered reports of Old Order correspondents from across the continent. *Die Botschaft* only publishes letters from Old Order scribes. During the 1980s it increased its circulation noticeably, and in some places is more widely read than *The Budget*. From about 1920 to 1980, however, *The Budget* was the most important weekly among the Old Order Amish.

See David Luthy, "A History of *The Budget*," *Family Life* (June 1978): 19-22; (July 1978): 15-18; Elmer S. Yoder, *I Saw It in The Budget* (Hartville, Ohio: Diakonia Ministries, 1990); and Harvey Yoder, "*The Budget* of Sugarcreek, Ohio, 1890-1920" *The Mennonite Quarterly Review* 40 (January 1966): 27-47.

traditional "Nebraskans," to Somerset County Old Orders who met in meetinghouses and used new hymnals, the spectrum—though not terribly wide—was broader than many observers realized. Although decidedly conservative in their outlook and world view, the Old Order Amish were not a homogeneous, uniform group.

The "Strict Shunning" Controversy

In the minds of many Old Orders, not every aspect of life and thought was negotiable. During the 1890s an important debate erupted in the church regarding the practice of excommunication and shunning. The doctrine of Christian avoidance of unrepentant sinners had always been a defining mark of the Amish church. It gave integrity and seriousness to church discipline, and in many cases, proved redemptive.

In the last years of the nineteenth century serious questions arose over the relationship between the Old Order Amish and the Amish Mennonites. Ever since the sorting out of tradition-minded and change-minded Amish during and after the *Diener-Versammlungen*, the two groups which emerged had maintained an uneasy, but cordial, relationship. Persons who left the Old Order Amish church as members in good standing and joined the Amish Mennonites were not excommunicated or shunned by the conservative group.[28] For their part the Amish Mennonites did not meddle in Old Order church discipline. If someone left the Old Order Amish on bad terms, the Amish Mennonites would not accept that one as a member until the errant one had made peace with his or her former church district. In short, persons quietly leaving the Old Order church found a welcome among the Amish Mennonites, but the progressive church would not accept those who left the Old Orders in anger or in disobedience.

An incident involving Old Order Amish Preacher Moses Hartz, Sr. (1819-1916), and his wife Magdalena Nafziger Hartz (1822-1901) challenged the two groups' delicate balance.[29] Hartz had been a German orphan who had found work and a home in the Conestoga Amish community of Lancaster and Berks Counties, Pennsylvania.[30] Joining the group as a young man, Hartz eventually received the church's ordination and served faithfully for many years. During the Amish Mennonite-Old Order Amish division of the 1870s, he remained with the conservative group.[31]

After 1894 trouble erupted in the Hartz home. Their son,

Moses Hartz, Jr. (1864-1946), took a job as a traveling mechanic for a millworks company. The nature of the assignment forced Hartz to miss a good number of Sunday morning church meetings, and to wear clothing out of line with church understandings of appropriately modest and simple dress. Instead of listening to church counsel and finding another job, Moses, Jr., simply left the church. But he had trouble finding another church home. The more progressive Amish Mennonites denied him membership. Finally Hartz affiliated with a local Mennonite congregation which accepted him, despite his admittedly irregular participation in church life.

Unlike joining the Amish Mennonites, taking membership with the Mennonites was considered a breaking of one's baptismal vows. When the younger Hartz joined the Mennonites, his action immediately excommunicated him from the Old Order church and called for his shunning by that group. But Preacher Moses, Sr., and Magdalena announced that they would not shun their son.

Now two generations of Hartzes were being disobedient—the

The children of Moses and Magdalena Hartz in 1934. David (1860-1959), Mennonite; Rebecca (1854-1946), Amish Mennonite; Jacob (1857-1936), Amish Mennonite; and Moses, Jr. (1864-1946), one-time Mennonite, by 1934 a member of the Religious Society of Friends (Quakers). In the 1890s the "strict shunning" controversy had swirled around Moses, Jr., and his parents.

younger Hartz had left the church entirely and now the parents refused to put into practice a key church teaching because of family favoritism. Eventually the elder Hartz's congregation silenced him from preaching. The Hartzes did not want to be cut off from their son, nor did they want to lose contact with their other Old Order family and friends. They devised a way around their unique situation: they would simply apply for membership in the nearby Amish Mennonite church. By quietly joining the Amish Mennonites, they could leave the Old Order church without being excommunicated themselves, and once they were Amish Mennonites, they would not need to shun Moses, Jr. (the Amish Mennonites had abandoned the practice of social avoidance).

The Old Order Amish were faced with a dilemma: should they discipline the elder Hartzes? Some argued that so long as the couple were joining another nonresistant, somewhat plain, Amish-related church, the ban and avoidance were unnecessary. Another sub-group stood for what became known as *streng Meidung* ("strict shunning"). Advocates of "strict shunning" felt that excommunication and avoidance should be practiced in all cases in which Old Order members broke their baptismal vows and left the tradition-minded group. The "strict shunning" position was not a new idea. A decade earlier, some Old Order leaders had proposed its practice, but the Hartz family incident became the point which tested the issue.

A series of Amish Mennonite-Old Order Amish joint meetings and church negotiations including Amish leaders from Ohio, failed to settle the matter. Under the false impression that the Old Order Amish would not object to the Hartzes becoming Amish Mennonites, the progressive church finally accepted them as members. But apparently the Old Orders had not yet made their final decision. A year later, in 1897, at a special gathering of conservative Amish leaders, the Old Order church decided that it would not accept the Hartzes becoming Amish Mennonites; the traditionalists would shun the couple for their disobedience. Moreover, no one else would be permitted to slip into the Amish Mennonite meetinghouse from an Old Order church district without also facing excommunication and avoidance.

The two groups which had maintained their tenuous connection for two decades had grown too far apart to maintain close fellowship. The change-minded and tradition-minded Amish were finally going their separate ways. The adoption of "strict shunning" marked a sharper break between the Old Order Amish and the Amish Mennonites.

Not all Amish communities chose the path of "strict shunning." A situation in the Arthur, Illinois, Amish church concluded differently than did the Hartz incident. In the mid-1890s in Moultrie County, Illinois, Joni (1865-1937) and Anna Yutzy (1864-1919) Helmuth found themselves excommunicated from the Old Order Amish church.[32] About the same time, in 1897, a new Amish Mennonite congregation formed in that area and the Helmuths soon began attending its Sunday school and applied for formal membership.[33] Most of the new group's members had grown up in Old Order Amish homes, but few were actually Amish church members. For the Helmuths, the situation was different—they had been church members and had then been disciplined.

When the new Amish Mennonite church took the Helmuths as members, some Old Order Amish suggested that their excommunication be lifted and the shunning ended. After all, the couple were now members in good standing of another Amish-related church. Others in the community felt that the ban must remain in place. In their minds, the Helmuths had both made solemn baptismal vows before God that they would give and receive church discipline. Now they had broken that promise, and their excommunication could not be forgotten until they confessed the wrong.

In the end both groups got their way; the Arthur community compromised. Those who felt that the ban should be lifted acted as though it was. Other Old Orders who wished to continue practicing shunning did as they saw fit. Amish leaders from other communities who came to mediate the situation agreed that such a compromise was best. Although one leader thought that a continent-wide Old Order ministers' meeting should discuss the whole matter of "strict shunning," no such gathering ever took place.

The "strict shunning" question did not go away. Into the twentieth century it lingered in some areas. It demonstrated the continued importance which the doctrine of social avoidance played in Amish church life two centuries after Jacob Ammann and Hans Reist had first debated the issue. It also illustrated the seriousness with which many Old Order persons regarded baptismal vows and the sin of disobedience.

Henry Lapp and Barbara Ebersol: Amish Folk Artists

Despite their physical challenges, both Henry Lapp (1862-1904) and Barbara Ebersol (1846-1922) were well-known folk artists and contributing members of Old Order Amish society.

Henry Lapp was nearly deaf from birth and always partially mute. Nevertheless, as an adult he established a small hardware store of his own near the village of Intercourse, Pennsylvania. He sold paint and other carpentry supplies at the shop. A creative and inventive man, Lapp once received a patent for a shutter bolt which he had developed. Lapp was best known for his own cabinetry work. Using a wind-powered saw and lathe, Lapp produced fine furniture, carriages, sleighs and even wooden toys. Traveling often to Philadelphia, Lapp absorbed

(left) A page from Henry Lapp's furniture sketch book showing two of his designs. (right) The fraktur book plate which Barbara Ebersol painted for her own Ausbund.

some of the feel of that city's tastes. His furniture incorporated latter nineteenth-century Philadelphia styles along with more traditional Pennsylvania-German patterns.

Lapp took orders using his own custom-designed notebook. In the book, Lapp painted pictures of his furniture and other creations. Using the book and pointing to the pictures and colors, he was able to overcome his speech and hearing limitations, take requests and successfully fill commercial orders.

Lapp also produced a series of wonderful animal and floral watercolors for his nieces and nephews. Both these pictures and his catalog book are now considered folk art treasures. The catalog-notebook is part of the collection at the Philadelphia Museum of Art and has been reproduced for sale to collectors.

Barbara Ebersol also lived in Lancaster County. Barbara was a dwarf. Later in her life she also experienced difficulty in walking and had to use crutches. She lived her entire life with four of her unmarried siblings. Affectionately nicknamed "Bevlie," Barbara spent much of her time working as a seamstress. In the evenings she relaxed with family or friends and smoked homemade cigars. Like Lapp, Ebersol joined the Old Order Amish and remained a member of church for the rest of her life.

Some of Ebersol's first artwork was her fancy needlework with which she embellished towels and pillow cases. Ebersol's specialty and most renowned artwork were her fraktur bookplates. "Fraktur," or Pennsylvania German illuminated manuscript, was an art form used to create decorative certificates, family records and bookplates. Ebersol's work has been dated as early as 1859 and as late as 1918.

Ebersol loved to paint flowers in her work, but some pieces include stars and other geometric shapes. One very rare painting included a man dressed in a military uniform astride a horse. Creating such a human likeness—and a martial one at that—is not easily explained in Amish art work.

Many of Ebersol's pieces still exist. Often she would lacquer her finished fraktur work to protect it. Because she was careful to date many of her illustrations, critics have been able to study her style and its evolution through her lifetime. A most unusual and free-spirited Amish woman, Ebersol was limited only by her physical body; her artwork carried her far beyond its boundaries.

See Beatrice B. Garvin, ed., *A Craftsman's Handbook: Henry Lapp* (Intercourse, Pa.: Good Books, 1991); David Luthy, "Henry Lapp: Amish Folk Artist and Craftsman," *Pennsylvania Mennonite Heritage* 11 (October): 2-6; Daniel McCauley and Kathryn McCauley, *Decorative Arts of the Amish of Lancaster County* (Intercourse, Pa.: Good Books, 1988); David Luthy, "Amish Folk Artist: Barbara Ebersol (1846-1922)," *Pennsylvania Mennonite Heritage* 14 (April): 2-7.

Depression Politics and the Amish

But Old Order Amish life was certainly not limited only to church affairs. Although appearing to be largely withdrawn from the goings-on of larger American society, the Old Order Amish were never unaware of, or unaffected by, happenings in their surrounding host societies. In the 1890s many Amish faced harsh economic realities along with their non-Amish neighbors. The economic depression of 1893-1897 was the worst that the United States had experienced until that time. During 1893 alone, 500 banks failed and 16,000 businesses closed their doors in bankruptcy. Probably twenty percent of the work force was unemployed for some part of those bleak years.[34]

The farm economy was particularly hard hit, especially in the midwestern and plains states. Serious drought conditions in some areas added to the problems. Commodity prices dropped sharply and land values plummeted. In spite of lower land costs, many of the farms for sale were still too expensive for young farm families attempting to set up business on their own. Hard-pressed farmers moved in search of cheaper acres. Amish were a part of that migration. In all, eleven new Old Order Amish settlements began during the depression years. The young communities were scattered in Illinois, Kansas, Michigan, Minnesota, Mississippi and North Dakota. Other Amish moved from older settlements in Indiana and Ohio to less expensive, more marginal land in those same states. Not all of the new settlements survived. Often the depression which gave them birth eventually forced them to dissolve.[35]

The Old Order Amish became involved in another important event of the depression years—the famous U.S. presidential election of 1896. That year's bid for the White House pitted Ohio's Republican Governor William McKinley against the thirty-six-year-old spell-binding orator and Nebraskan Democrat William Jennings Bryan. The campaign generated more attention and interest than any since before the Civil War. The depression colored all the issues and debates. McKinley stood for fiscal conservatism and gold-backed currency. Bryan countered with demands for lower interest rates, government regulation or purchase of utilities and railroads, and other seemingly radical economic measures. Even the candidates' personalities were a study in contrast. While McKinley calmly campaigned for office from his home in Columbus, Bryan canvassed the country, making hundreds of speeches and meeting thousands of people.[36]

In studying the Amish response to the 1896 election, Old Order Amish historian David Luthy has concluded that many Amish probably sympathized with Bryan.[37] "Amish people, generally not involved in political affairs, were caught up in the debate and suspense of this election," Luthy discovered. Bryan "had great sympathy for the farmers and the working-class people," Luthy notes. "He appealed to the common man and thus to the Amish." Bryan was well-known as a sincere and theologically conservative Christian, which may have also increased his standing among the Amish. It is unclear how many Amish voted, but in communities in which some most likely did, Bryan was the runaway winner. In Holmes County, Ohio, for example, the Nebraskan received a 2,300-vote majority.

But Bryan lost the election. The new President McKinley took office and promised that public confidence would bring back prosperity. When conditions for farmers only worsened after McKinley's election, many farmers became angry and resentful. McKinley seemed to be only a friend of big business and the urban rich; farmers felt abandoned. Old Order Amish persons writing in *The Budget* shared the sentiments of other rural folks. An Indiana Amish farmer noticed a *Budget* piece in which the writer had applauded McKinley's victory. The Indiana man replied, "That hurrahing [for McKinley] was rather out of place for this part of the globe, because corn has dropped 3c a bu[shel] since the election." A Nebraskan Amishman agreed, saying sarcastically, "Prosperity is here and corn has advanced from 10c to 9c. If it keeps on it will soon go up to 5c a bu[shel]. Hurrah for McKinley." Other Amish writers were equally bitter.

After 1897, the economic picture began to brighten. By 1900, farmers who had made it through the depression years were pulling their operations together and looking toward perhaps turning a profit. The election of 1900 brought little reaction from the Amish. Bryan once again challenged McKinley, and once again lost. The incumbent President received another four-year mandate. The Amish had chosen to involve themselves in the American politics of the 1890s. In the years which followed 1900, the nation itself would increasingly draw the Amish into its political, military and economic affairs—whether the Amish wanted to be involved or not.

As the 1800s drew to a close, the Amish found themselves in circumstances far different from those which had begun the century. A new wave of immigration in the early nineteenth century had dramatically increased the Amish population as well as settled the church more firmly in the Midwest and Ontario. By mid-century, deep differences within the group led some leaders to propose a series of unity meetings—which ended in permanent division. As the majority (Amish Mennonites) slowly moved toward merger with the Mennonites, the smaller (Old Order Amish) branch of the church struggled to define and maintain itself in a world obsessed with scientific progress and change. The Old Order Amish did not reject anything and everything that was new, but they did try to be selective and careful in what they adopted into their homes and communities. While the pace of change seemed rapid enough during the last quarter of the 1800s, it only increased after the new century began.

— 10 —

Challenges of a New Century, 1900-1945

> "If the world should stand another century, who can tell what it might bring forth."
> — *a Missouri Amishman, 1900*

The Robust Twentieth Century

"There isn't a man here who does not feel 400 percent bigger in 1900 than he did in 1896," New York's Senator Chauncey Depew declared as his country entered a new century.[1] Throughout most of the Western world a progressive optimism encouraged such wildly positive thoughts. Each year more phonographs, telephones, electric lights and other household gadgets appeared in American homes. Since 1898 a few of the nation's rich had even toyed with automobiles, and some futurists predicted the eventual appearance of "aeroplane" travel. Just two years before, the United States military had defeated Spain in a quick, calculated war. America had suddenly become something of a world power with new territorial holdings in Puerto Rico and the Philippines. Despite the fact that some forty percent of Americans lived in poverty, many felt that the country was on the verge of a new era of prosperity—symbolized very nicely by the transition from 1899 to 1900. The twentieth century was the future become the present.

Nor was the excitement and uniqueness of the times lost on North America's Amish readers. A February 1900 notice in *The Budget* from an Ontario scribe reported a recent quilting party. Tongue-in-cheek, the writer noted that "It was the largest quilting party ever heard of in the present century[!]"[2] Although other Amish readers corrected the writer and explained that the new century did not really begin until the first day of 1901, all agreed that there was a feeling of anticipation as the calendar changed. "Many wonderful inventions were made during the past century,"

213

A picture postcard produced about 1910 showing an Amish family on the streets of Ephrata, Pennsylvania.

a Missouri *Budget* scribe noted, "and if the world should stand another century who can tell what it might bring forth."[3]

Before long the answer to the scribe's question would be all too clear. The new century brought a staggering number of social and community changes, all promising to make the world a better place. But improved communication, intriguing inventions and scientific discovery did not do away with war and economic depression. By some accounts the new technology only hastened the break-up of community and family life during the next decades. The Amish faced this new era determined to be selective in what they adopted from larger, secular culture. Faith in God offered more assurance than trust in human progress.

The new century also saw the beginnings of another future phenomenon—the Amish as a motif for commercial literature and business. The roots of public interest in the Amish found fertile soil in the early 1900s. In 1905, prolific American author Helen Reimensnyder Martin published a 233-page novel *Sabina: A Story of the Amish*, based on popular, if not fully accurate, conceptions of Amish life.[4] In the city of Lancaster, Pennsylvania, a tobacco shop owner, Isaac Steinfeldt, sold Amish picture postcards, some of which were mailed and post-marked as early as 1915. Over the years, Steinfeldt also began marketing Amish-picture matchboxes, booklets on the Amish and "True To Life

Berenice Steinfeldt's 1940 booklet was one of the first publications for tourists interested in the Amish.

Amish Dolls.["5]

During the first few years after the turn of the century the Old Order Amish themselves were actively founding a number of new settlements. New permanent communities sprang up in Kansas, Ohio, Michigan, Iowa and Oklahoma. Amish families moved to Kent County, Delaware, in 1915, taking their church to that state for the first time.[6] Between 1900 and 1915, other Old Order church districts organized in Alabama, Arizona, California, Colorado, Georgia, Montana, Texas, Virginia and Wisconsin, but these did not survive for long. So while the Amish church spread geographically during this period, it still remained concentrated in the rural parts of the Midwest and Pennsylvania.

Technology, *Ordnung* and Division

In rural America, the young twentieth century was also promising a brighter economic future. With the depression of the 1890s behind them, farmers looked to better days ahead. Those days were not long in coming, as farm profits increased almost annually; the years 1910-1914 were the most profitable in American farm history. Part of the reason for the improved agricultural picture was the general strength of the larger economy. But new technology also contributed. That new technology, and the appearance of many more inventions and gadgets, caused some concern in the Amish church. Materialism lurked in enticing mail-order catalogs.[7] Neighborly cooperation and the value of extended family suddenly became endangered when single-operator machinery replaced community "work frolics."

Another convenience of the twentieth century's first quarter, the increasingly popular automobile, promised what its name suggested—"automatic mobility." For a people who valued community, mutual accountability and simplicity, cars symbolized the worst of worldly American culture. Increased autonomous travel weakened family ties and encroached on time spent at home. Moreover, the expense of the vehicles and the way in which different types of cars quickly gained recognition as economic status symbols made them incompatible with Christian stewardship and humility. It was natural for the Old Order Amish to reject ownership of automobiles even while acknowledging that, in some instances, car travel was beneficial. Thus the Amish would ride in cars if circumstances required it. The advent of American automobile culture was gradual enough that most Old Orders were able to carefully respond to its coming.[8]

Yet in some places the coming of new technology seemed so sudden and forceful that the Amish divided in their response to it. The years 1909-1914 saw a small wave of dissension roll through a number of Amish communities. During the fall and winter of 1909-1910 in Lancaster County, Pennsylvania, about one fifth of the Old Order Amish withdrew from their church. Nicknamed the "Peachy Church," this withdrawing group organized a new fellowship under the leadership of sympathetic Mifflin County, Pennsylvania, Bishop John P. Zook (1855-1942). According to the seceders, the chief source of contention between themselves and the Old Order was the practice of "strict shunning." Many of those who withdrew were still upset about the old Moses Hartz incident. In September 1909, they issued a plea for the adoption of more tolerant shunning practices. The local bishops turned down the request, and by February of the next year the dissatisfied members had left the church and were holding their own worship services.[9]

But the disagreement over excommunication practices was only one part of the story. In addition to favoring a more lenient church discipline, the new group also approved of the ownership of telephones in homes and alternating current electricity in houses, barns and shops. The quick adoption of such technology on the part of the break-away 1910 group seems to have pushed the Old Order church to more firmly oppose such innovation as dangerous to community and church stability. Before 1910, the Old Order Amish in Lancaster had in many cases not finally decided how much of the century's new gadgetry they would accept. The choices of the "Peachy Church" seem to have helped the larger, more conservative Amish body to decide against them. Technological disagreements hardened the Old Order and "Peachy Church" schism.

During the early 1900s, for example, telephones had come into limited use among the Old Order Amish of Lancaster County. After serious community problems erupted from gossip spread over the lines, the church decided to take a stand. By 1910 the Lancaster County Old Order Amish prohibited convenient in-home telephone ownership (telephone use itself was never forbidden). Modern means of communication might prove necessary in an emergency, but easy access to private conversation would only lead to trouble, the church was sure. The

Amish Communities in 1900

A Old Order Amish
M Amish Mennonite--Conferences (Eastern, Western, Indiana-Michigan)
I Amish Mennonite (Independent)
S Stuckey Amish--Central Illinois Amish Mennonite Conference
Є Egly Amish (Defenseless Mennonite Church)
G General Conference Mennonite Churches of Amish Background
○ More than one congregation in a community

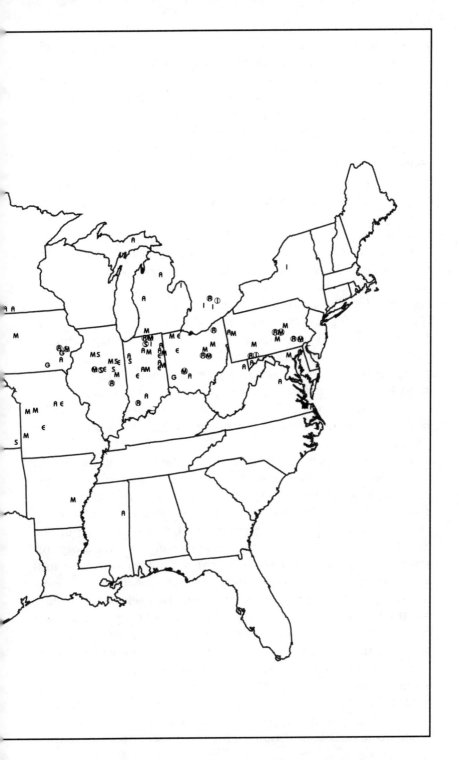

break-down of face-to-face conversation and community, which rode on the coattails of every-home phone ownership, could not be tolerated in a church which placed the quality of human relationships above personal luxury or individual convenience. Old Order Amish families who had purchased phones removed them and church *Ordnung* prohibited any other members from buying them in the future. However, the 1910 "Peachy Church" immediately adopted in-home telephones, further galvanizing Old Order opposition to the device.[10] The withdrawal of a minority group of Lancaster progressives helped to unite the Old Order majority on a decidedly conservative course.

Not all the early twentieth-century Amish groups which withdrew from their local districts over matters of technology were progressives. In Iowa, an Amish minority in Washington and Johnson Counties separated from the larger church in order to maintain a more traditional congregational, farm and family life. The Upper and Lower Deer Creek Old Order Amish church districts there had been hovering on the brink of major change during the last decade of the nineteenth century. In 1890 both groups built meetinghouses and gave up singing from the *Ausbund* in favor of a new hymn collection which included fewer Reformation-era songs. By 1910, the two districts seemed to be slowly but steadily moving toward affiliation with the progressive Amish Mennonites.[11]

Several families were displeased with the trend. Especially in Lower Deer Creek (the relatively more liberal of the two), some households were resistant to the church's progressive "drift." It seems that the factions within the congregation acted in reaction to one another: the more change-minded the majority of the members became, the more conservatively the minority responded. In 1914 seven traditionalist families withdrew and moved north to Buchanan County, Iowa, and established a new Old Order district there. Although they themselves had used a meetinghouse for nearly a quarter of a century in their old community, after moving to Buchanan the new group reverted to gathering in homes on Sunday mornings. (The conservatives had correctly sensed Lower Deer Creek's future. In 1917 the congregation allowed members to install telephones in their homes, broke all ties to the Old Order church and within four years affiliated with a Mennonite conference.)

The new Buchanan County church quickly gained a reputation for being a very conservative community—even by Old Order standards. Their acceptance of new technology was quite limited. Soon a number of Amish families from Kansas, Wisconsin and Indiana joined the Buchanan group. The arrivals from other states were also concerned that their local Old Order districts were toying too much with worldly farm and home inventions. The unique mix of Old Order Amish, all eager to maintain a strict *Ordnung* and highly suspicious of the supposed benefits of "progress," gave the Buchanan County Amish community a special flavor. The Old Order Amish there developed into an especially tradition-sensitive church. They became a conservative conscience within the larger Old Order Amish fellowship.[12] Buchanan County showed that the church could still thrive without striking too many compromises with American culture.

About the same time the Buchanan group formed, another conservative reaction within the Old Order Amish community fractured the Holmes County, Ohio, church. The precise issues at the time remain unclear and debated, but after 1913 an ultra-traditional Amish group took shape around the church district of Bishop Samuel E. Yoder (1872-1932). These so-called "Swartzentruber Amish" (nicknamed for a later leader), represented a distinct sub-group within the Holmes County Old Order Amish church. During the next decades, as most Old Order Amish in their area adapted, in a limited and modified way, some of the century's new technology, the Swartzentrubers did not. The Swartzentrubers, for example, rejected pressure naphtha lamps and indoor bathrooms, virtually all changes in clothing patterns and carriage styles, and non-electrical appliances such as natural gas refrigeration. The belt power of stationary tractor engines also found no place on Swartzentruber farms.[13]

Both the Buchanan County and Swartzentruber Amish signaled the growing variety within the Old Order church itself. These ultra-conservatives along with the older "Nebraska" group in Mifflin County, Pennsylvania, resisted most of the changes brought on during the 1900s. The majority of Old Order church districts began the twentieth century on a course characterized by limited and selective borrowing from surrounding society. While things which undermined and broke down family and community ties—such as automobiles, public utility electricity and telephones—remained taboo for all Old Orders, most saw the need to adapt some of the new century's wonders. Beginning in

Patriotic neighbors vandalized the Metamora Amish Mennonite Church building during World War 1.

the latter nineteenth century, for example, many Amish farmers had been deriving belt power from stationary steam engines in order to operate threshing machines and other equipment. In the early 1900s, some began using smaller stationary tractor engines to produce such power. While all the Old Order Amish purposely remained out of step with larger North American society, some—like the "Nebraska," Swartzentruber and Buchanan County Amish—were even more disciplined than the rest. Before long, the coming of World War 1 tested the discipline commitment of all of North America's Amish.

War Fever

Amish church members in Canada faced the prospect of war after 1914. Canada's involvement in World War 1 started that year, although the Dominion did not begin drafting young men until late summer of 1917. Even after conscription started, officials freely gave agricultural releases to the Amish.

Easy deferment did not last, and the next spring Ottawa suddenly canceled all draft exemptions. After April 1918, no one could claim conscientious objector (CO) status in Canada. Instead, each Amish man (or other CO) joined the army and waited. Government directives suggested that commanding officers then quietly issue the COs indefinite leaves of absence. Most Amish did, in fact, receive this second-hand military deferment, but the situation was not satisfactory to the Amish since it meant that their members were officially enlisted soldiers, even if they returned home. But before anything could be done to change the arrangement, the war ended.[14] The First World War experience of Canadian Amish was not ideal, but it turned out to be far better than what happened south of the border.

America's spring 1917 entry into World War 1 came as a surprise to many Americans.[15] All the while Europe had been at war, American politicians had preached non-involvement and peace. America would remain "neutral in fact as well as in name . . . impartial in thought as well as in action," President Woodrow Wilson had assured the country.[16] The United States had no stake or interest in what was going on in Europe, Washington repeatedly said. So, when the country did suddenly enter the fray, the federal government mounted a swift and massive public propaganda campaign to rally national support. Although many Americans were skeptical of the war effort at first—still sure that the affair was none of their business—the posters, rallies, war bond sales and organization of patriotic citizen groups soon enlisted broad popular sympathy. In a systematic way, the government also used churches and church periodicals to stir up war fever.[17] The American Amish, however, would not be stirred.

The first test for many young Amish men came with the military draft. Because of early public opposition to conscription, no draft law immediately followed the declaration of war. Later in the spring, however, Congress did pass a national conscription law. The act included a very vague provision for religious conscientious objectors, and some COs decided to try to gain exemption or deferment from military training. In Mifflin County, Pennsylvania, active Amish layman John S. Peachy (1873-1929) worked tirelessly as a draft counselor for the Amish youth in his area. Peachy kept abreast of changes in conscription regulations, learned how to properly fill out government forms and met with Mennonite leaders to discuss questions of draft exemption or deferment. Occasionally Peachy was successful, yet even when young men did receive formal recognition as conscientious objectors from their local draft boards, they often had to report to an army camp anyway.[18]

But once COs arrived at their assigned military posts, there were no specific guidelines explaining what they were supposed to do, nor what the military was to do with them. The army planned to send all men to training camps and sort out the CO question there. Once COs were in the camps and part of the

"I Make This Humble Plea"

Old Order Amish woman Rosa Bender Bontrager (1895-1918) wrote the following letter to Secretary of War Newton D. Baker a month and a half after her husband, Gideon J. Bontrager (1893-1947), received his World War I draft call and went as a CO to Camp Taylor, Louisville, Kentucky.

Shipshewana, Indiana
August 12, 1918

To the Hon. Secretary of War, Baker
Washington, D.C.

I am informed that the administration does not favor the practice of taking registrants for military service whose wives have no means of support other than their own labor. I therefore take the liberty to present my case to you and humbly plead that you may consider it.

I am a child of an orphan's home. I have no money of any kind and have no inheritance to expect.

I was married on January 25, 1917 at the age of 21 to Gideon J. Bontrager. He was called to camp on July 2, 1918, leaving me alone without any means of support other than my own labor. We have no home of our own and I am compelled to work out[side of the home] for my living. We failed to state all these facts fully when my husband filled out his questionnaire.

I may further state that my husband is a so-called conscientious objector and cannot because of conscientious scruples render any service under the military establishment, and must therefore also refuse to accept any pay from the government, and neither can I as his wife accept any money from the government for my support.

Because of these facts I make this humble plea to you, trusting that you may consider it and give instructions to the effect that my husband may be returned to me.

Your truly,
Mrs. Gideon Bontrager

Tragically, Rosa received her wish. In October 1918, she became very sick with Spanish influenza. Gideon had not yet received a release, but due to her illness he did obtain a leave of absence for October 16 to 27. On the 25th, Rosa died. Gideon had to report back to Camp Taylor the day of her funeral. One month later he was given the farm furlough which his wife had requested.

The complete story is found in Nicholas Stoltzfus, comp. *Nonresistance Put to Test* (Salem, Ind.: Nicholas Stoltzfus, 1981), pp. 25-27.

military routine, the War Department hoped that the men might forget their scruples and join the regular forces. Peer pressure and separation from their parents and church leaders would weaken young conviction, the army hoped.[19]

In some cases the military strategy worked. Of the dozens of young Amish men drafted and sent to camps, a few did join the fighting corps. The pressure to stand alone in a martial environment was simply too great for young men facing a threatening and harsh military establishment. Amishman Enos Stutzman (b. 1896), of Bucklin, Kansas, gave in to the pressure but took a noncombatant roll. Stutzman became a bugler.[20] Others even accepted regular infantry positions. Although Secretary of War Newton D. Baker had told a Mennonite leader, "Don't worry. We'll take care of your boys,"[21] the army's policy became one of intimidation and threats in an effort to force all drafted COs to take up a rifle.

But the army's tactics did not always produce Amish soldiers. Drafted in October 1918, Holmes County Amish farmer Rudy Yoder (1894-1968) reported to Camp Jefferson, Jefferson City, Missouri. Scared and tired, he tried to explain that he was a CO. Under pressure, he agreed to don a uniform, march with the other men and wait for word on his status from the commander. After several weeks it became obvious that no directive would come, and he was about to begin rifle training. Yoder decided that he would stop wearing his uniform and would withdraw from the regular camp activities in which he had slowly become involved. The decision was momentous and could have brought a court martial trial. Army officers took him outside the camp to what looked like three new graves. Menacingly brandishing pistols, the officers told Yoder he would be in the fourth grave if he did not put on his uniform the next morning. After a sleepless night, Yoder reported for breakfast in civilian clothes. Although other types of abuse continued, the officers never carried out their death threat.[22]

Unlike Yoder, most Amish men refused to participate in the army from the moment they reported to camp. Despite the threats and pressure, young Amish draftees remained unwilling to fight, wear military uniforms or perform certain jobs which they felt were aiding the army's war-making ability. At times the army kept COs separate from each other in an attempt to wear down their resolve. In other camps, the COs were crowded together and dealt with as a group.

Amish conscientious objectors (along with many other COs) received verbal abuse, beatings and wire-brush treatments. In addition, soldiers sometimes forcibly shaved the beards of the Amish. Many COs were made to stand for long periods of time in the sun without refreshment. Those who refused to wear military uniforms were at times left in cold, damp cells with no clothing at all. Officers occasionally "baptized" Amish COs in camp latrines in mockery of their Anabaptist beliefs. COs were stuck in abusive camp situations from the time of their induction until well after the war was over and demobilization began. For the Amish men who endured World War 1 camp experiences, the memories were powerful and unforgettable.[23]

Pro-Germanism?

Not only were the men in army camps tested by the country's war fever; but other, older Amish persons also ran into trouble when officials charged them with being German sympathizers. After all, the Amish spoke a German dialect, would not fight in the United States Army and, in almost every case, refused to buy war bonds.[24] The conclusion seemed inescapable to many: the Amish (and other ethnic-German peace churches such as the Mennonites and Brethren) wanted Germany to win the war. To those promoting the war effort, the mere possibility of such sentiment was intolerable.[25] Citizens' groups regularly hounded Amish and Mennonites who would not buy bonds or otherwise financially support the war effort. Two Mennonite meeting-houses were torched by patriotic neighbors.[26] In some cases Amish Mennonite meetinghouses were vandalized or community

A pen and ink drawing by Amish Bishop Manasses E. Bontrager.

civic groups posted American flags in front of them.[27] Not having church meetinghouses, the Old Order Amish escaped such attacks, but they were the subjects of other official government observation during the war.

Throughout the conflict the War Department's Military Intelligence Division kept Mennonites and Amish under surveillance. A lengthy Division memorandum (prepared in final form after the war was over) detailed the domestic spying. Most of the government's information apparently came from articles in the 1911 *Encyclopedia Britannica,* but the document also included original espionage material which the Division had collected during the war. Names, addresses and information on church leaders

suddenly appeared in War Department files. But the decentral-
ized Old Order Amish church was a frustration to the Division.
Amish congregationalism left no one single leader or denominational office for the Division to target. About the Old Order
Amish, Military Intelligence could only note: "No organization.
Services generally held in German."[28] Nevertheless, Washington
officials were watching the Amish.

When Old Order Amish Bishop Manasses E. Bontrager (1868-
1947) of Ford County, Kansas, wrote a lengthy letter for publication in *The Budget*, federal officials caught wind of its content.
In the letter, Bontrager urged Amish not to buy federal war
bonds. He chided those who voted in the elections which brought
the current administration into office. But he also praised the
Amish young men who were remaining steadfast in their refusal
to join the armed forces—steadfast even to the point of spending
time in army prisons. "What would become of our nonresistant
faith," Bontrager wrote, "if our young brethren in camp would
yield? From the letters I receive from brethren in camp, I believe
they would be willing to die for Jesus rather than betray Him."
The bishop urged his readers to muster the same resolve: "Let
us profit by their example they have set us so far, and pray that
God may strengthen them in the future."[29]

Two and one half months later, Bontrager was arrested on the
grounds that his *Budget* piece was "inciting and attempting to
incite insubordination, disloyalty and refusal of duty in the
military and naval forces of the United States."[30] Bontrager
appeared for trial in Cleveland, Ohio, the jurisdiction of the
paper's home state. He and *Budget* Editor Samuel H. Miller were
convicted and fined $500 each. Loose words were dangerous in
a nation at war.

School Problems

Conflicts with state authority did not end with Armistice Day
in 1918. The return to post-war "normalcy" brought its own
share of difficulties. One of the first post-war incidents involved
the Ohio Old Order Amish and that state's public school system.

The Amish had never opposed education as such, but many
in the Old Order church were wary of the so-called higher
education offered by high schools and colleges. Learning that
had no practical purpose for Amish life seemed to be not only a
waste of children's time, but also a danger to young minds.

Competition and individual self-improvement were important values in high school curricula. "Worldly wisdom" which went beyond the practical knowledge of reading, writing and mathematics posed a real threat to the Amish way of life and to church teaching on humility, simplicity and mutual aid. Spending time in school for nine months a year with teachers who were hostile to Amish beliefs and traditions was not something that Amish parents wanted for their young people.

Formal education should be basic, the Amish believed, in harmony with the church and the home. It should be only *one part* of a more complete education which included developing work and vocational skills on the farm or in family businesses. Learning how to live with one's family, church and community were skills missing from the new, expanded school studies. And with an ever longer school year, children had less and less time to be at home in that important learning environment. Formal education in the twentieth century was definitely becoming more problematic for the Amish.[31]

Already in 1914, Geauga County, Ohio, school officials had fined Amish parents whose children had stopped attending school after completing eighth grade before age sixteen.[32] But it was Ohio's post-war Bing Act of 1921 which brought into the open the smoldering Amish resentment of the encroaching school system. The Bing Act required compulsory school attendance through age eighteen. Under limited circumstances, a few children could receive work permits and leave school at age sixteen, provided they had completed seventh grade. Considered a major reform bill in Columbus, the Bing Act was no favorite among the Amish of Holmes and Wayne Counties. When some Amish children did not show up for classes, or refused to read some of the objectionable content in high school social studies and hygiene texts, the state stepped in. In January 1922 officials arrested five Amish fathers on charges of neglecting their children's welfare. Most of the men's school age children then became wards of the court. Authorities sent them to an orphanage and would not allow them to wear their Amish clothes, dressing them instead in more fashionable current styles.[33]

Distressed parents decided that keeping their families together was more important than opposing the Bing Act; they gave in and promised to comply with the law. Two weeks later the state released the children and collected fines and penalties from the parents. The Amish were resigned to make the best of the situation. All Amish teens would apply for work permits at sixteen. Hopefully the state would be generous.

For some Amish, the school difficulties were enough to start them thinking about leaving the United States entirely. First the military draft and now the schools were troubling the Amish church. The ever-encroaching American society seemed set on forcing all of its members into one mold. When word arrived in Wayne County that cheap, productive land was available in northern Mexico, some Amish persons decided to move south of the border. Just then some very conservative Canadian Mennonites were also moving to Mexico to avoid new Manitoba higher education statutes.

In the fall of 1923, ten Amish men signed a contract for the purchase of 5,000 acres of land in Paradise Valley (now Sacodell Valley), Nuevo Leon. Eventually eleven Amish households moved to Paradise Valley. Most were from Ohio, but several came from Missouri, looking for better farms. Traveling by rail, they took their household goods and animals with them. The land in Mexico was very fertile, and with some irrigation proved quite productive. The Amish built mud-brick homes and regularly traveled the sixty miles to town to buy and sell. And of course, they were free from Ohio school laws—they could have their own private school without state interference.

Although the settlement had the potential for economic growth, it did not last long. A promised railroad connecting Paradise Valley with other communities never materialized. Then too, the smoldering guerilla war in northern Mexico caught Amish families in waves of troop pillaging. Perhaps most importantly, no Amish church ever developed there. No church leader moved to Mexico and no ordinations ever took place. Without the formation of a more stable spiritual base, the community found life very discouraging. By 1929 all the Amish had left Mexico, returning either to Ohio or to a new settlement in North Carolina.[34]

A Legal Battle in Pennsylvania

In eastern Pennsylvania, school problems similar to those in Ohio erupted about a decade later. Since 1925, Pennsylvania law required school attendance until age fourteen, but often school boards (some of which had included elected Amish mem-

The Smoketown, Pennsylvania, consolidated public elementary school, built in 1937. Local Amish were opposed to the new building.

bers) gave work permits to Amish youth who left the classroom before that age. By the mid-1930s, an important change was taking place in the very structure of Lancaster County schools. School districts began to close rural one-room schools and consolidate students into larger buildings. This system involved the busing of children out of their immediate communities, making the school more distant from the home and family and lengthening the school day. In 1937 school consolidation came to involve the area in central Lancaster County in which many Amish lived. The resulting public protest on the part of the Amish was unprecedented in Amish history.

In 1937 East Lampeter Township announced plans to close ten township schools and replace them with one large consolidated institution in central Smoketown. Amish and a few non-Amish friends hired Philadelphia lawyers and received a court order halting construction of the school. A higher court later overturned the injunction and the building went up, but the Amish had shown their resolve to keep local education in parental hands.[35] Being a nonresistant people who avoided the violence of the court system, the Amish church did not approve of the lay members who hired lawyers and fought the state. Nevertheless, the majority of church members seemed set against the new school. Many would not send their children to it.[36]

A present day Amish parochial school in Trumbull County, Ohio.

For a time, Pennsylvania Governor George H. Earle promised to keep all the one-room schools operating for the Amish, but in the end only one of the schools kept its doors open. Additionally, the state passed new legislation in the summer of 1937 raising the age from fourteen to fifteen at which students could leave school on work permits. Now even the church's eight Lancaster County bishops sent a petition to the legislature. A 130-foot-long letter containing the signatures of 3,000 residents (many of the signers were Old Order and conservative Mennonites) went to Harrisburg, asking the state to rescind the new requirement.[37] An Amish committee known as the "Delegation for Common Sense Schooling" worked with legislators to reach a compromise. The Delegation reported that they did "not wish to withdraw from the common public schools," but they said that "at the same time we cannot hand our children over to where they will be led away from us."[38]

As matters grew more tense during the autumn of 1937, Amishman Aaron King (1899-1986) spent a night in jail for not sending his daughter to high school.[39] The Lancaster County Amish began to consider withdrawing from the public education system entirely and opening their own private schools.[40] (The small Old Order Amish settlements in Delaware, North Carolina and Mississippi had already established parochial schools in their own communities.[41]) In November 1938 the first two Lancaster County Amish schools opened.[42] New petitions arrived at the Capitol asking for relief from the age fifteen requirement.[43] The state attorney general agreed to draft a bill allowing fourteen-year-olds to withdraw from school on work permits. By the end of that school year, the Pennsylvania legislature rolled back the compulsory attendance age to fourteen. The Amish had succeeded in forcing the state's hand. Still, they had not obtained everything for which they had hoped. Their children still might have to attend consolidated public high schools until their fourteenth birthday if they completed eighth grade before that age. Not satisfied with the agreement and fearful that it would not last, some families left Pennsylvania. Beginning in 1940 a number of Amish households moved to Saint Mary's County, Maryland, where that state's government was more ready to work with the church.[44]

The Beachy Amish

During the 1920s and 1930s the Amish needed to react not only to changes in state law, but also to shifting loyalties within their own ranks. After 1927 an important new Amish group emerged—the Beachy Amish (also called the Beachy Amish Mennonites). The new church had roots in the "strict shunning" controversies of the 1890s. In Somerset County, Pennsylvania, the Amish faced the issue of what to do when members wished to leave the church and affiliate with the relatively more progressive Conservative Amish Mennonite congregation just to the south in Garret County, Maryland. Before 1895 the Somerset and Garrett people had been one congregation and there were still numerous friendly and family connections between the two groups. That complicated matters for church leaders who needed to deal with the requests of Old Order Amish who asked for membership transfers.[45]

For just over two decades, the authority of Somerset Amish Bishop Moses D. Yoder (1847-1927) muted the controversy. Yoder held to "strict shunning" and required Amish members to socially avoid all those who left for the Maryland church. After 1916, however, things changed. That year the ordination of Moses M. Beachy (1874-1946) as associate bishop with Yoder seemed to open the door for some change. Beachy let it be known that he would not excommunicate or shun those Old Order Amish who became Amish Mennonites. Attempts at mediation

The Beachy Amish Fellowship of Churches—Some Important Dates

1909-1910	Thirty-five families withdraw from the Lancaster County Old Order Amish community, objecting to the practice of "strict shunning." They are nicknamed the "Peachy Church."
1926	John A. Stoltzfus becomes bishop of the Lancaster County "Peachy Church."
1927	The Somerset County, Pa., Old Order Amish community divides. Moses Beachy and the progressives reject "strict shunning." Moses Yoder leads the remaining Old Orders.
1928	(October) Lancaster County Stoltzfus Church permitts automobile ownership
1928	(December) Somerset Beachy Church permitts automobile ownership
1929	Leaders from the Beachy Church and Stoltzfus Church begin exchanging fraternal visits.
1930	Lancaster group under Stoltzfus' leadership begins holding Sunday morning services in the Weavertown Meetinghouse. (They are thereafter often nicknamed the "Weavertown Amish.")
1930s	Both Moses Beachy and John A. Stoltzfus help organize congregations in other states. These congregations all recognize one another, forming the nucleus of an emerging Beachy Amish fellowship of churches.
1940	Nappannee, Indiana, Bishop David O. Burkholder leaves the Old Order Amish and helps form a church very much like that of Moses Beachy. (The Beachy Amish in Indiana are thereafter often nicknamed the "Burkholder Amish.")
1950	The Somerset, Pa. Beachy congregation and the Weavertown, Pa. Stoltzfus congregation officially join in full fellowship and affiliation
1952	Beachy Amish Mission Interests Committee formally organizes
1955	Amish Mennonite Aid, a Beachy Amish mission, relief, and service organization forms
1970	The Beachy Amish open Calvary Bible School, Calico Rock, Arkansas.
1970	The Beachy Amish begin a monthly church periodical, *Calvary Messenger*.

by visiting Amish leaders failed. In June 1927, in the last summer of his life, old Moses Yoder and those Amish who wished to maintain a position of "strict shunning" against those who left the church quietly separated from the rest of the Amish and began holding their own worship and communion services. The majority of the church continued under Beachy's leadership.[46]

The issue of shunning soon became a background matter. From Old Order Moses Yoder's point of view, the Beachy church's loose application of avoidance only symbolized a deeper loss of congregational nerve. Soon Beachy's congregation had adopted progressive Sunday schools and members were wiring their homes for alternating current electricity. Within a year and a half the group was tolerating automobile ownership and use. Somewhat relaxed dress standards and fully automated farming practices soon followed. The Beachy Amish experienced a number of rapid changes in the few years following their abandonment of "strict shunning." The Beachy Amish did maintain some traditionally Amish patterns of church worship and relatively conservative clothing requirements. Still, their use of motor vehicles and other innovations clearly set them apart from the Old Order Amish.[47]

Under Beachy's leadership, his change-oriented congregation attracted the fellowship of like-minded Amish in other parts of North America. After 1930 a progressive Amish group in Lancaster County (which had adopted automobiles at nearly the same time as Beachy's church), unofficially affiliated with Beachy's Somerset group. Under the leadership of Bishop John A. Stoltzfus (1870-1957), these Lancaster families represented nearly all of those "Peachy Church" members who had withdrawn from the Lancaster Old Order community in 1909-1910 during the "strict shunning" controversy there. The Stoltzfus congregation eventually began meeting in a church building—further distinguishing themselves from their traditional Amish neighbors.[48] Through the 1930s, '40s and '50s, new Beachy Amish congregations formed in central Pennsylvania, Ohio, Ontario and Indiana.[49] The Beachy churches liked to emphasize the renewed spiritual life and vigor which they saw in their congregations as the reason others joined them. Those less sure of the group's virtues saw only a church-sanctioned chasing after material things on the part of those Old Orders who joined the Beachy fellowship.

Beachy Amish congregations meet for Sunday morning worship in simple church meetinghouses such as this one in Kansas.

The Beachy Amish church remained loose in organization and structure. While preserving some key Amish beliefs and practices, the Beachy Amish represented a marked departure from many traditional Amish church and community understandings. The number of differences between the Old Order and the Beachy churches only increased through the twentieth century. The Beachy Amish came to serve a unique function as a "halfway" church between the Amish and the Mennonites. The Amish Mennonites had earlier played such a role, but with their total absorption into the Mennonite churches, no middle group existed any longer. Throughout the twentieth century, the Beachy Amish would gather many members from Old Order homes. But the Beachy churches also won converts of non-Amish background who were attracted to the group's strong evangelical faith and commitment to daily discipleship.

The Great Depression

While the Beachy division had affected some Amish communities, the financial squeeze of the Great Depression troubled all the Amish. America's farm and small-town families felt the effects of the October 1929 stock market crash as much as did the nation's city dwellers. Perhaps the most noticeable effect which the Depression had on the Amish was that of nearly bringing to a halt the founding of new Old Order Amish settlements. Of the few settlements begun during the Depression years, none ultimately survived. Economic hardship and the need for cheap land did lead to the formation of several new Amish settlements in Arkansas, Indiana, North Dakota, Oklahoma and Pennsylvania. The same harsh financial realities which brought the new communities into existence also caused most to quickly fail. (Three Depression-era Amish settlements later disbanded for other than economic reasons.)

Despite the tough times, some Amish believed that the lack of material things during those years caused the church to especially deepen its spiritual roots. "The Depression years were such times when we all needed to look to a Higher Power," one Amish minister thought. He was impressed with "how some people could have patience with each other, the creditor with the debtor."[50] Other members recall how few controversies and debates surfaced during those years as church districts pulled together in the face of an uncertain future. Christian mutual aid and sharing of scarce resources became a much stronger reality.[51]

In 1931, one anonymous Amishman's diagnosis of the country's economic ills found its way onto the front page of the Lancaster, Pennsylvania, *Intelligencer Journal.* Under the title, "Adoption of Too Many Labor Saving Devices Blamed for Depression," the author argued that "Extremity Is Cause of Many Ills Today."[52] Mechanized farming practices, which increased agricultural production faster than the growth of population, were the root of Depression problems, he was sure. If only farmers and other business leaders would have been satisfied with less, they would surely have avoided the troubles brought on by too much borrowing and debt, he claimed. The use of so-called labor saving machinery simply threw hard-working people out of a job. The greed of manufacturers and large-scale farmers seemed unquenchable. "They made a profit before they used labor saving-devices," the Amishman charged, but the desire for more had led business down the road of bankruptcy.

Soon the Amish lost the freedom to reflect philosophically on the causes of the economic downturn; the growing harshness of the times brought the reality home. By 1933 American farm income had fallen more than sixty percent on average.[53] In the

United States the federal government took drastic steps to stabilize the rural economy. The most famous measure was President Franklin D. Roosevelt's Agricultural Adjustment Administration (AAA). Of the many facets of the AAA program, the one which drew the greatest response from the Amish was the provision for paying farmers to reduce the number of acres they put into production. An attempt to boost prices by sharply reducing the supply, the tactic seemed foolish to most Amish— especially when they heard stories of starvation in America's cities. Said one Amishman, "We felt this was a cruel way to get money into circulation again, being so many people were going hungry."[54] While Amish farmers did reduce their planting in line with AAA guidelines, virtually all refused the government's reimbursement.[55] "I don't think it's right to take money that isn't earned," one Amish farmer told a *Philadelphia Inquirer* reporter. "That means, if you come down to it," he continued, "that a farmer is being paid to not work. Then there's farmers that don't tell the truth about their acreage [to get a greater subsidy]. That isn't right. That's just not right."[56]

The Amish also took no part in the new 1935 Social Security program (known then as Old Age and Survivors Insurance). The public pension plan was optional for those who were self-employed, and the Amish chose to opt out. Taking care of orphans, the poor and the elderly was the duty of the church—a duty that the Amish church refused to shirk. To the Amish, the surrender of God-given responsibilities to the secular state was a sure sign that Christianity in America had lost its moral resolve. The pressure to become a part of various government farm and social welfare programs would grow after 1935, but the Amish had already begun to resist that pressure. The 1930s proved to be merely the first round.

For the church itself, the Depression years did see the beginning of an important Amish publication—the extremely popular almanac from Raber's Bookstore, Baltic, Ohio. In 1929 bookstore owner and Amish deacon John A. Raber (1885-1967) announced his intent to issue an annual publication, *Der Neue Amerikanische Calender* (since 1970 also issued in English as *The New American Almanac*). Appearing the next year, the almanac quickly became a yearly Amish favorite. The most important feature of the *Calender* was its directory, which listed all Amish leaders' names, addresses and years of birth and

An Old Order Amishman discusses the World War 2 military draft with Major General Lewis B. Hershey, Director of Selective Service, as three Mennonites look on.

ordination. Raber's almanac became an important source of information and community connectedness for the Amish across North America. Son Ben J. Raber (b. 1923) took over publication of his father's almanac and ably continued the Raber tradition. The Rabers published and sold many other books over the years, but their *Calender*—a product of the Great Depression—has been their most important.[57]

A World at War

As the economic depression began to fade, new trouble surfaced on another horizon. Rumbles of war in Europe and the Pacific rim grew louder and closer. Beginning in 1939 Canada became involved in the Second World War and two years later the United States entered the global conflict. Already during the 1930s, leaders of the Religious Society of Friends, Brethren and Mennonites had been at work with government leaders on both sides of the border in an effort to avoid repeating the First World War's CO experience.[58] Although no war was threatened at that

Jonathan B. Fisher: Traveling Amishman

One of the most adventuresome Amish persons of all times was Jonathan B. Fisher (1878-1953) of Bareville, Pennsylvania. As a farmer, cheesemaker and farmers' market merchant, Fisher led a rather typical Old Order Amish life. But Jonathan Fisher also had an intense desire to explore the world around him. He traveled often as an young man and adult to various places in the United States, Canada and Mexico.

Fisher also took several longer trips and wrote two books about his adventures. In 1908 Fisher sailed for Europe, both to sightsee and to learn about European methods of cheese production. He visited England, France, Switzerland, Germany, Denmark and the Netherlands. Among his other activities, he rode to the top of the Eiffel Tower and went on a Alpine mountain climbing expedition. Upon returning home he published *A Trip to Europe and Facts Gleaned on the Way*, a 346-page book detailing his excursion. The book's back cover promised that the contents were "interesting reading matter for both young and old; teachers or pupils; country and city folks."

In 1934 Fisher set off again—this time on an around-the-world tour. Always curious, Fisher left with hopes "to take a peep into foreign lands, to note the customs of their natives, the beauty of their sceneries; [and] also, to glean about facts one may learn on the way." By the time he left on this second voyage Fisher was married, but according to a contemporary newspaper account his wife, Sarah Farmwald Fisher (1888-1976) "elected to stay at home." Fisher sailed from New York City, down the east coast to Cuba, then through the Panama Canal and north to Portland, Oregon. Turning west, his ship headed for Japan, then China, Singapore and Indonesia. After crossing the Indian Ocean and visiting Sri Lanka and India, he traveled through the Red Sea and the Suez Canal to Egypt. Fisher decided to remain in the Holy Lands for six months of touring biblical sites. Eventually he had to head for home, but not without stops in Italy, Spain, Portugal, Morocco and England. In every place his ship docked, Fisher spent days observing the people and cities he encountered, asking questions and writing in his diary.

Fisher kept two thick "autograph books" while on his world tour. People from many countries signed their names and addresses, and penned short sayings for him—often in their native language and script. Fisher described this second journey in *Around the World by Water and Facts Gleaned on the Way*. He noted the local history and architecture of places he visited, as well as his impressions of other cultures and ethnic groups. For example, the tea produced in Indonesia was superb, he thought, and the traveler in Japan was safer than in many parts of the United States.

Even at age 74, Fisher could not be kept at home. In 1952 he again went to Europe, this time under the auspices of the Christian relief organization Church World Service. Fisher oversaw a ship-load of livestock which the group was sending to the Continent. While in Europe, Fisher attended the Mennonite World Conference held that year in Basel, Switzerland. He was the only member of the Amish church to attend.

Jonathan and Sarah had three daughters and a foster son. The family also included a live-in house guest for many years—a homeless woman from the city of Reading, Pennsylvania, whom the Fishers had met at the farmers' market and offered a place to stay. Jonathan was always interested in learning about other people, but he also shared his own Old Order beliefs. He regularly "carried religious pamphlets, which he gave to everyone he met," and while on his global trip he visited the U.S. Navy base in San Diego and engaged some officers in a discussion of peace and conscientious objection to war.

A truly remarkable man, Jonathan Fisher loved people and deeply enjoyed learning about other ways of life. In sharing his travels with others through his books, Fisher enriched the lives and widened the perspectives of many other Amish as well.

See Jonathan B. Fisher, *A Trip to Europe and Facts Gleaned on the Way* (New Holland, Pa.: Jonathan B. Fisher, 1911); Jonathan B. Fisher, *Around the World by Water and Facts Gleaned on the Way* ([Bareville, Pa.]: Jonathan B. Fisher, 1937). Both of these books also appeared as serials in *The Budget*. See also H. Harold Hartzler, *Amishman Travels Around the World: The Life of Jonathan B. Fisher* (Elverson, Pa.: Mennonite Family History, 1991).

time, the groundwork laid made negotiations easier when conscription did begin. On the American side, twenty-two Old Order Amish bishops from Indiana, Kansas, Michigan and Pennsylvania signed a letter in 1939 declaring their support of a Mennonite statement entitled "Peace, War, and Military Service."[59] In offering their approval of the document, the bishops wrote that they were not only expressing their own personal convictions and beliefs, but also "that of the entire membership" of their whole church.[60]

The statement to which the bishops affixed their names was one which explained Christian nonresistance and denounced military involvement. It did offer to Washington a willingness "at all times to aid in the relief of those who are in need, distress or suffering, regardless of the danger in which we may be placed in bringing such relief."[61]

The draft alternatives which the state offered COs were significantly different from those of World War 1. The programs of 1939 and 1941 put Mennonites and Amish to work instead of sending them to military camps or jail. Ottawa and Washington established manual work programs in which the COs provided free labor for various government projects. The Canadian Alternative Service Work (ASW) and American Civilian Public Service (CPS) enrolled the efforts of thousands of conscientious objectors. ASW men worked in Canadian national parks as ground crews and forest fire fighters. Others staffed psychiatric hospitals and cleared land for the future Trans-Canadian Highway. Additionally, some Canadian Mennonite and many Amish COs received farm furloughs and worked at home.[62]

The CPS program provided similar jobs for its American participants. In addition to forestry and hospital assignments, some COs worked in social work programs or agricultural experimentation stations. While most CPS men lived in government-regulated camps, the sponsoring peace churches managed and funded nearly the entire program. Thus, while the Amish had refused government farm subsidies and social security payments during the Depression, they later helped to subsidize the government itself by providing free labor for various state and federal projects. Although men in CPS camps at times felt local community hostility towards their peace stance, they were not subject to the physical abuse which had plagued World War 1 COs.[63]

During the Second World War, 772 Old Order Amish received

U.S. draft calls. Twenty-three enlisted in regular army service, twenty-seven chose non-combatant military assignments and 722 declared themselves conscientious objectors.[64] While some Amish COs received farm or other deferments, at least six hundred Amish served in CPS and performed a wide variety of work assignments.[65] Most Amish CPS men served in Mennonite sponsored camps; however, the Amish church did operate one camp of its own—an experimental farming station near Hagerstown, Maryland. The Amish bought the farm in 1942 and managed it under U.S. Soil Conservation Service supervision. The camp had only about thirty-five COs at any one time, but it received widespread support from the Amish church. The Amish CPS camp newsletter *The Sun Beam* had an extensive circulation to Amish homes.[66]

Life in Mennonite CPS camps was a unique experience for many young Amish men. There, among fellow COs, the Amish were in an environment sympathetic to their historic views and peace teaching. Yet being in Mennonite camps was sometimes a challenge. Often Mennonites were unfamiliar with specific Amish customs or traditions. Mennonites also tended to look upon the Amish as "backward" or uneducated. When a few Amish decided while in camp to leave their church and join the Mennonites, relations were strained on all sides.[67] In general, Amish experiences in CPS were positive and men felt the support and encouragement of their friends and family back home. Lagrange County, Indiana Bishop Eli J. Bontrager (1868-1958) made a special effort to visit all Amish CPS men. Criss-crossing the country, Bontrager once traveled more than 16,000 miles (mostly by rail) in only five months.[68] Draftees deeply appreciated Bontrager's visits and encouragement. Amish families and church leaders often visited their drafted relatives and neighbors who were in CPS. Many Amish church members visited or wrote letters to Amish COs even if they did not personally know them.

Those relatives and friends were having enough problems of their own on the home front. In an especially troublesome situation in Reno County, Kansas, five Amish families lost their farms to the U.S. Navy Department. The Amish-owned acres were part of a four square mile tract taken over by the government to establish a navy pilots' training base.[69]

The war-time economy produced other problems. Many Amish refused to use the ration stamps distributed by the government for the purchase of food and other necessities. The stamps bore the images of tanks, cannons, air corps planes, navy ships and torpedoes. Many people could not use such ration booklets in good conscience. Moreover, the very idea of state regulation of commerce troubled some. Amish families who decided not to participate in the ration program provided their own food and simply did without other scarce material goods.[70] Their war-time thriftiness became their trademark. In a 1942 *New York Times* article, one reporter called the Amish "models for the nation's consumers."[71] By declaring themselves conscientious objectors and refusing to use war-glorifying ration stamps, the Amish had ironically became "models" for patriotic citizens. But in a world turned upside-down by depressions, dictators and atomic bombs, irony no longer seemed quite so strange.

When the war was over, some young Amish men signed up for extended voluntary service as "Sea-Going Cowboys." The Allied relief and rehabilitation of Europe involved the sending of hundreds of horses, cattle and donkeys to the Continent. The U.S. merchant marine needed people with experience in animal handling to watch over and take care of the livestock during the Atlantic passage. After a successful voyage and unloading of the livestock, these adventuresome Amish youth were often able to do a bit of European sightseeing before returning home.[72]

Sightseeing in Europe was a very different way for an Amish teen to spend part of a summer. But after 1945 the Amish were living in a very different world. The turbulent first four and one half decades of the twentieth century had left western society reeling. Despite their efforts to remain aloof from the chaos which surrounded them, the Amish were caught up in many of the events of those troubled years. The pressures of a changing economy, a growing welfare state, military conscription and ever-encroaching urbanization would continue to challenge Amish peoplehood in the second half of the twentieth century.

— 11 —

Peoplehood in a Changing World: Amish Life Since 1945

> "The Amish people feel that their mission is to lead an humble life that needs no publicity."
> — *An Amish farmer, 1978*

The Amish and Post-War America

With the ending of the Second World War the thoughts of many Americans turned homeward. Reunited families took vacations again and states and cities scrambled to capture a share of America's growing leisure time and tourist dollars. The Pennsylvania State Department of Commerce issued an advertisement encouraging would-be visitors to take a "post-war vacation." The ad included a large picture of an Amish horse and buggy, and bore the caption "Pennsylvania's Plain People." While the piece did not specifically mention the Amish by name, the picture clearly implied that the Old Order folks should be a part of every family's excursion fun.[1]

But for the Amish, life after 1945 was no vacation. Growing social, political and economic pressures only increased as the war ended. A rapidly-changing America challenged the Amish way of life. For much of 1946 and 1947, a severe economic recession and high inflation plagued the United States, but the country soon settled in for a long and steady period of economic growth and an accompanying baby boom. Prosperous middle class families entered a new golden age of consumerism. In the four years from 1946 to 1950, for example, the number of households owning television sets skyrocketed from a mere eight thousand to nearly four million.[2] Soon the new interstate highway system, sprawling suburbs and shopping malls further encouraged American mobility and changed spending habits. People lived farther from their jobs and spent even more time each day on the road. And as household income continued to rise

A few Old Order Amish church districts permit the use of tractors for field work. Here a Hartville, Ohio, Amishman also uses his tractor for a local shopping trip. The vast majority of Old Orders prohibit tractor use in the field and on the road.

each year, more and more gadgets offered themselves for sale.

To all of this hurried buying, selling, suburbanizing and expanding, the Amish remained quite distant. Yet maintaining a traditional way of life in a world fascinated by progress was not always easy. In the spring of 1946 federal agents publicly urged Amish farmers to give up horse-drawn farming practices and begin using tractors so as to boost American agricultural exports. "By hitching them [tractors] to the plow and harrow they will be serving not only the needs of their owners, but will help to sustain life among the hungry nations in Europe," the federal agents stated in their appeal. Amish farming practices were simply outdated and unscientific, the government was sure. The Amish needed to mechanize, the Agriculture Department said, or the Old Order church would not survive economically.[3]

But the Amish persisted in their use of horse-drawn equipment and reserved their tractor engines for stationary belt power. Fully automated farming destroyed the need for working together, and the Amish valued group cooperation. After the Second World War non-Amish "neighbors went for bigger tractors and combines and more modern ways of farming," one Amishman remembered, "until no one seemed to have any use for his neighbors anymore."[4]   Maintaining horse-based farming kept operations small and more labor-intensive. Also, tractors were too much like cars and Amish groups which approved tractor use in fields were soon driving automobiles on the road. In rejecting the government's plea, the Old Order Amish chose to maintain the way of tradition in the midst of post-war America.[5] (Several Old Order Amish communities have adopted the use of tractors for field work, but the vast majority have not.)

In some Amish communities, the pressures of life in post-war America were simply too great. As late as 1952 the long shadow of the atomic mushroom cloud fell across a newly established Amish community in Pike County, Ohio. That year the federal government announced its intention to build a nuclear power plant in the area. Plans called for tripling the County's population, which would in turn raise land prices considerably. While the project was a boon to some land-owning locals, it marked the demise of the young Old Order settlement. The area's winding roads would become too crowded for safe buggy travel, farmland

Conservative Amish Mennonite Conference women chat with a Mennonite delegate from the Netherlands during the 1948 Mennonite World Conference, Goshen, Indiana.

quickly became too expensive to own, and observers (mistakenly) expected that the entire area would become a highly secret military district. Within a year the Amish began moving away. Most emigrated to Ontario. One of the reasons the Pike County families chose Canada was because that country had no military draft. By then, military participation was again an issue in the United States.[6]

Alternative Service

Only in 1947 had the U.S. military finished demobilizing all of World War 2's conscripted men. But nearly as soon as the old Selective Service system completed its business, a new draft program took its place. The escalating "Cold War" between the United States and the Soviet Union persuaded Congress to establish a large peacetime standing army. In 1948 conscription began again in an effort to raise troops for home defense as well as for the ongoing occupation of West Germany and Japan. Amazingly, the new laws granted complete and total exemption to conscientious objectors. However, such deferment lasted only a few years. After 1950 the coming of the Korean War turned public opinion against COs, and the government demanded some type of alternative service. Beginning in the summer of 1952, objectors served two-year terms in an alternative work program commonly known by its Selective Service code "1-W."[7]

The 1-W program employed COs in hospitals or other non-profit organizations. Most of the hospital assignees worked as orderlies, cooks and maintenance personnel and many public institutions benefited from the inexpensive labor 1-W men supplied. The men needed to work outside of their home communities, but the government applied few other restrictions. The work was civilian-directed. The COs often lived on their own in private apartments, had total charge of their off-duty hours and many even received some payment for their labor. While such conditions seemed at first to be ideal when compared with those of World War 1 or even World War 2, the Amish church was not pleased with the arrangement. The easy money, unmonitored free time and urban lifestyle of the 1-Ws disturbed Amish parents. Because most of the men worked in cities, it was often difficult for Amish family members to visit them.[8]

Some Amish 1-Ws had difficulty adjusting to their new surroundings. Working in large, impersonal institutions, with no family and few friends, many became terribly lonely and even depressed. Raised in strong extended family and church communities, Old Order youth were often shocked by the individualistic and selfish attitudes of their co-workers and superiors. Others reacted by escaping into the surrounding culture. Frequenting popular city night spots, dating non-Amish hospital employees and discarding their traditional Amish garb, many Old Order Amish 1-W assignees lost themselves in contemporary American society; some Amish 1-Ws never returned to their home communities. Others did come back but did not return to active church membership. They had felt terribly out of place in the work assignments, but having spent two years in the city, many were no longer comfortable at home, either. A number returned home emotionally damaged by culture shock.

In time, some Amish youth simply refused to work in city hospitals. In 1955 three Indiana Amishmen received five-year prison terms and $2,000 fines for refusing 1-W induction.[9] Incarcerated in Mill Point, West Virginia, the men could not wear their Amish clothes and refused to put on the prison uniforms. Prison officials would not admit them to the dining hall, but after four weeks of resulting malnutrition, the warden adapted clothing requirements to suit both the state and the men.[10] Soon the government brought other Amish to trial. In 1957 Joni L. Petersheim of Hazelton, Iowa, received a two-month jail sentence along with a $5,000 fine for refusing 1-W work.[11] During the next several years a number of other Amish were convicted of refusing induction. Several of the trials became Associated Press newswire items which appeared in papers across the country.[12] In 1960 the *New York Times* ran an article on Holmes County Amishman Aden A. Miller's sentencing to three years in a federal work camp prison for rejecting city 1-W employment.[13]

Other media notoriety was more troubling for the Amish. At times local police would arrest rowdy Amish teens for disturbing the peace or underage drinking. In the wake of such news stories, public outcry often demanded that older Amish youth not receive conscientious objector status. After police arrested three Lagrange County, Indiana, Amish young people for public intoxication, the county's draft board president declared, "If they [the three Amish youth] can do things like that [i.e., drink] . . . I don't see how they can refuse to carry a gun in defense of their country."[14]

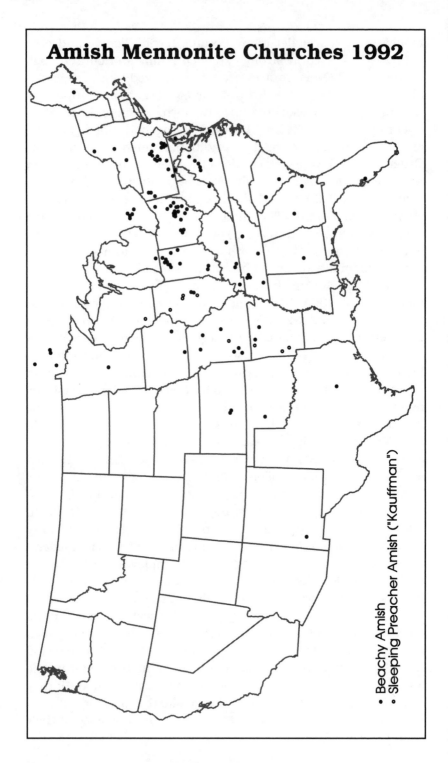

Amish Mennonite Churches 1992

• Beachy Amish
○ Sleeping Preacher Amish ("Kauffman")

Old Order Amish Communities
1992

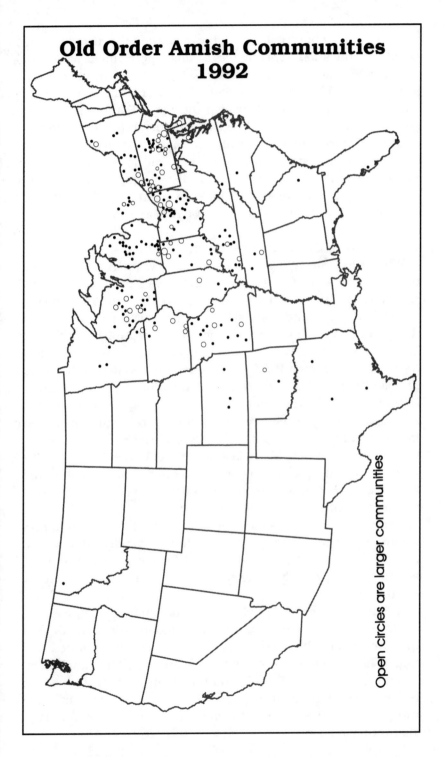

Open circles are larger communities

While such charges ignored the fact that the three young people in question represented a small percentage of Amish youth, such stories were embarrassing. As a result, church leaders worked harder to keep teens' behavior in line. Yet, Amish parents were limited by their own theology. Parents needed to give each child the choice of church membership and discipline, or a life of worldliness. After all, an Anabaptist understanding of believers' baptism included the very real possibility that not everyone would take up the way of discipleship. Some Amish children would not live as their parents might hope, but that did not invalidate the convictions of those Amish who did.

Tragedy and a Christian Response

While the military draft controversy drew the Amish into the national limelight of newspapers, magazines and courthouses, the church found itself in the press again—this time applying the principle of peace and nonresistance in a different situation. As the result of a terrible tragedy, the Old Order Amish offered the larger world a clear, though painfully difficult, witness of forgiveness. On a summer 1957 evening, two non-Amish youth, Cleo Eugene Peters, 19, and Michael G. Dumoulin, 20, met in Holmes County, Ohio. The two had earlier become acquainted in prison and upon their release, rendezvoused to celebrate their new freedom. Randomly targeting the Mount Hope, Ohio, home of Old Order Amish Paul M. and Dora J. Yoder Coblentz, the youths robbed the couple of nine dollars, molested Dora and shot and killed Paul. The Amish apparently offered no resistance. Their nineteen-month old daughter was unharmed.

Using a stolen car, Peters and Dumoulin then fled to Illinois where they shot a sheriff's deputy before surrendering to arrest. Returned to Ohio, the two stood trial for the Coblentz murder. Peters was eventually convicted and sentenced to death by electrocution.[15]

Still in deep pain and grief over the sudden tragedy, the Amish community found itself in a unique situation. Since the days of the early Anabaptist leader Menno Simons, Mennonites and Amish had taken a decided stand against capital punishment. Human life was too valuable and the chance for repentance too real for Christians to approve of executions, they believed. But rarely had the issue been so immediate for the Amish. How would they respond?

God's forgiveness needed to be extended to all, they reasoned. Letters offering forgiveness and promising prayer arrived at Peters' cell from Amish communities as far away as Iowa. Even the young victim and widow, Dora Coblentz, wrote to him. Amish families invited his parents into their homes for meals and Amish church leaders visited Peters in prison.

Next, the Amish community set out to call for a stay of execution. Wrote one Ontario Amishman, "Will we as Amish be left blameless in the matter if we do not present a written request to the authorities, asking that his [Peters'] life be spared"?[16] Individual letters and petitions arrived at the office of Governor C. William O'Neill until the November 7, 1958, date of execution. Seven hours before the scheduled electrocution, the governor commuted Peters' sentence.

The whole event had a marked impact on the Holmes County Amish community. "God has been speaking to many of us Amish people through this act," several Old Order church leaders wrote to Peters. "We believe that God allowed this, especially to call us back to Him in the work of winning souls to His kingdom."[17] In the midst of national conscription and Amish conflict with federal authorities, the Coblentz tragedy cut through the confusion, complication and bureaucracy, and brought the most important issue into clear focus: the church was to offer and demonstrate forgiveness and peace in a broken world.

The Draft Continues

Meanwhile as the 1-W program moved into its second decade, problems remained. After 1962 some Amish continued to refuse work in alienating urban environments and received fines or prison terms. But other Amish considered the program worthwhile. "I have worked in a hospital as an orderly for two years and I have not lost my Amish faith," one 1-W wrote to *The Budget*. There certainly were "temptations in these hospitals," he acknowledged, but that did not mean that everyone who went to the city would leave the church.[18] Yet by the mid-1960s some Amish leaders reported that only about half of their drafted men ever returned home. Many Old Order and Beachy Amish were coming to agree that something needed to be done.

The Beachy Amish attempted to address the problems of the 1-W plan by creating their own church work programs. The Beachy Amish established retirement homes in some five states and staffed them with their Beachy Amish 1-W men. Their COs were then able to serve in a non-secular institutional setting. Meanwhile a church-wide Beachy Amish spiritual revival had sparked the 1952 formation of a Mission Interests Committee, and three years later an organization known as Amish Mennonite Aid. Both groups worked on behalf of the evangelistic, mission, war-victim relief, and service goals of the Beachy Amish church. The Beachy Amish developed mission programs in Europe and among Native peoples in Canada and Latin America.[19] Some Beachy Amish 1-W men received government approval to work in the North American offices and warehouses of these new Beachy organizations.[20]

The Old Order Amish tried several different approaches to improve the 1-W program for their men. One positive response of the church was the beginning of an Old Order Amish magazine *Ambassador of Peace*. Beginning in 1966, each Amish CO received the *Ambassador*, which contained stories by various 1-W participants, as well as doctrinal articles and church news items from Amish leaders.[21] The magazine was the brainchild of Sarah M. Weaver (1921-1991), an Ohio Amish woman who was physically limited by muscular dystrophy.[22] Weaver spent a great deal of time thinking about the 1-W program and ways to improve it. She suggested that a regular Amish periodical might be a real encouragement to her church's COs.[23]

But by that time, other Old Order leaders were beginning to discuss working a completely new draft deferment arrangement. In November 1966 eighteen Amishmen gathered in Washington, D.C., to discuss proposed changes in the country's conscription laws. The group appointed a three-member National Amish Steering Committee to represent the church in all future dealings with the government. Three months later, at a Holmes County meeting of more than 100 church leaders from nine states, the Steering Committee received broad support from the wider church.[24]

For the Old Order Amish, forming the Steering Committee was a new step, indeed. Strongly congregational, the church had never had a national hierarchy or single spokesperson. The Committee's officers were laymen, which helped to ensure that their authority was limited to Steering Committee work, and would not spill over into matters of church practice or doctrine. Such decisions would remain in the hands of the local church district.

Amish fathers being released from Lancaster County Prison during the early 1950s. The men had been jailed for violating compulsory school attendance laws.

The next month Committee Chair Andrew S. Kinsinger (b. 1920) of Lancaster County met with officials from Selective Service and asked that all Amish COs receive farm deferments instead of city work assignments. By 1969 the Steering Committee and the government had reached a legal compromise whereby Old Order Amish young men could perform farm labor in lieu of their military service. Under the terms of the agreement, the church leased privately owned Amish farms for twenty-six month periods and hired each farm's owner as farm "manager." Drafted Amish men then worked on such farms for two-year periods. During the last few years of conscription, most Amish chose such farm work, although a few still took city hospital jobs. Even after the draft ended, the National Amish Steering Committee continued to meet on a regular basis as other church and state conflicts drew its attention.[25]

More School Difficulties

A major source of contention between the Amish and the state continued to be the proper education of Amish children. The Amish refusal to send their children to large, consolidated elementary schools, or to high schools of any variety, resulted in repeated run-ins with the law.[26] During the late 1950s and '60s, more private Amish schools open their doors. Throughout the period, Amish parents found themselves before local magistrates, paying fines and even serving jail terms. From Kansas to Pennsylvania, and most states in between, school difficulties plagued Amish communities.

In some areas, local officials and the Amish quietly reached compromise agreements which allowed the Amish to operate their own private schools without interruption, or tailored special rural public schools to meet Amish needs. In some instances Amish children remained in the public instruction system, but also attended church-run afternoon "Sunday schools." Different from their Protestant counterparts, Amish Sunday schools, or "German schools," taught German reading and writing along with a mix of biblical and doctrinal material. (As early as the 1890s, Amish school teacher Samuel D. Guengerich had advocated special "German schools" as a necessary Amish supplement to public instruction.)[27] And in a few cases Amish children took correspondence courses in an effort to meet state education requirements and yet avoid the secular influences of the modern high school.

In 1955 the Amish in Pennsylvania worked a unique compromise with the state. After completing eighth grade, Amish youth were free to work at home, but reported to a special "vocational school" one morning per week until they reached the age of fifteen. Here they continued their practice of basic skills, turned in required weekday work journals, and reported on independent projects on which they had labored. The compromise vocational school satisfied both state officials and Amish families. Several other states later copied its method. After 1967 in Ontario, the government also granted the Amish the right to establish and manage their own schools apart from provincial regulations.[28]

In other places working agreements were elusive. For years some communities suffered repeated conflicts. One of the best-known cases of such conflict occurred in Iowa.[29] After the 1947 school consolidation around the town of Hazelton in Buchanan County, Iowa, the local Old Order Amish community withdrew from most aspects of public school participation. They retained

Amish children in Buchanan County, Iowa, flee from authorities attempting to take them to a consolidated public school in 1965.

the use of two soon-to-be-abandoned one-room schools, hired teachers and maintained the facilities to their own standards. Fourteen years later, residents around Hazelton and another town in the neighboring county voted to further consolidate their

BERRY'S WORLD

© 1965 by NEA, Inc

"Let's skip the Viet Cong for a moment—what are we gonna do about the Amish school kids in Iowa?"

already consolidated school systems. Many Hazelton citizens were very upset by the merger and resented having their high school moved to the next county. Because the Amish believed that the new super-consolidated district would allow them to continue their own educational system, a number of Amish had voted for the merger. In fact, the Amish votes may have been decisive. Local Hazelton citizens angry about the new school consolidation bitterly resented the Amish voting for a joint district in which the plain children presumably would not participate anyway.

In the end it was the Amish who stood to lose the most. The new two-district school conglomerate had no intention of allowing the Buchanan County Old Orders free reign to manage their own schools. Officials visited the Amish schools and declared them too primitive for long-term use. The Amish could attend the one-room buildings for only two more years, and then only through sixth grade. Seventh- and eighth-graders would need to travel to Hazelton's junior high school.

The Amish balked, and in the fall of 1962 opened their two buildings with their own uncertified Amish teachers. Locals promised to take action against the schools for failing to meet state instructional standards. But the Amish schools were not unusual. Amish schools like those condemned in Buchanan County routinely received state approval to operate in other parts of Iowa. Nor was the use of uncertified teachers particularly uncommon. At the time, half of all Iowa's *public* secondary schools employed some uncertified teachers. What was unique in Buchanan County was civic emotion which forestalled all compromise.

For the next two school years the local controversy smoldered. State involvement only angered local leaders who felt as though they were handling the situation adequately. In the fall of 1965, public school and county officials were set to close the Amish schools and transport all of the Amish children to the Hazelton Elementary School. The Amish use of uncertified teachers served as the basis for the government's action. On the morning of November 19, 1965, school officials arrived at one of the Amish schools intent on quietly loading the students on a bus and transporting them to the public elementary building. While the children walked in an orderly way to the bus, one Amish adult shouted "Run!" in German, and the children dashed for the

Old Order Amish Parochial Schools, 1925-1991

Many Old Order Amish and Old Order Mennonite school teachers and directors subscribe to *Blackboard Bulletin*, a magazine devoted to supporting and strengthening private Old Order schools. *Blackboard Bulletin* attempts to contact all Old Order schools. Each year the magazine publishes a school directory. In November 1991 the publisher knew of 749 Old Order Amish schools, founded from 1925-1991:

Date	Number of Current Old Order Amish Schools Founded During Each Decade
1920s	1
1930s	3
1940s	9
1950s	46
1960s	148
1970s	173
1980s	198
1990-91	44

surrounding fields. The resulting mayhem left only a few children in police hands and the rest scurrying for home. Press photographers on hand captured images of fleeing children and angry officials. The day's events found their way to newspapers around the country.[30]

The next school day public education and police authorities arrived at the second Amish school, only to repeat the chaos of the Friday before. Instead of running, the children sang "Jesus Loves Me" at the top of their voices, while mothers cried and stern-faced fathers stood in protest by the doorway. Iowa's Governor Harold E. Hughes declared a three-week suspension on interference with the Amish, temporarily bringing the situation under control. National sympathy began to consolidate around the Amish. Private contributions arrived in Buchanan County to pay for Amish fines and penalties. Governor Hughes appealed to the state legislature to address the situation. Although rejecting the governor's own proposal, in 1967 the General Assembly granted state education officials the power to exempt all Amish (who had been in the state for at least ten years) from Iowa public education standards. The Buchanan County Amish could now manage their own schools with their own teachers, just as the Amish did in other parts of Iowa.

Supreme Court Resolution

The Buchanan County incident attracted wide public attention during the mid-1960s. One person who took special interest in the story was Iowa native Reverend William C. Lindholm.[31] In 1965 Rev. Lindholm was pastor of Grace Lutheran Church in East Tawas, Michigan. He believed that the situation involved a clear violation of Amish religious freedom. Rev. Lindholm contacted the Religious Liberty Office of the National Council of Churches of Christ, which in turn encouraged him to take action. In March 1967 he attended a University of Chicago conference on state regulation of non-public schools, where he called for all those interested in working for Amish civil rights to organize. The National Committee for Amish Religious Freedom (NCARF) formed as a result, with Rev. Lindholm chairing the group. Members included lawyers, academics and Christian and Jewish religious leaders.

By the time the group formed, the Iowa conflict had calmed considerably, but new problems surfaced. The state of Kansas had convicted Hutchinson Amish resident LeRoy Garber of not sending his daughter to the local high school. (She was carrying a ninety-five percent average on her American School of Chicago high school correspondence course.) Kansas had also declared the Pennsylvania-style "vocational school" compromise illegal in the Sunflower State. The U.S. Supreme Court refused to review the case.[32] NCARF discussed the situation, but could do nothing without the chance to argue a federal appeal.

Meanwhile the Garbers and other Old Order Amish decided to leave Kansas. The decision to migrate had always been an option for Amish facing inflexible state laws. The Adin Yutzy family had left Buchanan County, Iowa, during the height of that controversy, and had moved to Green County, Wisconsin.[33] Begun in 1964, the Green County Amish settlement drew families from various parts of the Midwest. Then in the fall of 1968, two Old Order Amish fathers and one Amish Mennonite father found themselves under arrest in Green County, charged with not

Amishmen ascending the steps of the United States Supreme Court. The Court ruled in favor of Amish schools in 1972.

sending their children to high school. Ironically, one of the men was Adin Yutzy, who had faced the same situation in Iowa.

On Christmas Eve 1968, NCARF's Rev. Lindholm called Harrisburg, Pennsylvania, attorney William Bentley Ball and discussed the Wisconsin situation. The two wrote to the state of Wisconsin asking for Amish exemption from state school codes. The state refused and Ball began to prepare a case on behalf of the defendants. In the spring of 1969 the NCARF lost its case in Green County Court.[34] Although the court acknowledged that the government had violated Amish religious liberty, the decision held that a "compelling state interest" overshadowed any religious rights. On appeal the Wisconsin Supreme Court reversed the ruling and decided in favor of the church and parents. No such "compelling right" existed in this instance, the justices said. The church posed no significant threat to society by choosing an eighth grade education.[35]

The case was not exhausted, however. Wisconsin appealed its state's high court verdict to the U.S. Supreme Court. In December 1971 Ball and the NCARF argued persuasively in Washington, D.C. The following spring the Supreme Court handed down its now famous decision in *Wisconsin v. Yoder, et al.*[36] (see excerpts of the decision, p. 274). The Court ruled that the government does not have reason to deny the Amish their right to practice their faith and teach their children—even if such teaching included no certified high school work. Lack of formal secondary education has not made the Amish a social or economic "burden" to American society, Chief Justice Warren E. Burger reasoned in his majority opinion.[37] For Attorney Ball, the ruling was more than just a victory for the Amish; it also strengthened the cause of religious freedom for all Americans. "The results of the decision not only helped the Amish people everywhere," Ball later commented, "but the terrific emphasis on religious liberty and parental rights is just golden."[38] Since 1972 hundreds of other court decisions have cited the Amish case. Other Amish and Old Order Mennonite groups have also received the same educational rights under the 1972 ruling. Nearly all Beachy Amish children, for example, attend private Beachy Amish schools, and most do not complete high school.[39]

Since *Wisconsin v. Yoder*, all states must grant the Old Order Amish the right to establish their own schools (should they choose) or to withdraw from public institutions after completing eighth grade.[40] In some communities Amish parents have continued to send their children to public elementary schools even after *Wisconsin v. Yoder*. In most places tensions eased considerably after the Supreme Court ruling, although certain difficulties remained for those Amish living in Nebraska. Not interested in any more court cases, the Amish finally left that state in 1982.[41]

Church Life at Mid-Century: Conservative Dissent and the "New Order" Amish

Questions of church and state certainly did not occupy all the time and attention of the Amish. Other concerns weighed heavily, as well. At mid-century, the Old Order Amish found themselves in the midst of a number of debates and discussions concerning important Christian doctrines and church order. While the resulting conversation fostered healthy thought and reflection for many Amish church members, in several communities it also sadly ended in division. Again, one of the important matters concerned the practice of shunning. During the 1950s several Old Order Amish communities, including the important Holmes County settlement (the largest in North America), decided that in many cases social avoidance should only be a temporary provision. If an excommunicated Old Order church member later affiliated with another nonresistant, "plain," Amish-related church, the Old Order group would suspend its shunning and restore fellowship with the formerly errant one. This new provision sparked a strong reaction within the Ohio community.[42]

By 1955-1957 a group of church districts who wished to continue "strict shunning" withdrew from the larger Holmes County Old Order fellowship. Known locally as the "Andy Weaver Amish" (one of the group's influential leaders was Bishop Andrew J. Weaver), the group also rejected changes in farm and household technology which seemed to be quietly creeping into other Old Order homes. A related conservative Old Order sub-group formed in the Lagrange County, Indiana, Amish community and relocated in Ohio. There were similar divisions in other communities and new settlements formed which attracted these especially conservative Amish.[43] These groups represented one of the streams which flowed through the larger Amish church during the 1950s—church renewal inspired by increased attention to personal and group discipline.

But other streams were flowing, too. Also during the 1950s, identifiable currents of change and new patterns of emphasis appeared in certain Old Order Amish circles. Some Amish began to testify of deeply personal—for them, very meaningful—encounters with God. Proponents called the movement a "spiritual awakening" and celebrated its popularity among Amish youth. Those less sure of the new spirituality's merits feared that it substituted an emotional and subjective human experience for the serious reality of life-long discipleship. Was the new movement the result of a powerful and supernatural working of God, or did it represent another human attempt to try and somehow find God?

Perhaps the most debated issue among the movement's supporters and detractors concerned the Christian doctrine of salvation. Citing Jesus' teaching in Mark 13:13 that "He who endures *to the end* will be saved," the Amish had traditionally taught that eternal life was God's gift to those who persevered in a life-long reliance upon God's grace. In this life Christians had only the *hope* of salvation, conditioned upon their continued trust.[44] As the apostle Peter had warned the early church, anyone could be "led away with the error of the wicked" and "fall from . . . steadfastness" (2 Peter 3:17). To publicly announce that one was *absolutely certain* of one's standing in God's eyes smacked of both spiritual pride and ultimate human arrogance, traditional Old Orders believed.

Those who espoused the new teaching emphasized that any Christian could be sure of his or her salvation. This "assurance" teaching also found support in scripture, its proponents believed. Among these was the New Testament's First Epistle of John which assured the church that the presence of both the Holy Spirit and Christian love evidenced the real presence of God's salvation. The Christian entered into a knowable saving relationship with God in this life, and then received the full gift of God after death.

The new movement stirred controversy in a number of communities. Advocates of the teaching traveled, spoke and spread the debatable doctrine. One of the most active was Preacher David A. Miller (b. 1910) of Thomas, Oklahoma. Miller became something of a traveling Amish evangelist. He preached tirelessly, on Sundays, weekdays, mornings, afternoons and evenings—sometimes for several days in a row. Miller delivered sermons wherever he received a hearing: in a house, a front lawn or a barn. Often hosts needed to move the meetings to larger spaces as crowds—some very sympathetic, others more skeptical—gathered to hear his teachings on "assurance" and other topics. Among other places, Miller gained a special hearing in Holmes County, Ohio, and Lancaster County, Pennsylvania. In 1952 after spending a week and a half in the Lancaster area, Miller found himself excommunicated by the Lancaster church for insisting too strongly on the controversial ideas.[45] That action and Miller's later leaving the Old Order church entirely for the Beachy Amish fellowship symbolized the seriousness with which both sides approached the new movement.[46]

Although the heated controversy died somewhat after 1960, it did not go away. Soon advocates of the revised doctrine also agitated for private, in-house telephone ownership and fully-automated tractor farming. Such a material agenda on the part of the innovators seemed to confirm conservatives' fears that claims of renewed spiritual life could easily become excuses for neglecting stewardship, family and community life. Mechanized farming broke down the need for family teamwork and cooperation and convenient access to private telephones actually destroyed close community by extinguishing face-to-face relationships.

But, the change-minded Old Orders responded, their goals were definitely not material. They strongly advocated moral, family-centered living. Their members did not merely practice temperance when it came to tobacco and alcohol use (as many Old Orders did), but outright abstinence. Moreover, they enforced a stricter discipline with their teens, and did not tolerate the occasional rowdiness which some conservative parents did.

During the 1960s tensions grew as some Lancaster Amish adopted farm equipment which was not approved by the larger church. As conservatives moved to force the innovators to get rid of their purchases, the church severed. In February and April 1966 about one hundred families withdrew from the Lancaster County Old Order fellowship and formed two new church districts, dubbed "New Order Amish."[47] (The conservatives did not shun the seceders, however.[48]) During the next three years the Holmes County community also divided, but for somewhat different reasons. The number choosing the so-called "New Order" was much larger in Ohio. Scattered Old Order Amish in other states identified with this movement or formed new districts. Some of the New Orders chose the designation "Amish Brotherhood."[49]

All of the New Orders were in agreement on such things as stressing high moral standards regarding courtship practices and tobacco use. They also established Sunday schools and church-centered activities for their youth. But they differed a great deal on questions of technology. The Lancaster County group eventually allowed public utility electricity, in-home telephones and tractor farming. The majority of the Holmes County New Order Amish did not allow any of these innovations.[50]

The New Order Amish attempted to remain close to their Old Order roots while implementing selected doctrinal and technological changes. Even those adopting tractors in the fields still make use of horse-drawn buggy transportation for family travel, and continue to hold German-language worship services in private homes (a few have built meetinghouses). The Amish Brotherhood has produced a number of very articulate tracts and books outlining their beliefs and practices.[51] They remain a loose, yet defined fellowship, balancing what they see as the strengths of Old Order life with new spiritual insight.[52] The New Order Amish are generally considered a sub-group of the Old Order Amish and are usually not listed separately in tabulations of Old Order Amish communities. Since 1966 numerous other groups have splintered from the New Order Amish in Lancaster County. These churches have rapidly adopted automobiles, church meetinghouses and other innovations. Some have affiliated with the more progressive Beachy Amish.[53]

Amish in Latin America

In the midst of all the 1960s church controversy and division, another significant movement was afoot among the North American Amish. Increasing pressure from the surrounding culture had led some Amish to consider leaving their host society. The failed Mexican settlement of the 1920s had not deterred others from dreaming of a thriving Amish community in Latin America. As early as 1951 Samuel Hertzler, Sr. (1887-1972), of Saint Mary's County, Maryland, considered beginning an Amish community in Honduras. Hertzler and two sons traveled to New Orleans and then by boat to the Central American nation in order to determine its suitability for settlement. The men reported that "it might be an ideal place for Amish to get away from the turmoil of our modern country including [the military] draft, unreasonable school laws and high land prices."[54] The Hertzlers returned to Maryland, however, and nothing came of their Central American dreams.[55]

In 1967 another Amish family with a vision for an Amish church witness in Latin America, Peter (1912-1971) and Anna Wagler (b.1912) Stoll, of Aylmer, Ontario, traveled south to visit Latin American countries in search of a new home. They stopped in Belize and traveled as far as Costa Rica looking for available land.[56] They decided that Honduras would be the best place to begin. The next year the Stolls and several other families moved to farms near Guaimaca, Honduras. Within four years, sixteen families from Ontario, Indiana and Pennsylvania were part of the new community. The group had a solid core of resident church leaders, with a bishop, two ministers and a deacon as a part of the settlement.[57]

Agriculturally the region was nearly everything for which the Amish hoped. The new settlers adjusted to the climate, soil and new crops. Yet the group had its difficulties, too. Mastering Spanish was a challenge for many. One of the largest issues the church faced was that of the surrounding Native poverty. In North America the Amish had lived a much simpler lifestyle than most of their neighbors. In Honduras, by contrast, the Amish were considered somewhat wealthy—they owned land, horses and homes. "We have been challenged," wrote one Amishman from the Honduran community, "to live less luxuriously as we have come face to face with the poor and hungry."[58] Already by 1970, one family had adopted an Honduran orphan. Other families soon did the same. In 1974, the Guaimaca Amish built a small cement block school for the local Native children. An Amishman served as the teacher for the indigenous students, some thirty of whom had enrolled by the second year.[59]

But the major difficulty for the Honduran Amish resulted from tensions within their church itself. From the beginning, the group included both New Order and Old Order Amish persons. A unique cooperative venture at its start, the partnership soon proved problematic. When lifestyle changes came more and more quickly through the years, a number of the settlers became uneasy. By 1977 some families returned to North America. The next year almost all of the Old Order Amish resettled in Aylmer, Ontario, and several of the New Order members moved to central Ohio. Those New Order Amish who remained in Honduras continued to rapidly modernize their homes and farms, and most eventually affiliated with the Beachy Amish.[60]

While some Amish were moving from North America to Honduras, other Old Order Amish families were packing their bags for Paraguay. In 1967 seven families from Orange County, Indiana, moved to a community in Paraguay's Chaco region. The area was already home to a sizable group of conservative Mennonites, and the new Amish arrivals settled near these spiritual cousins. Six more families arrived in the next twenty-four months and the settlement seemed off to a good start. Bishop Noah J. Coblentz (b. 1897) of Lakeside, Ontario, a man of amazing energy, traveled twice by ship from North America to Paraguay and helped organize the church and ordain resident leaders. The aged bishop's long journeys and deep interest seemed to be strong symbols of northern faith in and support of the new group.[61]

The prospering Paraguayan farms produced milk, beef cattle, dates and fruit. By 1977 the group had its best year ever and was improving economically beyond everyone's expectations. But the Paraguayan Amish never formed a spiritually stable congregation. The next year nearly all the settlers sold their property and returned to the United States. A few families stayed and joined their neighboring conservative Mennonites. Others tried to keep the Amish church going, but with the departure of most of the members and all of the leaders, the remnant was hard put to continue. The few Amish who remain in Paraguay use no motor vehicles, hold their church meetings in Spanish and English, and worship in meetinghouses. They have no official contact with any other Amish group.[62]

One of the Old Order Amish leaders who did settle in Latin America for a time admitted that "it is only honest" to realize that the risks involved were great. "But then," he continued, "it was also a bit risky for our forefathers to leave Europe, cross the Atlantic, and face the American wilderness." The Latin American settlements have not thrived as Old Order Amish communities in the way that they had in the "[North] American wilderness," however.[63] Without a more sizable flow of emigrants from Canada and the United States and the establishment of stronger church foundations, the small Latin American congregations were doomed to fail.

Life in the Welfare State

Back home in the United States, life had been changing, too. One of America's most far-reaching twentieth century social and political developments had been the rise of the welfare state. In broad terms, welfare state philosophy called for the government's deliberate and planned involvement in national affairs so as to encourage a better life for all of its citizens. Rooted in turn-of-the-century Progressive thought, the welfare state took on identifiable shape during President Franklin D. Roosevelt's response to the stark economic realities of the Great Depression. Positive public action on behalf of the unemployed, the poor, the aged and the physically challenged were becoming standard public fare by the 1940s and '50s. In the decades which followed, welfare state activities did not stop with aiding the retired, disabled and lower class, but grew to include such diverse programs as farm commodity subsidies, college tuition student loans, federal funding of airport construction and pollution control laws. From "the cradle to the grave" Americans now encountered a host of programs, institutions and activities designed to better their lives.[64]

For the Amish, the reality of the welfare state caused serious conflict. The "better life" toward which the system strove was not at all like the Amish ideal. Government-directed programs seemed to destroy community-based mutual aid. Church-centered care and extended family responsibility tended to become irrelevant in the face of public intervention and activity. Moreover, the welfare state's promises of upward social and economic mobility were not important goals for the Amish. Since the mid-1950s, confrontation between the Amish and the government's many public service programs have occurred often. Ultimately, the Amish have been rather successful in limiting the state's encroaching tentacles of power and influence. But the Amish right to care for themselves has not been an easy privilege to gain. The Amish story proved to be one small chapter in the larger U.S. civil rights movement of the time.

One of the first conflicts erupted in 1955 when Congress extended the Social Security program to include self-employed farmers.[65] Self-employed Amish had never taken part in the twenty-year-old program, but suddenly participation became mandatory. Many Amish would not voluntarily pay Social Security taxes, and Internal Revenue Service (IRS) agents had to collect funds through Amish bank accounts. A few Amish closed out their accounts and made it very difficult for the state to tap their resources. In 1958 the government foreclosed and sold several Amish farms in order to recover lost Social Security funds. During the next two years the IRS forcibly collected from 130 other Amish households.[66] However, such action did not stop Amish opposition to involvement in a system which they saw as misdirected and wrong.

The spring of 1961 saw the most dramatic encounter between the Amish and the IRS. Two years before, the federal government had officially placed a lien on the work horses of Amishman

Amish men wait outside the office of the Internal Revenue Service. Social Security taxes have caused great concern among the Amish.

Valentine Y. Byler (b.1913). The New Wilmington, Pennsylvania, self-employed farmer had not paid his Social Security taxes and the government intended to collect. The next summer authorities arrested Byler after he failed to appear in court. Although the judge immediately released him, tension mounted. The following April, 1961, agents arrived at Byler's farm while he was involved in spring plowing. Walking through the fields, the men stopped Byler, unhitched three of his horses and led them away as confiscated property. The government later sold the animals to recover Byler's unpaid Social Security taxes. While officials also seized the horses of other Amish, Byler's case became the celebrated incident.[67]

Since the government's method of recovering the funds also deprived the Byler family of its livelihood, Byler sued Washington for damages. He withdrew his case, however, in the face of strong Amish opposition. The church rejected Christians using the force of the court system to take revenge. But non-Amish public outcry did cause the IRS to declare a moratorium on collecting Social Security from the Amish.[68] In the summer of 1965 Congress addressed the problem as a part of the nation's

Old Order Amish and Old Order Mennonites appear in an Ontario courtroom for a hearing on provincial education laws, July 1968.

new Medicare bill. A subsection of that measure exempted self-employed Amish from both the Medicare and Social Security systems.[69]

But Amish employers and employees were still liable for all Social Security taxes. In 1982 the Supreme Court upheld the necessity of such payment, but six years later Congress sided with the church and passed another exemption. Since 1988, if Amish employees work for Amish employers, neither party needs to pay Social Security pay-roll taxes.[70] The IRS still requires one group of Amish to participate in the social insurance program: Amish persons working for non-Amish employers must contribute their full Social Security liability; however, they continue choosing to forfeit virtually all benefits of the system.

In addition to Social Security tax laws, the Amish have responded to portions of the 1970 Occupational Safety and Health Act. Amish men employed in construction work rejected the hard hats stipulated under the law, in preference for their own black felt or summer straw hats. In 1972 the federal government granted Amish workers a head-gear exemption. Workers Compensation Insurance, farm commodity subsidies, Medicare programs, U.S. Department of Agriculture dairy herd reduction plans and other welfare state activity have caused special problems for the Amish. Much publicity resulted from the opposition of a few ultra-conservative Amish to the bright orange slow-moving vehicle signs required on Amish carriages. At times the National Amish Steering Committee and the National Committee for Amish Religious Freedom have become involved in negotiations with the government.[71]

In Canada, too, welfare state policies resulted in conflict with the church.[72] Ironically, in 1953 it was Canada's relative dearth of welfare entanglements which in part enticed American Amish to move to Ontario. The rapid rise and spread of Canadian social programs soon followed, and the Old Order Amish found themselves confronted by their new home's National Pension Plan. By 1967 Revenue Canada officials were invading Amish bank accounts and garnering wages in an effort to collect unpaid Pension Plan taxes. Finally in 1974 self-employed Amish received exemption from the system. The situation for Amish employees and employers remains problematic. Some Amish businesses have become multi-member partnerships so that each employee becomes a self-employed part-owner. In the end, all Canadian Amish accepted Social Insurance numbers, but their digits are such that they cannot be used to receive any benefits.

Canadian milk marketing regulations have also been difficult for the Amish, with the result that since 1977 there has been a decline in the number of Canadian Amish-owned dairy operations. Many Canadian Amish have moved into other types of farming and non-farming work, or returned to the United States.

Economic Diversity

During the second half of the twentieth century non-farming jobs became more and more common among the Old Order Amish in the United States. Especially during the 1960s, '70s, and '80s, Amish employment patterns shifted noticeably.[73] At times the scarcity and high cost of farmland prohibited some Amish families from owning farms. Earlier in their North American experience, the Amish had moved in search of more or cheaper land. While the church continued such a strategy after 1960, its members adopted another approach as well. Amish who could not obtain farms remained in established Amish communities and took other jobs. At times the jobs were agriculturally-related, but often they were not.

Various types of non-farming jobs became popular. In some communities, like Lancaster, Pennsylvania, increasing numbers of Old Order Amish established home businesses, or "cottage

Supreme Court of the United States: State of Wisconsin, Petitioner, v. Jonas Yoder, Adin Yutzy, and Wallace Miller. On Writ of Certiorari to the Supreme Court of Wisconsin. [May 15, 1972], No. 70-110.

Excerpts from the landmark 1972 United States Supreme Court case *Wisconsin v. Yoder, et al.* The seven members of the court unanimously sided with the Amish defendants. Chief Justice Warren Burger wrote the majority opinion. (Justice William Douglas dissented in part from Warren's opinion, but agreed in the main. Several other justices wrote concurring opinions.)

"Amish objection to formal education beyond the eighth grade is firmly grounded in . . . central religious concepts. They object to high school and higher education generally because the values it teaches are in marked variance with Amish values and the Amish way of life. . . . The high school tends to emphasize intellectual and scientific accomplishments, self-determination, competitiveness, worldly success, and social life with other students. Amish society emphasizes learning-through-doing, a life of 'goodness,' rather than a life of intellect, wisdom, rather than technical knowledge, community welfare rather than competition, and separation rather than integration with contemporary worldly society.

"As the record so strongly shows, the values and programs of the modern secondary school are in sharp conflict with the fundamental mode of life mandated by the Amish religion; modern laws requiring compulsory secondary education have accordingly engendered great concern and conflict. The conclusion is inescapable that secondary schooling, by exposing Amish children to worldly influences in terms of attitudes, goals and values contrary to beliefs, and by substantially interfering with the religious development of the Amish child and his integration into the way of life of the Amish faith community at the crucial adolescent state of development, contravenes the basic religious tenets and practices of the Amish faith, both as to the parent and the child. . . .

". . . The State's requirement of compulsory formal education after the eighth grade would gravely endanger if not destroy the free exercise of respondents' religious beliefs.

"The State attacks respondents' position as one fostering 'ignorance' from which the child must be protected by the State. No one can question the State's duty to protect children from ignorance but this argument does not square with the facts disclosed in the record. Whatever their idiosyncrasies as seen by the majority, this record strongly shows that the Amish community has been a highly successful social unit within our society even if apart from the conventional 'mainstream.' . . .

"It is neither fair nor correct to suggest that the Amish are opposed to education beyond the eighth grade level. What this record shows is that they are opposed to conventional formal education of the type provided by a certified high school because it comes at the child's crucial adolescent period of religious development. . . .

"We must not forget that in the Middle Ages important values of the civilization of the western world were preserved by members of religious orders who isolated themselves from all worldly influences against great obstacles. There can be no assumption that today's majority is 'right' and the Amish and others like them are 'wrong.' A way of life that is odd or even erratic but interferes with no rights or interests of others is not to be condemned because it is different. . . .

By the Court: Chief Justice Warren E. Burger, Justices Harry A. Blackmun, William J. Brennan, Jr., William O. Douglas, Thurgood Marshall, Potter Stewart, and Byron R. White. (Justices Lewis F. Powell, Jr. and William H. Rehnquist took no part in the consideration or decision of the case.)

industries." These family-centered enterprises thrived and served both Amish and non-Amish clientele. Often the business involved the work of entire families—even extended family—in a way similar to that of operating a family farm. Businesses included a wide range of services. Greenhouses, grocery stores, print shops, dry goods stores and cabinetry shops became common Amish enterprises. Along with more traditional Amish work such as blacksmithing and carriagemaking, these new jobs became the source of income for increasing numbers of families. Amish construction crews, house painters and lumber workers also became common.

Not only were men involved in home businesses, but also many Amish women supplemented family income through the sale of quilts or other crafts. Some women developed networks of "putting out" materials for products such as quilts. Various Amish households might work on certain parts of the quilting process (cutting, piecing, quilting, etc.) The organizing woman coordinated the whole process and found retailers for the finished products. Such a system of household-managed production was an early part of the Western world's Industrial Revolution, but was soon replaced as concentrated business interests monopolized manufacturing. The Amish have preserved this early form of division of labor.[74]

Another arena into which the Amish have ventured for jobs off the farm has been industrial occupations. Especially in Indiana's Elkhart and Lagrange Counties and Ohio's Geauga and Trumbull Counties, Amish heads of household work in the manufacturing industry. Many Indiana Amish find work in the assembly of recreational vehicles and mobile homes, while the northeastern Ohio settlement includes numerous persons whose work weeks are spent in commercial rubber manufacturing. In a detailed study of the northern Indiana Old Order Amish community, sociologist Thomas J. Meyers discovered that in 1988 a full forty-three percent of Amish heads of household under age sixty-five held factory jobs. Only thirty-seven percent were engaged in farming.[75]

A similar 1981 study of the Holmes County, Ohio, Old Order Amish community found forty-two percent of heads of household involved in full-time farming, while twenty-one percent held factory positions, and twenty-eight worked in carpentry, construction or traditional trades.[76] By contrast, in 1986 the majority of married male Old Order Amish in Lancaster County, Pennsylvania, continued to farm but a growing number of others worked in carpentry or home-based shops. Almost none were employed in factories.[77]

Will the move away from farming prove detrimental to Amish society, supported so long by an agrarian family base? Sociologist Donald B. Kraybill has suggested that large numbers of Amish working in non-Amish-owned factories could, in fact, threaten the church's life together. In the larger world, industrialization ultimately results in smaller families, increased individualism, upward social and economic mobility, and some degree of cultural alienation. Work environments profoundly shape people. Impersonal, secular, industrial jobs simply do not fit with Amish beliefs and lifestyle choices, Kraybill has said. In the long run, moving work out of the environment of the home and family and into large-scale commercial factories might prove detrimental to the Amish. Home-based cottage industries in which the Amish are better able to control their work environment would be a safer choice for those Amish who leave the farm.[78]

Meyers cites the experience of the northern Indiana Amish who have successfully maintained their Amish faith identity, family structures and church connectedness while holding industrial manufacturing jobs.[79] The Old Order Amish are able to adapt to new work environments, Meyers believes. Only the choices of future generations of the Amish church will determine whether the move from farm to factory was a benign solution to farmland shortages, or a dangerous temptation to dissolve into mainstream American culture. Either way, the Amish move away from farming occupations toward home-based or factory occupations remains a new and growing reality.

The Impact of Tourism

Another reality of latter twentieth century Amish life was the rise of tourism and popular interest in Old Order Amish communities. As Amish society diverged more and more from mainstream North American culture, fascination with the Amish church grew slowly but steadily. The impact of tourism challenged the Amish. In some places the Amish lost the ability to be fully private citizens, as each year their lives became the focus of attention for millions of interested and inquisitive visitors.

Old Order Amish Settlements With Ten or More Church Districts, 1991

Location	Church Districts
Holmes/Wayne/Tuscarawas Counties, Ohio	145
Lancaster/Chester Counties, Pennsylvania	103
Elkhart/Lagrange Counties, Indiana	78
Geauga/Trumbull Counties, Ohio	54
Berne, Adams County, Indiana	22
Nappanee, Marshall/Kosciusko Counties, Indiana	20
Arthur, Douglas/Moultrie Counties, Illinois	18
Mifflin County, Pennsylvania	16
New Wilmington, Lawrence County, Pennsylvania	12
Allen County, Indiana	11
Daviess County, Indiana	11

Source: "David Luthy, "Amish Settlements Across America: 1991," *Family Life* 25 (April 1992): 19-24.

Under careful eye and camera lense, the Amish have become one of the most closely examined people in America.

The 1930s Pennsylvania public school controversy brought the first extended media attention of the Amish into American homes. *Time, Literary Digest* and *The New York Times* were among those national publications which featured the Amish during the troubled 1937-1939 school years.[80] In the 1950s, articles on the Amish and military conscription also found their way into newspapers around the country, as did stories of other confrontations between the Amish and the state.

Such increased public notice, coupled with a growing American post-war penchant for travel and vacation, naturally led to the development of Amish-related tourism. Lancaster County, Pennsylvania's close proximity to several major metropolitan centers made it one of the early destinations of middle class vacationers wanting a glimpse of Amish life.[81] In 1946 a major Lancaster City hotel began offering bus tours of its surrounding Amish farming country. By 1950 the New York City-based Parker Tours provided regular trips to the Lancaster Amish community. Picture books prepared for visitors soon appeared in local shops and restaurants. Travelers could also tour an area farm house which non-Amish entrepreneurs had furnished as an authentic Amish home. Opened in 1955, The Amish Farm and House was probably the first paid-admission Amish attraction.[82]

Soon Amish themes appeared in wider American popular culture. Secular writers and producers used the Old Order Amish as characters in books, films and on Broadway. Even young children learned about the Amish. Marguerite de Angeli's 1944 story of a little Amish boy, *Yonie Wondernose*, received a wide audience after winning the American Libray Association's Caldecott Honor for outstanding children's book illustrations.[83] Throughout the 1950s a number of other stories for teens and adults—including a popular Nancy Drew mystery, *The Witch Tree Symbol*—further popularized Amish images, settings and plots.[84] In 1955 Twentieth Century Fox released an Ernest Borgnine film, *Violent Saturday*, in which criminals hid on an Amish farm. Earlier that year the Mark Hellinger Theatre in New York City opened *Plain and Fancy*, a wildly popular Broadway musical centering on a young Amishman's adventures in the city.[85] While some credited the show with creating popular interest in the Amish, it actually only contributed to an already present and growing popular fascination.[86]

Meanwhile as the number of annual visitors to Lancaster County approached one million, the local Chamber of Commerce and Industry established a Tourism Committee to coordinate and promote travel to the area. Begun in 1957, the Committee developed into a Visitors' Bureau which handled tourists' questions and lodging arrangements. The Bureau quickly grew and became an independent, self-supporting organization fifteen years later.[87]

By that time, other Amish communities were also beginning to receive noticeable numbers of visitors. A June 1967 article in *Travel: The Magazine that Roams the Globe* briefly suggested visiting northern Indiana's Old Order Amish community.[88] A year later the same periodical included a piece on the Holmes County, Ohio, Amish settlement.[89] While Amish-related tourism in Ohio was a much smaller enterprise than in eastern Pennsylvania, since 1960 organized tours had been bringing visitors to Holmes County. Amish-theme restaurants and other Amish-related attractions soon opened their doors in both Ohio and

The Old Order Amish, Number of Church Districts, 1974 and 1991

Location	1974 Church Districts	1991 Church Districts
Canada		
Ontario	16	17
Honduras	1	—
Paraguay	1	—
United States		
Delaware	5	8
Florida	1	1
Georgia	—	1
Illinois	12	20
Indiana	91	155
Iowa	15	23
Kansas	4	5
Kentucky	3	19
Maryland	3	6
Michigan	9	40
Minnesota	3	9
Missouri	19	32
Montana	—	1
New York	5	29
North Carolina	—	1
Ohio	136	253
Oklahoma	1	4
Pennsylvania	104	216
Tennessee	4	6
Texas	—	3
Virginia	1	1
Wisconsin	11	48
TOTAL	**444**	**898**

Old Order Amish total membership, 1992: approx. **63,000**
Old Order Amish total population (including children), 1992:
approx. **135,000.**

In older, established Amish communities, each church district typically includes 125-175 people (adult members and children). In newer, smaller settlements, districts often include fewer than 100 people.

Source: David Luthy, "Old Order Amish Settlements in 1974," *Family Life* 8 (December 1974): 13-16; and David Luthy, "Amish Settlements Across America: 1991," *Family Life* 25 (April 1992): 19-24.

The Beachy Amish, Congregations and Membership, 1971 and 1991

Location	1971 Congregations	Members	1991 Congregations	Members
Belize	2	33	5	126
Canada				
Ontario	4	324	8	382
Costa Rica	—	—	6	217
El Salvador	1	19	4	133
Paraguay	1	18	2	38
United States				
Alabama	—	—	1	35
Arkansas	1	10	2	38
Florida	1	41	1	166
Georgia	1	177	3	198
Illinois	1	74	2	169
Indiana	10	662	11	764
Iowa	2	179	2	199
Kansas	1	176	3	281
Kentucky	—	—	5	279
Maine	—	—	1	12
Maryland	1	31	2	94
Michigan	1	26	1	42
Minnesota	1	39	2	66
Missouri	—	—	3	130
New Mexico	—	—	1	6
New York	—	—	1	50
Ohio	12	664	18	1230
Oklahoma	1	42	1	43
Pennsylvania	13	1129	12	1393
South Carolina	2	76	2	166
Tennessee	—	—	6	416
Texas	—	—	1	57
Virginia	5	304	6	498
TOTAL	**61**	**4024**	**112**	**7228**

In 1971 the Beachy Amish also sponsored mission churches in West Berlin (Germany) and Washington, D.C. Both of these congregations are still in existence, but no longer have formal ties to the Beachy Amish Church.

Source: *Mennonite Yearbook* 1972 and *Mennonite Yearbook* 1992.

Indiana.[90] Amish communities near Kalona, Iowa, and Arthur, Illinois also developed a variety of tourist-related businesses.[91] Meanwhile many of the newer, smaller Amish settlements, along with several older, more secluded communities, escaped the influx of visitors.

Tourism has affected the Amish in a number of ways.[92] A few Amish moved away from areas which they felt were becoming too busy and crowded. However, most Amish who lived in heavily visited areas chose to remain. Often these Amish adapted to crowded roads, clicking cameras and persistent questions. A number of Amish have taken jobs in businesses which primarily serve tourists. In addition, many Amish women supplement their family's income through selling quilts or other craft items to visitors. Few Amish own or operate full-scale tourist-related commercial establishments. Most choose to offer their products to visitors through non-Amish stores and shops or sell their crafts from their own homes or small road-side stands.

While some members of the church have benefited enormously from the economic advantages which the influx of visitors has created, other Old Orders resent what they perceive to be an invasion of their privacy and a disruption of their way of life. At the same time, in some communities entire generations of the church have grown up surrounded by tourism and do not even realize its full impact. Some Amish have cooperated in producing accurate literature about their people in an effort to combat inaccuracy and myth which have worked into popular images of their church.[93]

Occasionally, offended Amish leaders have even voiced some protest against their people's portrayal in secular culture. When the 1984 filming of Paramount Pictures' *Witness* disturbed members of the Lancaster County Amish community, they addressed their concerns to Pennsylvania's state government. (*Witness* portrayed the Lancaster Old Order Amish innocently entangled in a fictional web of big city drug crime.) A delegation of Amish leaders, including three bishops, traveled to the state capitol to register their complaint. As a result Harrisburg promised not to encourage any future filming of motion picture or television scripts involving Amish themes.[94]

Despite tourism's pressures on Amish life, sociologist Kraybill has suggested that visitation strengthens, even "energizes" Amish life as it "galvanizes the cultural gap between the two

The Amish are a growing group as they enter the twenty-first century.

worlds and helps define Amish identity." In fact, growing public interest in the Amish bolsters popular sympathy for them and discourages the government from infringing on Amish rights or forcing them to move away. States are not eager to lose the handsome tax revenues which Amish-inspired tourism provides.[95]

Phenomenal Growth

Despite the twentieth-century pressures of tourism and repeated conflict with government, the Amish have remained a remarkably resilient people. While the larger Western world seeks peace in bigger weapons, happiness in newer, larger and ever more material things, and disregards extended family and community in the search for individual self-fulfillment, the Amish continue to espouse such unpopular values as "turning the other cheek," living with less and working for a common good. Faith in God and God's activity in the world through the church has marked Amish life as noticeably different from an American society bemused by "progress," but unable to find a purpose or meaning in the resulting activity.

To maintain such a different way of life for generations would be notable in itself, but the Amish have more than maintained themselves. Three hundred years after their beginnings, the Amish churches are growing at a remarkable rate. The Beachy Amish church has grown to include some 95 congregations in twenty-three states and one province, along with seventeen other congregations in Belize, Costa Rica, El Salvador and Paraguay. During the quarter century from 1966 to 1991 the group's total membership climbed 118 percent.[96]

The largest Amish body, the Old Order Amish, has increased in size as well. Although the Old Order church does not record membership statistics, it is clear that their numbers are growing. In only seventeen years, from 1974 to 1991, the number of Old Order Amish church districts rose 102 percent.[97] One Old Order Amish historian figures that "the Amish population doubles nearly every twenty years."[98]

Amish families establish new communities almost annually. Active church districts stretch from Dover, Delaware, to Rexford, Montana, and from Norfolk, New York, to Pinecraft, Florida. Of the 215 Amish settlements in existence at the beginning of 1992, only nineteen have histories which pre-date 1900. A full 136 (63%) of the current settlements have begun since 1970. While not every new community succeeds, most do survive and thrive. Twenty-two states and the province of Ontario are home to a growing number of Old Order church districts, with Wisconsin, Michigan and New York receiving the most new settlements. The Old Order Amish do remain rather concentrated in three states, with twenty-eight percent of all church districts in Ohio, twenty-four percent in Pennsylvania, and seventeen percent in Indiana.[99]

Of course, large families play an important part in Amish church growth since nearly all new members come from Amish homes. But another important factor also appears to be at work among the Amish—an *increasing percentage* of Old Order Amish children choose to join their parents' church. Sociologist Meyers' study of the Old Order community in Elkhart-Lagrange Counties, Indiana found that of those Amish children born in the 1930s, twenty-one percent did not join the Old Order Amish. Of those born in the 1940s, only fourteen percent decided against their parents' church, and of those born in the next decade, the drop-out rate dipped to ten percent. While later-born offspring were still too young to accurately complete the study, the trend seems to be continuing in that community. In each generation, a growing number of youth decide to become members of the Old Order church.[100]

Along with growth in membership, the Old Order Amish have also established a number of modest church institutions which bolster and help to define the community. A monthly Old Order Amish periodical, *Family Life*, and a teen magazine, *Young Companion*, support Amish values and teaching though stories, poems and editorials. Pathway Publishers of Aylmer, Ontario, and Lagrange, Indiana, provides family reading material, devotional and prayer books, as well as Amish school texts. The publication *Blackboard Bulletin* provides help and ideas for Amish school teachers. Several Amish communities have also established historical libraries to preserve a valued heritage and assist in passing on the faith. Some settlements have also adopted more extensive church trust fund systems which function as emergency insurance reserves in cases of liability or hospitalization (such plans remain controversial in some parts of the church, however, as they seem to be too much like commercial insurance). The small network of modest Old Order Amish institutions, along with older, informal vehicles of connection such as *The Budget*, or the more recent *Die Botschaft*, bring the Amish world closer together. Still locally organized and congregationally governed, the Amish church has created a greater and broader sense of unity and peoplehood which have balanced their phenomenal growth with an equally amazing continued commitment to one another.

Reflecting on the story of his own Amish people, their life and faith commitment to both God and each other, one Amish writer found himself at a loss for words. There simply was no logical explanation, he realized, "that can explain the basic fundamentals of their faith that was inherited from ancestors of many generations ago, which was granted to them through the grace of our Lord Jesus Chirst." Instead, the Amishman thought, his people had "cultivated as their every day mission" the task of Christian discipleship, and "feel that their mission is to lead an humble life that needs no publicity."[101]

And yet publicity comes. For such a life is so much at odds with the assumptions and values of western society, that many moderns are compelled to stop and think about Amish choices and decisions—watching, weighing and wondering—as the Amish story continues.

Notes

Chapter 1 Notes

1. Hartzler (1902).
2. Hartzler quoted Lamentations 3:22-23.
3. A fine introduction to the Anabaptist movement is found in Weaver (1987). The brief, classic interpretation of the movement is the 1943 American Society of Church History presidential address of Bender (1944). A comprehensive history of Anabaptism and related sixteenth-century groups is provided by Williams (1962). Introductions to Anabaptist thought include Friedmann (1973) and Klaassen (1981a). Selected Anabaptist primary sources appear in English translation as Klaassen (1981b).
4. For a good, in-depth look at the reformation theology of Luther, see George (1988). This very readable book also deals with the thought of Huldrych Zwingli, John Calvin and Menno Simons, and provides an introduction to late Medieval Catholic theology and piety.
5. The writings of this group, and especially those of one member of the group, Konrad Grebel, are available in English as Harder (1985). An accurate, easily-read book which tells the story of Anabaptist beginnings in Zurich is Ruth (1975). See also Blanke (1961) for the story of an early Anabaptist congregation at Zollikon, near Zurich.
6. Clasen (1972:437), documents 843 Anabaptists known to have been executed between 1525 and 1618 in Switzerland, the Rhine Valley, Swabia, Hapsburg territories, southeast Germany, Franconia and Thuringia-Fulda. The total does not include those Anabaptists executed in the Low Countries or England.
7. Violence against the Anabaptists in the Low Countries lasted only about 50 years. In Switzerland and south Germany, executions continued for approximately ninety years after 1525.
8. Yoder (1973:8).
9. The writings of Menno are preserved in English as Menno (1956).
10. Some of the many biblical citations used to support the practice of physical, social shunning were: Matthew 18:17; Romans 16:17; 1 Corinthians 5:9-11; 2 Thessalonians 3:6, 14, 15; 2 Timothy 3:2-5; Titus 3:10.
11. The doctrine of shunning was also tied theologically to the particular Christology of the Dutch Anabaptists, see Oyer (1984:222-24).
12. Bender (1927:57-66) and Gross (1991).
13. The most accurate translation of the *Dordrecht Confession* is Horst (1988). The text is also available in Leith (1982:292-308). See also Horst (1982).
14. Mast (1950b:58).
15. Mast (1950b:87, 88).
16. Scherer (1974:25).

17. Background to the Swiss Brethren migration to the Alsace is given in Seguy (1984:207-209).
17. Yoder (1973:9).

Chapter 2 Notes

1. Gratz (1953:37).
2. For social conditions of the Anabaptists in the Alsace, see Seguy (1980:2-9). For conditions in and around Bern, Switzerland, see Gratz (1953).
3. Scherer (1974).
4. MacMaster (1985:30).
5. Primary source material on the controversy between Jakob Ammann and Hans Reist, and the eventual schism, is contained in a set of letters as Mast (1950b). The letters appear in German in an issue of the Swiss Mennonite Historical Society periodical as "Briefsammlung" (1987:26-61). A narrative account of the Ammann-Reist division is presented in Bachman (1942:35-50) and in Yoder (1987a:43-59). Another complete narrative is Gascho (1937:235-66); Gascho, however, presents Jakob Ammann in an unfavorable light.
6. Leroy Beachy has suggested another reason for Ammann's suggestion of twice-yearly communion. Beachy has hypothesized that it may have been a reform aimed at including women more fully in church life. Both social custom and the limitations of travel and health care often forced pregnant women and new mothers to remain at home. Caught in the perpetual cycle of childbearing, some women had missed communion for years when it was held only annually. A more frequent observance would have permitted them more opportunities to participate in this important ordinance. See Yoder (1987a:55).
7. Mast (1950b:28).
8. Mast (1950b:29).
9. Mast (1950b:103).
10. Mast (1950b:71, 72).
11. Mast (1950b:72).
12. Mast (1950b:73).
13. Mast (1950b:74).
14. It was quite common for Swiss people to shorten their surnames by dropping the last syllable and adding an "i" with a long "e" sound. Thus, "Ammann" would probably have been said as "Ami" (Ah-mee). In this common form, the transition to the term "Amisch," or "Amish" is much more plausible. See Luthy (1978a).
15. Mast (1950b:49).
16. Mast (1950b:49).
17. The issue of salvation for the True-Hearted may have become more acute as the Swiss Brethren/Mennonites picked up themes and impulses from Continental Pietism. For one suggestion of such a connection, see Schelbert (1985:118-127).
18. On Ammann's followers in the Ber-

nese Oberland, see Gratz (1953:45-48).

19. Mast (1950b:86, 87).

20. Uli Ammann was apparently himself a somewhat tolerant and pastoral leader as evidenced in a letter he wrote to the church at Markirch, probably about 1720, Ammann (1977:2, 3).

21. Mast, (1950b:67).

Chapter 3 Notes

1. Quoted in Dyck (1983:3).

2. MacMaster (1985:53).

3. See examples in Gratz (1952:5-7). A 100-Taler reward went to anyone turning in an Anabaptist minister, fifty Talers for a deacon, twenty-five for a lay man and twelve and a half for a female member.

4. Gerlach (1990:3).

5. Correll (1955:70); Stoll (1974).

6. Gratz (1952:9).

7. This narrative is found in Gratz (1952:13-18); Smith and Krahn (1981:87-94); and Smith (1929:70-72).

8. See the memory recorded in Bachmann (1934), and Smith (1929:71, 72). Other authorities are less specific about the Mennonite refusal.

9. Smith and Krahn (1981:92-94, 134); and Gratz (1952:5-21).

10. Frost (1990).

11. Luthy (1988c:20). Hostetler (1980:65, n. 34). See also Hostetler (1980:56, n. 12).

12. MacMaster (1985:59).

13. MacMaster (1985:69, 70).

14. Guth (1986:9); Gerlach (1990:2).

15. Gerlach (1990:2-8).

16. The story of the Galician and Volhynian Amish and Mennonites is given most completely in Schrag (1974). See also Stucky (1981).

17. An introduction to Hutterite history, life and society is found in Dyck (1981:71-82, 236-45). A more comprehensive work is Hostetler (1974).

18. Wenger (1981); Beiler (1969). For a similar experience of Lutheran-turned-Amish Martin Bornträger, see Luthy (1991b:19).

19. Schrag (1974:44).

20. Gerlach (1990:2).

21. Correll (1928:66-79, 198-204). Guth (1987:130).

22. Correll (1928:200-204).

23. On the 1779 meeting and its written resolutions, see Amish Church (1970);

24. Correll (1928:200-204).

25. Kauffman (1979:16).

26. Amish Church (1930:140-48).

Chapter 4 Notes

1. A key source on the early Amish communities in colonial Pennsylvania is a series of articles by Joseph F. Beiler, titled "Our Fatherland in America," which appeared regularly in The Diary beginning in May 1972. See also Beiler (1976/1977). See also

Stoltzfus (1954). Recent secondary reviews of the settlements include Hostetler (1980:56-60) (including a map); MacMaster (1985:86-88, 125-27); Kauffman (1991:19-24). Also of interest are the maps and text of Early Amish Land Grants in Berks County, Pennsylvania (1991).

2. Beachy (1954).

3. Kauffman (1991).

4. Luthy (1981a).

5. On the debate over whether the Amish or the Mennonites should get to keep a certain European meetinghouse after the Ammann-Reist split, see Mast (1950b:62).

6. Luthy (1984b).

7. On the unique Chester County Amish community, see for example the thoughts of sociologist Mook (1955).

8. Brunk (1982).

9. Beiler (1974b:120, 119).

10. Beiler (1978). See also MacMaster (1985:151, n. 28).

11. MacMaster (1985:70-72, 86-88, 125-27).

12. Wenger (1937:399).

13. Beiler (1975a) gives some information, but suggests too strongly that Hertzler was the first Amish leader in America. On suggestions of Amish leaders who preceded Hertzler, see Kauffman (1991:20). Historian Leroy Beachy has also researched pre-Jacob Hertzler Amish church leadership.

14. Kauffman (1991:32).

15. For Gnage, MacMaster (1985:127); for Garber, Beiler (1976/1977:46); for Beiler, Stoltzfus (1954:240); for Blank, Murray (1981:16).

16. MacMaster (1985:97, 98).

17. Stoltzfus (1954:259-62).

18. Beachy (1954:265).

19. MacMaster (1985:101, and n. 47 Tully article).

20. MacMaster (1985:100).

21. MacMaster (1985:74). For a nineteenth century example, see Hostetler (1989:35).

22. For this whole period and the Amish and other peace church involvement, see MacMaster (1979:61-164).

23. Kauffman (1979:15).

24. On the Great Awakening in America, begin with a standard treatment in Hudson (1965:59-82). The Awakening in the Middle colonies (and more specifically among the German churches) had a slightly different emphasis than did its New England variety, however.

25. Beiler (1977c). Hostetler (1989: 199, 200). It is unknown when Drachsel was silenced and left the Amish church. However, he was preaching in non-Amish congregations by at least 1782. In 1789 he attended a conference of the United Brethren church held in Baltimore. In 1804 he moved from Lebanon County to Westmoreland County, Pennsylvania, where he died.

26. Hostetler (1983); Kauffman

(1991:31). For information on Brethren history, begin with Durnbaugh (1986).

27. The best source of information (both primary source material and narrative interpretation) is found in MacMaster (1979).

28. Durnbaugh (1978 : 9), esp. as, ". . . the neutrality of the German sectarians had a definitely pro-British tinge."

29. Ruth (1976:129).

30. MacMaster (1979:245, 246).

31. MacMaster (1985:254).

32. MacMaster (1979:474-77).

33. MacMaster (1979:464-66); Mast (1952).

34. Kauffman (1991:30, 31).

35. Kauffman (1979:16).

36. Beiler (1975b).

37. Beiler (1975b).

38. Gingerich and Kreider (1986:xiii). Also Yoder (1991:23, 25).

39. Kauffman (1979:13).

Chapter 5 Notes

1. Gerlach (1990:5, 6). Luthy (1986:288).

2. On the impact of the French Revolution and the Napoleonic era on the French Amish (and Mennonites), see Seguy (1984:212, 213).

3. Quoted in Correll (1955:72).

4. Correll (1956).

5. Smith and Krahn (1981:213).

6. Neff (1957).

7. A Mennonite congregation or two may have helped to pay the expenses of the delegates. One of the congregations which donated funds was the Donnersberger Gemeinde bei Mainz, which was most likely the Weierhof Mennonite community.

8. The final Conseil de l'Etat denial of their request for military exemption came on 21 April 1812. Chronology by Joe A. Springer; correspondence of 23 June 1992 cites Seguy (1977:368, 69).

9. Grieser and Beck (1960:34).

10. Luthy (1981b).

11. Luthy (1984c).

12. Schabalie (1975).

13. Catechism (1905).

14. Zijpp (1956) and (1957).

15. Schrag (1974:62-66).

16. Gingerich (1982:185).

17. Seguy (1973).

18. Varry (1984). See also Yoder (1954).

19. Guth (1986:10, 11).

20. Sommer and Hostetler (1957).

21. In 1832 some of the Hessian Amish who immigrated to Butler County, Ohio, brought pianos among their belongings. One is now in the Butler County (Ohio) Historical Society, Hamilton, Ohio. See Schlabach (1988:64).

22. Gerlach (1990:4).

23. Historical (1975:106).

24. Quoted in Smith (1983:78).

25. Quoted in Schwemer and Bender (1956).

26. Smith (1983:57).

27. Hostetler (1989:35).

28. Estes (1984:30).

29. See, for example, Gerlach (1990:2, 3).

30. Yoder (1964:41).

31. For a list of some of the Amish immigrants of the years 1804-1810, see Luthy (1988c:21).

32. Hostetler (1980:65). Gerlach (1990:3) lists Amish church membership statistics for the mid-nineteenth century (1855-1888). He estimates 1,659 to 1,859 Amish members total.

33. Luthy (1973:16).

Chapter 6 Notes

1. Stoltzfus (1954).

2. Luthy (1972a).

3. Schlabach (1978:1, 2), (1981:6-8). Kaufman and Beachy (1991:10-17). Luthy (1986:339-42).

4. Luthy (1986:411-18).

5. Page and Johns (1983:9, 10).

6. Lehman (1978:57).

7. Estes (1984:21). Luthy (1986:166).

8. Roth and Grant (1986:13-17). After Barbara's death in 1789, Christian married Elizabeth Becker.

9. Christian Troyer himself had come to Welland County, Ontario, from Bedford County, Pennsylvania, as early as 1786. He returned to Pennsylvania to bring other members of his immediate and extended family, and resettled in Norfolk County.

10. By the time the Christian Troyer family moved to Ohio, they had been living in York County, Ontario. Christian's son David Troyer (1784-1871) and his wife Catherine Hooley (1783-1847) remained Amish and also moved to Ohio. Other children and siblings of Christian Troyer who had joined other denominations remained in Ontario.

11. Gingerich (1972:27-31).

12. Luthy (1986:76).

13. Hostetler (1989:35).

14. There is some debate as to which Christian Zook this was. In the opinion of Steven R. Estes, it was Christian Zug/Zook (1758-1829) who married Magdalena Mast. Christian Zug/Zook who served as an Amish minister in the Chester County community died on 8 October 1826.

15. Mast and Mast (1982: 46, 47).

16. Hostetler (1989:27, 310) states that Nussbaum was Amish, and Stoltzfus (1954:249) implies the same. However, the editor of the original document doubted that Nussbaum was an Anabaptist of any sort. Others in his party were Mennonite. See Gratz (1953:129, 130, esp. n. 8). See also Lehman (1969:28).

17. Gratz (1953:137, 138).

18. Gingerich (1961a:108, 109).

19. Yoder (1940); Kauffman (1991:245-47).

20. Kauffman (1991:100-105).

21. Wenger (1961:328). On the Elkhart-Lagrange settlement beginnings, see Amish and Mennonites (1992:4-18).

22. Luthy (1991a:2-5).

23. Smith (1983:61) and Estes (1990:45, 46). Baechler was born in Europe.

24. Yoder (1991:118).

25. Luthy (1986:77).

26. Luthy (1986:118, 119).

27. Gingerich (1955b:12).

28. Luthy (1986:241).

29. Umble (1947:1)

30. Grieser and Beck (1960:26); Stoltzfus (1969:79, 80).

31. Miller (1971).

32. The eight Amish congregations were Partridge Creek, Busch Gemein, Dillon Creek, Mackinaw River, Rock Creek, Hessian, Bureau Creek and Ohio Station.

33. Umble (1948:103).

34. Estes (1982:11, 12).

35. Examples of Swiss Amish conservatism, even into the twentieth century, are detailed in Scott (1981:76-78); (1986:116); and (1988:63, 89, 101).

36. Stoltzfus (1954:252).

37. Bender (1934:93-95).

38. For more on the 1809 and 1837 meetings, see Bender (1934). On the 1849 meeting, see Gingerich (1965).

39. Yoder (1991:31, 32); Miller (1959).

40. Yoder (1991:121-34). For the later views of Lancaster County Deacon John Stoltzfus on the subject, see Yoder (1979a:41, 42, 44-47, 170-77).

41. The Amish of Chester County, Pennsylvania had a meetinghouse, but that group ceased to exist and its building seems not to have set a precedent for any of the later Amish church buildings. Likewise, the temporary log structure used by the Amish around Louisville, Stark County, Ohio, in the 1830s, and the log "cemetery chapels" in Ontario Amish graveyards as early as 1859, did not represent the same type of change-minded approach to church life which the meetinghouses built after 1851 did. The Chester, Stark and Waterloo Counties' meetinghouses/chapels were unusual, but not permanent.

42. Belcher (1859).

43. Umble (1941b:20, 21).

44. Umble (1963:1-8); Umble (1941b:16-28).

45. Umble (1933:82).

46. Kauffman (1991:118, 119).

47. Estes (1984:40, 41).

48. Gingerich (1972:41).

49. Luthy (1986:347).

50. The standard history of the Apostolic Christian Church is Klopfenstein (1984).

51. Yousey (1987:47-59).

52. Bender (1934:94).

53. Among those concerned were northern Indiana's John E. "Hansi" Borntreger (1988:12); Lancaster County, Pennsylvania's David Beiler, in Umble (1948); Iowa's Jacob Schwarzendruber, in Bender (1946). Political activism also took place among the Amish in Bulter County, Ohio, documented by Page and Johns (1983), and the large central Illinois community and in Mifflin County, Pennsylvania, documented below.

54. Ellis and Evans (1883:928, 932, 933). In 1849 the Pennsylvania Supreme Court finally ordered Upper Leacock Township to open public schools after the residents repeatedly stalled. Ebersol was elected a school director in 1858.

55. Kauffman (1991:144-47).

56. Hostetler (1964:280-84). For more on Zook, see Luthy (1989b).

57. Estes (1982:47-50).

58. Estes (1982:37, 47-50).

59. Estes (1984:85, 86, 88).

60. Estes (1982:50, 51).

61. Luthy (1989a) includes the story of two generations of the Graber family who received exemption from the Civil War draft.

62. Yoder (1991:95).

63. Bender (1946).

64. Yoder (1991:95).

65. Lehman (1978:58).

66. Luthy (1986:241, 242).

67. Yoder (1971:26).

68. Gingerich (1939:62-64).

69. Bender (1946:223-25).

70. Umble (1948:105).

Chapter 7 Notes

1. As early as 1831 Alexis de Tocqueville had noticed that individualism was a more important social value in America than in Europe.

2. Point made by Donald B. Kraybill in Yoder (1991:14, 15).

3. For a fine definition and explanation of *Ordnung* by a contemporary Old Order Amish leader, see Beiler (1982).

4. Gingerich (1986).

5. To avoid confusion, this chapter will identify two of the northern Indiana church districts by their home counties—Elkhart and Lagrange. In fact, the church district in Lagrange County was often called the Elkhart congregation because its members' farms were along the Elkhart River (in Lagrange County). See Yoder (1991:117-121).

6. Borntreger (1988:10).

7. Borntreger (1988:11).

8. Yoder (1991:130-34).

9. Umble (1948:105).

10. Yoder (1987c:37).

11. Yoder (1991:142).

12. Yoder (1987c:63-65).

13. Yoder (1987c:66).

14. Minutes ("Proceedings") of all seventeen *Diener-Versammlungen* sessions are available in German from many Amish and Mennonite historical libraries. This book cites historian Paton Yoder's preliminary English translation of those minutes. Steven R. Estes, Hopedale, Illinois, graciously loaned the translation. The translation runs 296 pages. Citations here will use both the original [German] year and page reference, and Yoder's translation page number. Hopefully Yoder and Estes will be able to publish these

important documents in English in the near future.

15. Proceedings, 1865, p. 3; Yoder trans. p. 2.

16. Proceedings, 1864, p. 7; trans. p. 52. Proceedings, 1864, p. 9; trans. p. 54.

17. For example, see Proceedings, 1863, p. 14; trans. p. 39.

18. Proceedings, 1863, p. 17; trans. p. 44.

19. Proceedings, 1862, p. 9; trans. pp. 8, 9. Proceedings, 1863, pp. 7, 8; trans. pp. 31, 32. Proceedings, 1864, p. 10; trans. p. 56. On these problems, see Yoder (1985:2-9).

20. In a letter of 12 February 1863, Shem Zook of Mifflin County, Pa., informed John Stoltzfus of Lancaster Co., Pa., that Bishops Jonas D. Troyer and John Schmucker ordained a bishop for the Hessian Amish congregation. Zook reported that this happened because "the [Hessians'] playthings [i.e., musical instruments] have been put away." See Yoder (1987c:101, 102).

21. Proceedings, 1862, p. 13; trans. p. 14. Proceedings, 1863, pp. 15, 16; trans. p. 41. Proceedings, 1863, p. 16; trans. p. 41. Proceedings, 1864, p. 14; trans. p. 60.

22. Proceedings, 1862, pp. 10, 11; trans. p. 10. Proceedings, 1863, p. 17; trans. p. 43. Proceedings, 1864, pp. 7, 8, 10, 13; trans. pp. 52, 53, 55, 59.

23. Proceedings, 1864, p. 11; trans. pp. 56, 57. Possibly, Proceedings, 1863, p. 15; trans. p. 40.

24. Umble (1948:107).

25. Yoder (1991:159-61).

26. Proceedings, 1864, p. 8; trans. p. 53.

27. Two English translations of the conservatives' statement are found as Bender (1934:95-98); and Yoder (1991:167, 168).

28. Proceedings, 1865, p. 5; trans. p. 73.

29. The Old Order Amish themselves used the self-designation *Alt Amisch* ("Old Amish"). The particular etymology of the title "Old Order Amish" is elusive. See Yoder (1991:261) for its discussion.

30. Proceedings, 1866, pp. 4, 5, 9; trans. pp. 79, 80, 83.

31. Proceedings, 1867, p. 4; trans. p. 91.

32. Proceedings, 1867, p. 8; trans. p. 94.

33. Procedings, 1868, pp. 5, 7; trans. pp. 101, 103.

34. Proceedings, 1875, pp. 19, 20; trans. p. 244.

35. Proceedings, 1875, p. 20; trans. p. 244.

36. A brief account of the Egly division, sympathetic to Egly, is Nussbaum (1976 or 1977). See also Yoder (1991:184-87).

37. Claudon and Claudon (1947).

38. Jacob Rupp (c.1801-1875) spoke for Egly. Proceedings, 1865, p. 6; trans. p. 73. Proceedings, 1866, pp. 6, 7; trans. p. 81. Proceedings 1870, p. 12; trans. p. 135. Proceedings, 1870, pp. 14, 15; trans. pp. 136, 137. Proceedings, 1870, p. 17; trans. p. 138.

39. "Henry Egly's Autobiography," Hist. Mss. 1-542, Henry Egly Papers, Box 1, folder

3 (English translation): 2, 3, Archives of the Mennonite Church (AMC), Goshen, Indiana. Document pointed out by Steve Estes.

40. One interpretation of the division is Estes (1982:66-68).

41. On the "Stuckey Division," see Estes (1982:83-86); Yoder (1991:187-94); Smith (1983:88-91).

42. Estes (1982:52).

43. Estes (1982:53).

44. Weaver (1926:72) contended that although Stuckey "was sometimes blamed for splitting churches," in fact "he was only trying to care for those who had left the old church and were without a leader."

45. Estes (1982:48, 49, 81).

46. Estes (1982:80, 81). See also Proceedings 1870, pp. 9, 11, 12; trans. pp. 133, 134, 135.

47. Proceedings, 1872, pp. 21, 22; trans. p. 179.

48. Proceedings, 1871, pp. 12, 13; trans. p. 154.

49. Proceedings, 1873, pp. 25-27; trans. pp. 206, 207. Estes (1982:70-86).

50. Estes (1982:94, 95).

51. Proceedings, 1871, p. 10; trans. pp. 95, 96.

52. Much biographical information on Yoder is found in Lehman (1978), esp. ch. 4. A brief biography of King is found in Stoltzfus (1969:77).

53. Proceedings, 1878, pp. 7,8; trans. pp. 289, 290.

54. Yoder (1991:196-201).

55. One small act of unity achieved by the ministers' meetings should not be overlooked. In 1874 the Mennonites living in Russian Volhynia immigrated in groups to South Dakota and Kansas. Some of these persons had been of Amish background, mostly the descendants of Amish from the Alsace and Montbeliard, France. While in Europe they had given up any distinctive Amish church life and had merged with their neighboring Mennonites. After settling in North America, however, one of the Volhynian ministers heard of the Amish *Diener-Versammlungen* and attended and registered as a fellow Amish minister. In 1875, 1876, and 1878, Preacher Johannes Schrag of Turner, Dakota Territory, participated in the gatherings. (Proceedings, 1875, p. 52; trans. p. 263. Proceedings, 1876, p. 34; trans. p. 286. Proceedings, 1878, p. 18; trans. p. 296.) The *Diener-Versammlungen* provided a means of uniting a scattered Amish family, divided geographically for three-quarters of a century. However, the Volhynian Mennonites of Amish background did not continue their connection with the Amish after the ministers' meetings discontinued. The Volhynians eventually found a church home with the General Conference Mennonite Church.

Chapter 8 Notes

1. C. B. Newhause, et al., "From Tennes-

see," *Herald of Truth* 8 (October 1871): 152.

2. Other early examples of Amish Mennonite and Mennonite cooperation as recorded in the *Herald* include: John Ringenberg, "Letter from Locke, Ind.," *HT* 1 (July 1864): 43; John M. Christophel, "Letter from Indiana," *HT* 2 (January 1865): 7; Daniel Brenneman, "A Visit," *HT* 4 (January 1867): 11, 12; G. Z. Boller, "From Noble Co., Ind.," *HT* 4 (February 1867): 25. Some letters and articles were also printed in the German-language companion paper *Herold der Warheit*, such as Ringenberg, above, *HW* 1 (July 1864): 43.

3. Yoder (1991:267).

4. Lind (1990): 45, 46.

5. Mahala Yoder Collection, Hist MSS 1-12, Small Collection, Long Box, 1871-76 Diary, AMC.

6. Yoder (1991:228-30).

7. Mast and Mast (1982:63-70).

8. The text of the 1889 sixteen-article Oak Grove discipline may be found in Lehman (1978:110, 111).

9. On the reaction of both first generation leaders like Stoltzfus and King, as well as the concerns of second generation Amish Mennonites surprised by the rapid pace of change in their fellowship, see the description in Yoder (1991:252-60).

10. Hiller (1968/1969); Gingerich (1971); Miller (1970). For an appraisal of the Spirit Preachers by C. Henry Smith (who witnessed spirit preaching as a boy), see Smith (1962:132-35).

11. Stutzman's relatives transcribed and printed her revelation as *Revelation* (n.d.).

12. Graber (1984).

13. See for example Presbyterian Spirit Preacher Constantine Blackmon Sanders (1831-1887) among others in Yoder (1968/1969). See also Schlabach (1988:220).

14. Gingerich (1959).

15. The Paper's masthead from April 1, 1893 until December 15, 1895.

16. Amish Mennonite leaders had met as early as 1882, but they did not organize a formal church body until 1890. For the story of the Western District Conference's formation, see Hartzler and Kauffman (1905:306, 307), and Weber (1931:187-96).

17. Historical (1975:379).

18. Lehman (1978:134, 135). Yoder (1991:231).

19. On Oak Grove Amish Mennonite, Smithville, Ohio, support for Elkhart Institute, see Lehman (1978:135-42).

20. Smith (1962).

21. For the biography of Smucker, see Yoder and Smucker (1990).

22. Lehman (1990:6-30).

23. See Yoder (1991:220-222), for examples of the last few Amish Mennonite attempts at shunning. Hartzler and Kauffman (1905:306-308) imply that the abandonment of the practice of shunning was a more formal decision on the part of the Amish Mennonites.

24. Yoder (1991:247).

25. Joseph Holdeman, "A Visit to Clinton and Haw Patch" *Herald of Truth* 8 (February 1871:25, 26).

26. J. D. Troyer, et al., "Correspondence," *Herald of Truth* 23 (1 March 1886): 73, 74.

27. Gingerich (1972:85, 88).

28. The classic history of the group is told in Wenger (1966). Recent revisions include Schlabach (1988) and Juhnke (1989), although these books are inter-Mennonite and include the history of other groups in addition to the "old" Mennonites.

29. For a chronology see Bair (1952).

30. Yoder (1991:17).

31. Yoder (1987a:83).

32. Erb (1974:468, 469).

33. Umble (1964).

34. Yoder (1991:17).

35. The standard history of the group is Miller (1985).

36. A standard history of the General Conference Mennonite Church is Pannabecker (1975).

37. Pannabecker (1968:18-22) and (1975:69).

38. Pannabecker (1968:18-22).

39. Gingerich (1942:14) reprints the newspaper article.

40. Pannabecker (1968:22-24) and (1975:71, 72).

41. Pannabecker (1968:24, 25) and (1975:72, 73).

42. There were other congregations of Amish background which joined the General Conference Mennonite Church. The GC Mennonite church at Ransom, Kansas, may have Amish background. See Haury (1981:54-56), although it does not match completely with Erb (1974:207-209).

43. Summaries of Stuckey Amish history include Weber (1931:435-536) and Smith (1983:88-110).

44. Yoder (1991:193).

45. General Conference Mennonite Church leader Christian Krehbiel (1832-1909) visited Stuckey hoping to persuade Stuckey to join the General Conference Mennonites. Krehbiel (1961:65, 66).

46. Estes (1982:93, 94).

47. Estes (1982:118-20).

48. Weaver (1926:94, 95); Weber (1931:485-96).

49. Juhnke (1979:67, 68); Weber (1931:377-92).

50. Weber (1931:519-25).

51. Weber (1931:402-11).

52. Weaver (1926:179-83).

53. See Nussbaum (1976/1977); Smith (1983:111-131).

54. Schlabach (1988:116).

55. Weber (1931:377-401).

56. For a history of the Missionary Church Association, see Lugibihl (1950).

57. Kauffman and Harder (1975:133, 134).

58. Estes (1990:42-46) documents this third wave of Amish immigration, especially as it related to the area around Chenoa, Ill. Estes cites an Amish immigrant as late as 1924. In every case these third wave immigrants joined progressive Amish Mennonite congregations once in North America.

59. Luthy (1986:290).

60. Gerlach (1990:2).

61. Neff (1959).

62. Gingerich (1982:182).

63. Seguy (1984:206-17).

64. Correll (1955).

65. Fretz (1957).

66. Yoder (1955).

67. Sommer and Hostetler (1957).

68. Gerlach (1990:8).

69. Hostetler (1955:212-19., esp. pp. 215, 218, 219).

Chapter 9 Notes

1. See United (1941:2:1005, 1006). The report includes numbers for 1906, 1916, 1926 and 1936. Statistics for the Old Order Amish may be a bit low due to some uncompleted questionnaires. The 1890 (United States) Federal Census gathered membership and congregational statistics on religious bodies including the Old Order Amish and Amish Mennonites, however, the numbers are incomplete, and additionally in a number of cases confuse known Old Order communities with decidedly progressive ones. The 1890 figures are only somewhat helpful at best.

2. For a careful comparison of Old Order Amish beginnings and that of other Old Order groups in America (Old Order River Brethren, Old German Baptists and Old Order Mennonites), see Hostetler (1992).

3. Smith (1983): 132, 133.

4. Luthy (1972/1973). The series of articles covers other time periods as well.

5. See Luthy (1986) for stories of numerous Amish settlements which began during this period and then dissolved.

6. Luthy (1978c); Yoder (1966); Yoder (1990).

7. Heritage Historical Library, Aylmer, Ontario, has several of these autograph books.

8. See letters from Isaac Ebersol to Sarah Lapp Zook, and Andrew Ebersol to Sarah Lapp Zook, in the Sarah Lapp Zook Papers, Custody of a relative, Lancaster, Pennsylvania (hereafter, SLZP).

9. Isaac Zook to Sarah Lapp, 8 January 1897, SLZP.

10. Sallie J. Fisher to Sarah Lapp, 23 December 1888, SLZP.

11. Bettsy Speicher to Sarah Lapp, 30 October 1891, and Speicher to Lapp, 2 March 1896, SLZP.

12. Rebecca S. Smucker to Sarah Lapp, 25 March 1896, SLZP.

13. Deeben (1992): 21-29.

14. Scott (1981:60, 72). Apparently Amish carriages in Pennsylvania were covered during at least the latter part of the nineteenth century, see Scott (1981:51, 55, 56).

15. The biblical text prescribing the prayer covering (or prayer veiling, head covering or devotional covering) is 1 Corinthians 11: 1-16. Scott (1986:98-103) gives more description and explanation. All of Scott (1986) is an excellent explanation on plain dress. Gingerich (1970) is also a standard work on dress.

16. Gibbons (1882:59).

17. See, for example, Luthy (1988b), and Luthy (1991a).

18. Swartzendruber (1950).

19. Samuel D. Guengerich, "Value of Education," Hist. Mss. 1-2, "Samuel D. Guengerich, 1836-1929," box 8, AMC.

20. Samuel D. Guengerich diaries, 10 March 1864, Hist. Mss. 1-2, "Samuel D. Guengerich, 1836-1929," box 1, AMC.

21. Hostetler (1989): 180-82; Luthy (1972/1973).

22. Luthy (1981c).

23. The Amish Aid Society began in 1885 according to Fisher (1978:335, 379). Amos J. Stoltzfus (1984:191, 192) cites apparently the same source as Fisher, but gives a date of 1875. Stoltzfus is to be preferred as the Heritage Historical Library, Aylmer, Ontario, has a printed policy for the "Amish Aid Insurance Compnany" dated 1879, as in Kraybill (1989:86, n. 18). Landis (1955) gives an overview of the program as it expanded into other communities, but gives too late a beginnning date. Gingerich (1955a) offers a description of a similar program among midwestern Amish, begun in the first part of the twentieth century.

24. Luthy (1981a). Later, about half of the community (mostly those living south of the Pennsylvania/Maryland border) left the Old Order church and affiliated with the Conservative Amish Mennonite Conference. The Old Order Amish in Somerset County, Pennsylvania, however, continue to use meetinghouses for their bi-weekly Sunday services.

25. Swartzendruber (1977): 12, 13.

26. Luthy (1986): 271-76.

27. Kauffman (1991): 118, 119.

28. Another method of handling such a situation followed this procedure: A baptized member of an Old Order church district would leave the church and join the Amish Mennonites. The Old Order group would excommunicate and shun the individual for a period of time. After the person had been a member in good standing of the Amish Mennonite congregation for a determined period of time, the Old Order church would "lift" the ban.

29. The story is recounted in Yoder (1991:266-73); Mast and Mast (1982:83-87); Hostetler (1980:278-80) and Yoder (1987a:103-106).

30. Mast and Mast (1982:37-39).

31. Mast and Mast (1982:57).

32. See Yoder (1991:273, 274). Other parts of the story were provided by Joni Helmuth's nephew, Orva Helmuth, Arthur, Illinois, in a phone interview, 14 May 1992. Orva made one correction to the story reported in Yoder and the document Yoder cites (p. 274, n. 38). Joni Helmuth's middle initial was "F." not "J." The tradition in most midwestern Amish families was for sons to have their father's first names as their middle names. Because Joni's father was Joseph, many assumed that Joni's middle initial was "J." The Helmuth family, however, had not followed that naming tradition. Joni Helmuth later left the Amish Mennonites, as well, and joined the Church of Christ.

33. Helmuth (1961); Smith (1983:141, 169). The Arthur Amish Mennonite Church functioned as a congregation from 1897 to 1914. It was a member of the Western District Amish Mennonite Conference.

34. Degler (1977:121, 122).

35. Luthy (1986:85-91, 134-39, 177-83, 213-18, 221-28, 305-32) for some of those stories.

36. Jones (1964).

37. The material on the Amish response, including quotations from *The Sugarcreek Budget*, comes from Luthy (1982:23-26).

Chapter 10 Notes

1. Quoted in Lord (1960:1). While not an academic history of the period, Lord's book does offer a helpful view of the popular press' view of the new century.

2. Quoted in Yoder (1990:332).

3. Quoted in Yoder (1990:332).

4. Martin (1905). The year before, Martin had published a novel whose main character was Mennonite, see Martin (1904). Martin probably had no intention of accurately portraying Amish or Mennonite life. Rather, she was interested in finding new or unusual ethnic characters for her stories. See Seaton (1980).

5. Luthy (n.d.); See also Kriebel (1910) for an early example of Lancaster tourism literature. The booklet makes brief mention of the Old Order Amish on p. 38.

6. Clark (1988:21-74) recounts the Amish move to near Dover, Delaware.

7. See the thoughts of Smith (1962:32) on the Montgomery Ward catalog. (Smith grew up in a progressive Amish Mennonite home.)

8. A fine description of the Lancaster County Amish reaction to, and negotiated use of, the automobile is Kraybill (1989:165-71). For an Old Order Amish discussion on the objections to car ownership, see Wagler (n.d.).

9. Yoder (1987a:106-110); and Lapp (1963).

10. For a good study from a sociological point of view as to how the technological decisions of the Old Order Amish and the 1910 "Peachy" Church affected each other and hardened those decisions on each side,

see Kraybill (1989, esp. ch. 7).

11. Gingerich (1939:311-14).

12. Schwieder and Schwieder (1975:98).

13. Information gathered in Ohio Amish communities by Stephen E. Scott while researching the historical chart in Ohio (1973:14-17). During 1917-22 the Swartzentruber Amish divided, leading to the formation of the Daniel Wengerd group. In 1934 the Wengerd group reunited with the majority Holmes County Old Orders. However, they were slightly more conservative than that group. Many of the former Wengerd people left the majority Old Orders again in 1955-57 with the conservative Andy Weaver group.

14. Interview with William Janzen, Mennonite Central Committee Ottawa Office. See also Epp (1982:365-89).

15. The only one-volume reference on Mennonites and Amish during the First World War is still Hartzler (1921). A complete book on the subject is being prepared by Gerlof D. Homan.

16. Quoted in Keim and Stoltzfus (1988:32).

17. See Abrams (1933).

18. Letter from Donella Clemens, 26 May 1992. Clemens is Peachy's granddaughter.

19. Keim and Stoltzfus (1988:46-52).

20. Juhnke (1989:236).

21. Quoted in Keim and Stoltzfus (1988:40).

22. Stoltzfus (1981:7-24).

23. Even years later the stories told by Amish men who lived in army camps as COs during the First World War are full of detail and emotion. Some men did not want the notoriety of being named with their stories, but they shared freely. See the collection, Stoltzfus (1981).

24. For one instance of the pressure to buy war bonds, see Swope (1969).

25. A good history of the Amish and Mennonite experience during World War 1 is Juhnke (1989:208-42).

26. See for example Homan (1990).

27. Examples include Mast and Mast (1982:132, 133); and Estes (1984:216-19).

28. Teichroew (1979:107).

29. Luthy (1972b).

30. Reason cited for arrest and conviction in File No. 186400-18, Department of Justice, Washington, D.C., as quoted in Luthy (1972b).

31. For a careful, articulate explanation of Amish obections to state-sponsored, formal higher education, see the essay by an Old Order Amish author, Stoll (1975).

32. Keim (1975:14, 15). For an annotated chronology of Amish school court cases, see Keim (1975:93-98). An updated, expanded annotated list is Place (1993).

33. Luthy (1986:513, 514).

34. Luthy (1986:514-21).

35. The school was originally slated to cost \$112,000, but the final cost increased to \$125,000. Of that sum, \$52,250 was Federal

Public Works Administration money. Some reporters marvelled that a people would reject government money for the construction of a new school when so many American communities were only hoping for increased funding from Washington.

36. "Education: Amish Folk Shun Their New PWA School," *Literary Digest* (4 December 1937): 32-34. A fine narrative of the events of 1937-1939 is found in Kraybill (1989:122-25).

37. This petition (with the names of all of the signers) is reproduced in Lapp (1991:141-67).

38. Text is Hostetler (1989:136, 137).

39. Keim (1975:94).

40. Keim (1975:94). A number of East Lampeter Township Amish families had not sent their children to school in 1937 and did not again in the fall of 1938. The boycott drew national attention as in: "Amish Loose Fight for Old Schools," *The New York Times* (28 June 1938): 22; "Amish Threaten School Secession," *The New York Times* (21 July 1938): 23; "New Amish School Strike Looms in Pennsylvania," *The New York Times* (5 September 1938): 15.

41. On the Delaware school, named Apple Grove School, see Clark (1988:195-206, 111-28), which lists enrollment in the various Delaware parochial schools through the years. Apple Grove opened in 1925. On the North Carolina school operated during the school year 1925-26, see Luthy (1986:299, 300).

42. "'Plain People' Win Right to Their Own Schools as Well as Way of Life," *Newsweek* (12 December 1938): 32. The article was more positive-sounding than the situation really was for the Amish. The school featured in the article was located on Horseshoe Road. The state had sold it at auction to Beradino Di Berardino for $890. The Amish rented the school building from Di Berardino. Mennonite Ella May Grove served as the teacher. See also "Amish Pupils Back in 1-Room School," *The New York Times* 29 (November 1938): 25. A history of the beginning of Amish parochial schools in Lancaster County, Pennsylvania, written by an Amish leader, is Esh (1977). See also Ferster (1983).

43. "Amish hit High School," *The New York Times* (21 September 1938): 26.

44. Amish Moving (1965).

45. Yoder (1987a:112-16).

46. Yoder (1987a:116-20) and Beachy (1955). For a description of the Beachy Amish/Old Order schism from a perspective very sympathetic to Beachy, see Mast (1950a).

47. Beachy (1955).

48. In 1928 two members of the group purchased the Weavertown meetinghouse in the hope that the group would use it in the future. In 1930 the group, under the leadership of John A. Stoltzfus, did begin meeting in the building. The structure is still being used in 1992. The building had been a Church of the Brethren meetinghouse, built in 1888. The Brethren had owned several meetinghouses in the area and had regularly held services in each of them on a rotating basis. During the first quarter of the twentieth century the congregation began meeting every Sunday in the same location, the Conestoga Church of the Brethren, Leola, Pa. See Hess and Fry (1983). Also Lapp (1963:9-11); and Yoder (1987a:110-12).

49. A chronology is given in Yoder (1987a:126, 127). See Yoder (1987a:128-38) for further discussion on consolidation and growth of the Beachy Amish.

50. An Amish minister writing anonymously, Amish Life (July 1971:20).

51. Amish Life (1971).

52. "An Amishman Speaks," Lancaster (Pa.) Intelligencer Journal (23 February 1931): 1.

53. Historical (1975:483).

54. Amish Life (August 1971:19).

55. "Amish Gratitude," *Time* (29 November 1937): 37. Article again mentions the Smoketown School controversy.

56. John M. McCullough, "Amish Curb Crops—But Not For AAA Pay" *Philadelphia Inquirer*, (2 April 1933).

57. Luthy (1984a).

58. For an in-depth look at the Historic Peace Churches in dialog with the United States government during the years between the world wars, see Keim and Stoltzfus (1988:56-102). For a brief review of the situation in Canada between the wars, see Janzen and Greaser (1991:44-46).

59. Peace (1937).

60. "Statement" (1939).

61. Peace (1937).

62. On the ASW program see Janzen and Greaser (1990:39-59); and Klippenstein (1979).

63. On the CPS program, see Wagler and Raber (1986); Keim (1990); Gingerich (1949); Hershberger (1951); and Keim and Stoltzfus (1988:103-26).

64. Unruh (1952:286).

65. See the Amish CPS directory which lists 600 men by name, address, and CPS assignment(s), in Wagler and Raber (1986:97-127). First person accounts of Amish who worked as forest fire fighters, on dairy farms, in psychiatric hospitals, in public health projects, in Puerto Rico, for the Fish and Wildlife Service, or as human guinea pigs for medical research, are also found in Wagler and Raber (1986). One of the best-known stories of Amish work in CPS is the rescue story, "The Tale of Doris Dean," Wagler and Raber (1986:28-33). Amish CPS men helped to find a little girl lost in the Blue Ridge Mountains of Virginia.

66. Huntington (1956:547, 548).

67. For a serious Amish critique of the Mennonite-administered CPS camp to which he was assigned, see Wagler (1991). Wagler

found the Mennonite camp administrators too liberal and out-of-touch with Old Order Amish values.

68. Bontrager (1956:23-25, 30-33); Wagler and Raber (1986:75).

69. Luthy (1978b).

70. "Rationing," file collection at the Heritage Historical Library, Aylmer, Ontario.

71. Dick Snyder, "Amish Undisturbed by the War Shortages, Have Always Done Without Autos and Such," *New York Times* (12 April 1942): II, 10.

72. Unruh (1952:227-29). See also "Sea-Going Cowboys" clippings file, Heritage Historical Library, Aylmer, Ontario.

Chapter 11 Notes

1. Luthy (1980b:33).

2. Historical (1975:796). Households with television sets in 1950 numbered 3,875,000.

3. "Urge Amish Use Tractors to Boost Yield of Wheat," a newspaper clipping dated Saturday, 27 April 1946, p. 5. Probably from a Lancaster, Pennsylvania, newspaper and pasted inside a copy of Steinfeldt (1937). This copy in the archives of the Lancaster Mennonite Historical Society Library and Archives, Lancaster, Pennsylvania.

4. Amish Life (1971:20).

5. A good description of the Lancaster County, Pennsylvania, Amish and the question of tractors for field use is found in Kraybill (1989:171-77).

6. Luthy (1986:366-69).

7. The story of the 1948 conscription law, the 1950 demand for alternative service from conscientious objectors and the development of the 1-W program is recounted in Keim and Stoltzfus (1988:127-46).

8. Not much published research has appeared on the negative side of the 1-W program. The negative points are hinted at in Keim and Stoltzfus (1988:146). Some of the negative implications of the 1-W program, especially as they relate to its Amish participants, are discussed in Keim (1993).

9. A fourth man received a suspended sentence and probation after he agreed to take a 1-W assignment.

10. The story is told in detail in Huntington (1956:579).

11. Associated Press story carried by the Lancaster, Pa. *Intelligencer* (28 June 1957).

12. Examples may be found, among other places, in the file "Amish," Clippings Collection, AMC. Many of the clippings are from *The South Bend* (Ind.) *Tribune*, but other newspapers are included as well. Stories of Amish convicted of refusing induction into the 1-W are also found in the pages of *The Reporter for Conscience Sake*, the official publication of the National Service Board for Religious Objectors (now the National Interreligious Service Board for Conscientious Objectors). A related item from the national press and the Amish peace position: In 1955 at the begin-ning of the draft controversy *The New York Times* ran a story which called the Amish "pacifists." "Amish Visit U.N. As Peace Symbol," *The New York Times* (25 May 1955): 35, reported that a group of Old Order Amish from Lancaster County, Pennsylvania, visiting New York City had toured the United Nations building. The group was led by 76-year-old Daniel Bawell, Bareville, Pennsylvania, and had come to bid farewell to a woman named Leah Fisher who was leaving for Europe. In an interview the Amish said that they specifically wanted to visit the U.N. because it works for peace. The reporter especially noted the nonresistant stance of the Amish.

13. "Amish Farmer Jailed," *The New York Times* (19 March 1960): 9. The story was a United Press Internation wire item.

14. *The South Bend* (Ind.) *Tribune* (28 October 1953): 1. This particular case drew special attention because the Lagrange County, Indiana, draft board halted all induction and demanded that state or federal officials take action against the Amish. No action was taken against the church, however, and Selective Service persuaded the draft board to resume its regular activity in spite of the events.

15. Information from the *Wooster* (Ohio) *Daily Record*, various articles, July 1957, file "Amish," Clippings Collection, AMC.

16. David Wagler writing to *The Budget*, quoted in Yoder (1990): 279.

17. Quoted in Yoder (1961:3).

18. The letter appeared in "The Editor's Corner," *The Budget*, 15 (April 1965: 6; however, the editor was clearly not the author.

19. For the story of the formation of these Beachy Amish relief and mission organizations, see Yoder (1987a:211-60).

20. Yoder (1987a:293-95); also described in Keim (1993).

21. Stoll (1966:1).

22. Anderson (1966:3).

23. Keim (1993).

24. The formation of the Steering Committee is described in Olshan (1993). The Steering Committee's first officers were Andrew S. Kinsinger, Lancaster County, Pa., chair; David Schwartz, Allen County, Ind., secretary; and Noah Wengerd, Adams County, Ind., treasurer. Kinsinger served as chair until 1989 when Christian Blank, Lancaster County, Pa., was elected to that position.

25. The primary sources detailing the events, meetings and farm labor program are found in Steering Committee (1966-1972).

26. One of many examples is "Caesar and God," *Time* (24 March 1958): 50. See also list of cases in Keim (1975:93-98) and Place (1993).

27. For the development of one Sunday school program, see Headings (1959). On Guengerich's views, see Stoll (1975:24-26).

28. Primary documents and newspaper articles recording the events in Pennsylvania

from 18 September 1950 until the vocational school compromise was in place (10 April 1956), appear in Lapp (1991:191-518). For narrative, see Kraybill (1989:128, 129).

29. The Hazelton, Ia., Amish school situation is best told by Erickson (1975b). Also see Schwieder and Schwieder (1975:94-127).

30. Also "The Old Order," *Newsweek* (6 December 1965): 38. (Article included a photograph).

31. The story of Rev. Lindholm's involvement in the Amish school issue and the subsequent formation of The National Committee for Amish Religious Freedom is detailed in Lindholm (1993).

32. Erickson (1975a); Keim (1975:97, 98).

33. Erikson (1975a:73).

34. Keim (1975:98, 114-23).

35. Keim (1975:98) and Ball (1975:120).

36. Supreme (1972). The text of the decision is also found in Keim (1975:149-81). For newspaper accounts of the Wisconsin case, see Lapp (1991:547-56).

37. Discussions of the case include Hostetler (1975) and Pfeffer (1975). Ball reflects on the implications of the Wisconsin case in Ball (1988) and Ball (1993).

38. Ed Klimuska, "A Harrisburg Attorney Won the Supreme Court Case for Amish," *Lancaster* (Pa.) *New Era* (26 May 1989): A-10.

39. Yoder (1987a:209, 210, 270, 271).

40. An excellent study of Amish parochial schools (history, operation and management, strengths and student performance), is Hostetler and Huntington (1992).

41. Fisher and Stahl (1986:18) and Luthy (1985:2,5).

42. First-hand information obtained by Stephen E. Scott from Old Order Amish persons in Ohio while researching historical section of Ohio (1973:14-17).

43. First-hand information obtained by Stephen E. Scott.

44. Emphasis added. Parallels in Matthew 24:13, Mark 13:22, Luke 21:19. See also Revelation 2:5.

45. Yoder (1987a:79, 80).

46. Miller and his congregation, named Zion Amish Mennonite, affiliated with the Beachy Amish Mennonite Church in 1957. In Mifflin County, Pennsylvania, John R. Renno (b.1924) was excommunicated for insisting too strongly on the assurance teaching. For his defense of the teaching, see Renno ([1976]).

47. Beiler (n.d.); and Kraybill (1989:182, 183).

48. The Old Order Amish did not shun those who left at that time because they considered the incident a church schism, and not an act of personal disobedience on the part of those who left.

49. Yoder (1987a:80).

50. Interview with Stephen E. Scott and Old Order Amish persons who wish to remain anonymous.

51. See for example, Beachy (n.d.); Burkholder (n.d.); Kline (n.d.a), (n.d.b); Miller (n.d.); and Truth (1983).

52. A current leader among the Amish Brotherhood church disctricts has written that "The early emphasis on an emotional, subjective experience has given way to the more traditional emphasis of discipleship, especially as our people learn more about church history and Anabaptist thinking." (Letter to the author, 29 June 1992).

53. Scott (1991).

54. Amish Moving (1965).

55. The Hertzler family kept Samuel, Sr.'s vision alive, however. Son Samuel, Jr. (b.1918) and his family were a part of the later Paraguayan Amish community from 1969-1975. Grandson Enos (b.1949) wrote a book about his life in Paraguay, see Hertzler (1985).

56. In 1949 eight Amish families from Michigan, Ohio, Indiana and Pennsylvania purchased 1,200 acres in Arkansas and began a settlement there. In 1966/67 this group of Arkansas Amish families moved by bus and train to near Cayo, British Honduras (now Belize). This community was the one in which the Stolls stayed. The settlement did not remain distinctly Amish for long, but blended with the conservative Mennonites living in the same area of Belize. The Arkansas group's leader was Bishop Harold Stoll. See "Amish Go to British Honduras, Fleeing Arkansas Materialism," *The New York Times* (25 December 1966): 51. A description of the group is found in Sawatzky (1971:363, 364). See also Warkentin (1987:300, 302).

Another, unrelated Amish move to Latin America, involved a move of two Amish families to San Luis Potosi, Mexico, during the 1960s. They joined a group of 400 Mennonites there and did not continue an Amish identity. See Landing (1969).

57. Stoll (1972).

58. Stoll (1972).

59. Honduras (n.d.).

60. Interview with David Luthy.

61. Fretz (n.d.). See also Mennonites (1968), (The Costa Rican group mentioned was Beachy Amish).

62. Fretz (1978). Interview with Stephen E. Scott and David Luthy. The Heritage Historical Library, Aylmer, Ontario, has a copy of a Paraguayan-produced Amish hymnal. It contains selected *Ausbund* hymns translated into Spanish.

63. Stoll (1972:198).

64. Graham (1976).

65. The story of the conflict between the Amish and the Internal Revenue Service is explained fully in Ferrara (1993).

66. "Unto Caesar," *Time* (3 November 1958): 21; Robert Metz, "The Amish and Taxes," *The New York Times* (22 May 1961): 45. The article attempts to explain the situation from the government's point of view.

67. "U.S. Sells 3 Mares for Amish Tax Debt," *The New York Times* (2 May 1961): 34.

The story was a United Press International wire item. Mark Andio of Youngstown, Ohio, bought Byler's animals; Robert Metz "The Amish and Taxes," *The New York Times* (22 May 1961): 45. Byler owed $308.96. The horses sold for $460. The auction costs were deducted at $113.15. The remaining $37.89 was refunded to Byler. See also Ferrara (1993), and Hostetler (1980:265, 266).

68. Hall (1962).

69. "Amish Are Granted Exclusion," *The New York Times* (31 July 1965): 8. The article was an Associated Press wire item. An earlier attempt was Pennsylvania's Rep. Richard S. Schweiker reported as "Bill Would Exempt the Amish," *The New York Times* (7 November 1963): 29. The story was an Associated Press wire item.

70. Ferrara (1993).

71. For complete treatment of the issues involved and the Amish response, see Olshan (1993); Zook (1993); and Huntington (1993). Also Hostetler (1980:267).

72. See Thomson (1993).

73. Beiler (1977b: unpaginated "Introduction"). Beiler believes that non-farming jobs were more common among the Amish in America until about 1830. Since the mid-twentieth century, non-farming jobs are becoming more common again, he asserts. Directory lists a variety of Old Order businesses (Amish as well as Mennonite), but is not geographically representative, as proportionately fewer midwestern firms are included. A large collection of catalogs of Amish-owned businesses are housed at the Heritage Historical Library, Aylmer, Ontario.

74. For a good description of the "putting out" (or "out work") system of early capitalism and its demise in the face of centralized manufacturing, see Clark (1990:176-91). (The book's examples are from New England.)

75. Meyers (1991): esp. Table 5, p. 315.

76. Troyer and Willoughby (1984:52-80, esp. 61).

77. Kraybill (1989:200).

78. Kraybill (1989:192-211).

79. Meyers (1991:317-21).

80. Of the many examples, see "Amish Gratitude," *Time* (29 November 1937): 37; "Education: Amish Folk Shun Their New PWA School," *Literary Digest* (4 December 1937): 32-34; "Amish Threaten School Sucession," *The New York Times* (21 July 1938): 23; and "New Amish School Strike Looms in Pennsylvania," (5 September 1938): 15.

81. A sociological study of the rise of tourism and its effects in Lancaster County, Pennsylvania, is Buck (1979).

82. Luthy (1980b:33, 34).

83. de Angeli (1944).

84. Keene (1955).

85. Burkhart (1957).

86. Luthy (1980b:34).

87. Currently, the working name of the agency is The Pennsylvania Dutch Convention and Visitor's Bureau (the organization is still incorporated under its old title). The organization acquired property and built a visitors center in 1967. (Interview with Harry L. Flick, Jr. president of the Pennsylvania Dutch Convention and Visitor's Bureau.)

88. Steinmeier (1967:30). The article mistakenly refers to the Elkhart/Lagrange Amish community as the second largest in the United States. At the time (and today) it was the third. See also Luthy (1991c).

89. Thomas (1968).

90. Luthy (n.d.).

91. On Iowa, see Schwieder and Schwieder (1975:48). On Illinois, see Smith (1983:143).

92. For the perspective of one Amishman on the rise and influence of tourism, see Fisher (1978:361-70).

93. See for example Fisher and Stahl (1986).

94. Kraybill (1989:223-27).

95. Kraybill (1989:227-34).

96. Mennonite Yearbook (1967:91, 92) and (1992:190-94).

97. Luthy (1974), (1985), and (1992). Figures on church districts could also be obtained from Raber (1930-). *Mennonite Yearbook* contains total membership figures for the Old Order Amish in North America; however, it is unclear how these numbers are arrived at, and often they seem not to have been updated regularly. Until 1967 *Mennonite Yearbook* also included a directory of ordained Amish leaders. *Mennonite Yearbook* continues to include a congregational and ministerial directory for the Beachy Amish Mennonites. Yoder (1987a): 307-400, includes a Beachy Amish congregational and historical ministerial directory as well.

98. Luthy (1992:19).

99. Luthy (1992).

100. Meyers (1991:313, 314). Neither are Old Order Amish communities static. For a look at changes in contemporary Amish communities, see Savells (1990). A comprehensive study of the Lancaster County, Pennsylvania, Old Order Amish settlement is Kraybill (1989).

101. Fisher (1978:320).

Bibliography

Archival sources, newspaper and news-magazine articles appear only in the end notes.

Abbreviations used in this bibliography:

AP   Ambassador of Peace, Amish-published periodical for their young men who performed alternative service in lieu of the military draft, 1966-1970. It was succeeded by the monthly Amish youth periodical *Young Companion,* 1971-present.

FL   Family Life, monthly magazine subscribed to by many Old Order Amish (and Old Order Mennonites), published by Pathway Publishers, Aylmer, Ont.

HT   Herald of Truth, semi-official "old" Mennonite paper, from 1864 published in Chicago, Ill., and after 1867 in Elkhart, Indiana, until 1908.

ME   The Mennonite Encyclopedia: A Comprehensive Reference Work on the Anabaptist-Mennonite Movement. Hillsboro, Kans.: Mennonite Brethren Publishing House; Newton, Kans.: Mennonite Publication Office; Scottdale, Pa.: Mennonite Publishing House. 4 vols.: 1955-59; Scottdale, Pa. and Waterloo, Ont.: Herald Press. vol. 5, 1990.

MFH   Mennonite Family History, a genealogical magazine which regularly includes articles on Amish families and communities in Europe and North America, published in Elverson, Pa.

MHB   The Mennonite Historical Bulletin, publication of the Historical Committee of the Mennonite Church, Goshen, Ind.

ML   Mennonite Life, a General Conference Mennonite Church historical journal, published by Bethel College, North Newton, Kans.

MQR   The Mennonite Quarterly Review, major journal of Anabaptist/Mennonite studies, published by The Mennonite Historical Society, Goshen, Ind.

MRJ   Mennonite Research Journal, formerly the publication of the Lancaster Mennonite Historical Society, Lancaster, Pa.

PHM   Pennsylvania Mennonite Heritage, quarterly journal of the Lancaster Mennonite Historical Society, Lancaster, Pa.

TD   The Diary, a monthly magazine preserving Old Order Amish history, published in Gordonville, Pa.

Abrams, Roy H.
1933   *Preachers Present Arms.* Philadelphia: Round Table Press, Inc.
Amish and Mennonites in Eastern Elkhart and LaGrange Counties, Indiana, 1841-1991
1992   Goshen, Ind.: The Amish Heritage Committee.

"An Amish Church Discipline of 1779"
1970   *FL* 3 (September): 21-23.
"An Amish Church Discipline of 1781"
1930   *MQR* 4 (April): 140-48.
"An Amish Congregational Discipline"
1975   *MHB* 36 (October): 4, 6, 7. The printed discipline of the Daviess County, Indiana, Old Order Amish community, dated 27 November 1871.
"Amish Life in the Great Depression, 1930-1940"
1971   *FL* 4 (July): 18-21; (August): 18-21.
The Amish Moving to Maryland
1965   Gordonville, Pa.: A. S. Kinsinger.
Ammann, Uli
1977   "Copy of a Letter Written by Uli Ammann to the Preachers and Elders of the Congregation at Markirch," *MHB* 38 (October). Ammann probably wrote the letter about 1720.
Anderson, Calvin E.
1966   "[Editorial] Introduction," *AP* 1 (February): 3, 4.
Aurand, Ammon Monroe, Jr.
1938   *Little Known Facts About the Amish and Mennonites: A Study of the Social Customs and Habits of Pennsylvania's "Plain People."* Harrisburg, Pa.: Aurand Press.
Ausbund, Das ist: Etliche schöne christliche Lieder
1991   Lancaster, Pa.: Lancaster Press. First edition was in 1564.
Bachman, Calvin George
1942   *The Old Order Amish of Lancaster County.* Norristown, Pa.: The Pennsylvania German Society.
Bachman, Peter
1934   *1784-1934, Mennoniten in Kleinpolen: Gedenkbuch . . . .* Lemberg: Verlag der Lemberger Mennonitengemeinde in Lemberg.
Bair, Ray
1952   "The Merger of the Mennonite and the Amish Mennonite Conference[s] from 1911 to 1928," *MHB* 13 (October): 2-4.
Ball, William Bentley
1975   "Building a Landmark Case: *Wisconsin v Yoder,*" in *Compulsory Education and the Amish: The Right Not to be Modern,* ed. by Albert N. Keim, Boston: Beacon Press.
1988   "An External Perspective: The Constitutional Freedom to be Anabaptist," *Brethren Life and Thought* 33 (Summer): 200-204.
1993   "First Amendment Issues," in *The Amish and the State,* ed. by Donald B. Kraybill, Baltimore: The Johns Hopkins University Press.
Beachy, Alvin J.
1954   "The Amish Settlement in Somerset County, Pennsylvania," *MQR* 28 (October):

263-92.

1955 "The Rise and Development of the Beachy Amish Mennonite Churches," *MQR* 29 (April): 118-40.

Beachy, Lester
n.d. *The Cross: Bitter or Sweet?* Baltic, Oh.: Amish Brotherhood Publications.

Beiler, Abner F.
n.d. "A Brief History of the New Order Amish Church, 1966-1976," unpublished paper, Lancaster Mennonite Historical Library, Lancaster, Pennsylvania.

Beiler, David
1888 *Das Wahre Christenthum: Eine Christliche Betrachtung nach den Lehren der Heiligen Schrift.* Lancaster, Pa.: Johann Baers and Sons. Doctrinal writings and exposition of scripture by an Old Order Amish bishop.

Beiler, Joseph F.
1969 "Two Hundred Years in America: The Stoltzfus Family," *TD* 1 (January): 6, 8.
1974a "The Amish in the Pequea Valley Before 1800," *TD* 6 (July): 162-64.
1974b "Landgrants," *TD* 6 (May): 120, 119.
1975a "Bishop Jacob Hertzler," *TD* 7 (July): 168, 165-67.
1975b "Revolutionary War Records," *TD* 7 (March): 71.
1976/1977 "Eighteenth Century Amish in Lancaster County," *MRJ* 17 (October): 37, 46; 18 (January): 1, 10; (April): 16.
1977a "Amish History in Lancaster County," *MRJ* 17 (April): 16.
1977b *Old Order Shop and Service Directory of the Old Order Society in United States and Canada.* Gordonville, Pa.: Pequea Publishers.
1977c "The Drachsel Family," *TD* 9 (March): 70.
1978 [land grant map including Christian Rupp parcel], *TD* 10 (January): 13, 32.
1982 "Ordnung," *MQR* 56 (October): 382-84.
1983 "A Review of the Founding of the Lancaster County Church Settlement," *TD* 15 (December): 17-22.

Belcher, Joseph
1859 *Robert Raikes: His Sunday Schools and His Friends, Including Historical Sketches of the Sunday School Cause in Europe and America.* Philadelphia: American Baptist Publishing Society.

Bender, Harold S.
1927 ed., "The Discipline Adopted by the Strasburg [sic] Conference of 1568," *MQR* 1 (January).
1934 ed., "Some Early American Amish Mennonite Disciplines," *MQR* 8 (April): 90-98.
1944 *The Anabaptist Vision.* Scottdale, Pa. and Kitchener, Ont.: Herald Press.
1946 ed., "An Amish Bishop's Conference Epistle of 1865," *MQR* 20 (July): 222-29.
1955a "Amish Division," S.v. in *ME*, 1: 90-92.
1955b "Amish Mennonites," S.v. in *ME*, 1:

93-97.
1955c "Ammann, Jakob," S.v. in *ME*, 1: 98, 99.

Blanke, Fritz
1961 Joseph Nordenhauge, trans. *Brothers in Christ.* Scottdale, Pa.: Herald Press.

Bontreger, Eli J.
1946 "Further Notes on Ordinations," *MHB* 7 (March): 4.
1956 "My Life Story," mimeographed autobiography housed at the Archives of the Mennonite Church, Goshen, Ind.

Borntreger, John E. (Hansi)
1988 Elizabeth Gingerich, trans., *A History of the First Settlers of the Amish Mennonites and the Establishment of Their First Congregation in the State of Indiana . . . .* Topeka, Ind.: Dan Hochstetler. First issued in German by Bontreger in 1907.

Braght, Thieleman J. van.
1990 *The Bloody Theater; or Martyrs Mirror of the Defenseless Christians.* Joseph F. Sohm, trans. Scottdale, Pa. and Waterloo, Ont.: Herald Press.

"Briefsammlung"
1987 *Informations-Blaetter/Feuilles d'Information: Schweizerischer Verein fuer Taeufergeschichte/Societé Suisse d'Histoire Mennonite* 10: 26-61. A German edition of the letters detailing the Amish schism of 1693-97.

Brunk, Ivan W.
1982 "Mennonites in the Carolinas," *PMH* 5 (January): 14-21.

Buck, Roy C.
1979 "Bloodless Theatre: Images of the Old Order Amish in Tourism and Literature," *PMH* 2 (July): 2-11.

Burkhart, Charles
1957 "The Amish Theme in Recent American Theatricals," *MQR* 31 (April): 140-42.

Burkholder, David G.
n.d. *The Inroads of Pietism.* Baltic, Oh.: Amish Brotherhood Publications.

Catechism, or Plain Instruction From the Sacred Scriptures
1905 Elkhart, Ind.: Mennonite Publishing Company. An English translation of the well-loved 1797 "Waldeck Catechism" of the Waldeck, Hesse, Amish. The Waldeck Catechism was itself originally the 1783 Elbing, Prussia, Mennonite catechism.

Clark, Allen B.
1988 *This Is Good Country: A History of the Amish of Delaware, 1915-1988.* Gordonville, Pa.: Gordonville Book Shop.

Clark, Christopher
1990 *The Roots of Rural Capitalism: Western Massachusetts, 1780-1860.* Ithaca, N.Y.: Cornell University Press.

Clasen, Claus-Peter
1972 *Anabaptism: A Social History, 1525-1618, [in] Switzerland, Austria, Moravia, South and Central Germany.* Ithaca, N.Y.: Cornell University Press.

Clauden, David N. and Kathryn Egly Claudon
1947 *Life of Bishop Henry Egly, 1824-1890.* n.p.

Correll, Ernst
1928 "The Value of Family History for Mennonite History, Illustrated from Nafziger Family History Material of the Eighteenth Century," *MQR* 2 (January): 66-79; (July): 198-204.
1955 "Alsace," S.v. in *ME*, 1: 66-75.
1956 "French Revolution," S.v. in *ME*, 2: 392.

A Craftsman's Handbook: Henry Lapp
1991 Intercourse, Pa.: Good Books.

Cronk, Sandra
1978/1981 "Gelassenheit: The Rites of the Redemptive Process in Old Order Amish and Old Order Mennonite Communities," *MQR* 55 (January): 5-44.

de Angeli, Marguerite
1944 *Yonie Wondernose.* New York: Doubleday.

Deeben, John P.
1992 "Amish Agriculture and Popular Opinion in the Nineteenth and Twentieth Centuries," *PMH* 15 (April): 21-29.

Degler, Carl N.
1977 *The Age of the Economic Revolution: 1876-1900,* second ed. Glanview, Ill.: Scott, Foresman and Company.

A Devoted Christian's Prayer Book
1984 Aylmer, Ont. and Lagrange Ind.: Pathway Publishing Corp. An English language translation of *Die Ernsthafte Christenpflicht.*

Dietrich Philip (Dirk Philipsz.)
1978 *Enchiridion, or Hand-book of the Christian Doctrine and Religion.* Aylmer, Ont. and Lagrange, Ind.: Pathway Publishing Corp. First appeared in Dutch in 1564, translated into English by Abram B. Kolb, 1910. An Anabaptist leader's writings kept in print by the Old Order Amish.

Durnbaugh, Donald F.
1978 "Religion and Revolution: Options in 1776," *PMH* 1 (July): 2-9.
1983 ed. *The Brethren Encyclopedia.* Oak Brook, Ill. and Philadelphia, Pa.: The Brethren Encyclopedia, Inc.
1986 *Church of the Brethren: Yesterday and Today.* Elgin, Ill.: Brethren Press.

Dyck, Cornelius J.
1981 ed., *An Introduction to Mennonite History: A Popular History of the Anabaptists and the Mennonites,* second edition. Scottdale, Pa. and Waterloo, Ont.: Herald Press.
1983 "European Mennonite Motivation for Emigration, 1650-1750," *PMH* 5 (October): 2-9.

Early Amish Land Grants in Berks County, Pennsylvania.
1991 Gordonville, Pa.: Pequea Bruderschaft Library.

Ellis, Franklin and Samuel Evans
1883 *History of Lancaster County, Pennsylvania, with Biographical Sketches of Many of its Pioneers and Prominent Men.* Philadelphia: Everts and Peck.

Epp, Frank H.
1974 *Mennonites in Canada, 1786-1920: The History of a Separate People.* Toronto: Macmillan Company of Canada.
1982 *Mennonites in Canada, 1920-1940: A People's Struggle for Survival.* Scottdale, Pa.: Herald Press.

Erb, Paul
1974 *South Central Frontiers: A History of the South Central Mennonite Conference.* Scottdale, Pa. and Kitchener, Ont.: Herald Press.

Erickson, Donald A.
1975a "The Persecution of LeRoy Garber," in *Compulsory Education and the Amish: The Right Not to be Modern,* ed. by Albert N. Keim, Boston: Beacon Press.
1975b "Showdown at an Amish Schoolhouse," in *Compulsory Education and the Amish: The Right Not to be Modern,* ed. by Albert N. Keim, Boston: Beacon Press.

Esh, Levi A.
1977 "The Amish Parochial School Movement," *MQR* 51 (January): 69-75.

Estes, Steven R.
1982 *A Goodly Heritage: A History of the North Danvers Mennonite Church.* Danvers, Ill.: North Danvers Mennonite Church.
1984 *Living Stones: A History of the Metamora Mennonite Church.* Metamora, Ill.: Metamora Mennonite Church.
1990 *From Mountains to Meadows: A Century of Witness of the Meadows Mennonite Church.* Chenoa, Ill.: Historical Committee of Meadows Mennonite Church.

Ferrara, Peter J.
1993 "Social Security and Taxes," in *The Amish and the State,* ed. by Donald B. Kraybill, Baltimore: The Johns Hopkins University Press.

Ferster, Herbert V.
1983 "The Development of the Amish School System," *PMH* 6 (April): 7-14.

Fisher, Amos L.
1984 "History of the First Amish Communities in America," *TD* 16 (September): 35-39.

Fisher, Gideon
1978 *Farm Life and Its Changes.* Gordonville, Pa.: Pequea Publishers.

Fisher, Jonathan B.
1911 *A Trip to Europe and Facts Gleaned on the Way.* New Holland, Pa.: Jonathan B. Fisher.
1937 *Around the World by Water and Facts Gleaned on the Way.* [Bareville, Pa.]: Jonathan B. Fisher.

Fisher, Sara E. and Rachel K. Stahl
1986 *The Amish School.* Intercourse, Pa.: Good Books.

Franck, Ira Stoner
1952 *A Jaunt into the Dutch Country: Part 1, Accent on the Amish.* n.p.: Ira Stoner Franck.
Fretz, Clarence Y.
1957 "Luxembourg," S.v. in *ME*, 3: 422, 423.
Fretz, J. Winfield
1978 "Witnessing a Community's Death." unpublished paper, Heritage Historical Library, Aylmer, Ontario.
n.d. "The Amish in Paraguay." unpublished paper, Heritage Historical Library, Aylmer, Ontario.
Friedmann, Robert.
1949 *Mennonite Piety Through the Centuries: Its Genius and Its Literature.* Goshen, Ind.: The Mennonite Historical Society.
1973 *The Theology of Anabaptism: An Interpretation.* Scottdale, Pa. and Kitchener, Ont.: Herald Press.
Frost, J. William
1990 *A Perfect Freedom: Religious Liberty in Pennsylvania.* Cambridge: Cambridge University Press.
Gascho, Milton
1937 "The Amish Division of 1693-1697 in Switzerland and Alsace," *MQR* 11 (October): 235-66.
Geiser, Samuel
1959 "Reist, Hans," S.v. in *ME*, 4: 281, 282.
George, Timothy
1988 *Theology of the Reformers.* Nashville, Tenn.: Broadman Press.
Gerlach, Horst
1990 "Amish Congregations in Germany and Adjacent Territories in the Eighteenth and Nineteenth Centuries," *PMH* 13 (April): 2-8.
"The German School Association of the Iowa Old Order Amish Mennonites"
1955 *MHB* 16 (July): 7, 8.
Getz, Jane C.
1946 "Economic Organization and Practices of the Old Order Amish of Lancaster County, Pennsylvania," *MQR* 20 (January): 53-60; (April): 98-127.
Gibbons, Phebe Earle.
1882 *"Pennsylvania Dutch," and Other Essays.* Philadelphia: J. P. Lippincott.
Gingerich, Hugh F. and Rachel W. Kreider
1986 *Amish and Amish Mennonite Genealogies.* Gordonville, Pa.: Pequea Publishers.
Gingerich, James Nelson
1986 "Ordinance or Ordering: *Ordnung* and Amish Ministers Meetings, 1862-1878," *MQR* 60 (April): 180-99.
Gingerich, Josef
1982 Elizabeth Horsch Bender, trans. "The Amish Mennonites in Bavaria," *MQR* 56 (April): 179-88.
Gingerich, Melvin
1939 *The Mennonites in Iowa.* Iowa City: State Historical Society of Iowa.

1942 "Amish Ministers' Meeting, 1874," *MHB* 4 (December): 1-4.
1949 *Service For Peace.* Akron, Pa.: Mennonite Central Committee.
1955a "Amish Aid Plan," S.v. in *ME*, 1: 89.
1955b intro. *Joseph Goldsmith (1796-1876) and His Descendants.* Kalona, Ia.: John W. Gingerich.
1959 "Sleeping Preacher Churches," S.v. in *ME*, 4: 543-44.
1961a "Mennonite Indentured Servants," *ML* 16 (July): 107-109.
1961b "A Note on the Diener-Versammlung of 1866," *MHB* 22 (October): 2.
1965 "A List of Amish Ministers in 1849," *MHB* 26 (July): 7.
1970 *Mennonite Attire Through Four Centuries.* Breinigsville, Pa.: The Pennsylvania German Society.
1971 "Sleeping Preachers," *MHB* 32 (January): 4-6.
Gingerich, Orland
1972 *The Amish of Canada.* Waterloo, Ont.: Conrad Press.
Good, Merle
1985 *Who Are the Amish?* Intercourse, Pa.: Good Books.
Good, Merle and Phyllis Pellman Good
1979 *Twenty Most Asked Questions About the Amish and Mennonites.* Intercourse, Pa.: Good Books.
Graber, O. A.
1984 "Gleanings from Yesterday," *Die Botschaft* (8 February): 14.
Graham, Otis, Jr.
1976 *Toward a Planned Society: From Roosevelt to Nixon.* New York: Oxford University Press.
Granick, Eve Wheatcroft
1989 *The Amish Quilt.* Intercourse, Pa.: Good Books.
Gratz, Delbert L.
1951 The Home of Jacob Amman [sic] in Switzerland," *MQR* 25 (April): 137-39.
1952 "Bernese Anabaptism in the Eighteenth Century, I," *MQR* 26 (January): 5-21.
1953 *Bernese Anabaptists and Their American Descendants.* Goshen, Ind.: The Mennonite Historical Society.
Grieser, Orland R. and Ervin Beck, Jr.
1960 *Out of the Wilderness: History of the Central Mennonite Church, 1835-1960.* Grand Rapids: The Dean Hicks Co.
Gross, Leonard
1978 "S. D. Guengerich's Five Cent Trip Around the World," *MHB* 39 (January): 1, 2.
1991 "The First Mennonite Merger: The Concept of Cologne," in *Mennonite Yearbook, 1991-1992.* Scottdale, Pa.: Mennonite Publishiong House.
Guengerich, Daniel P.
n.d. *An Account of the Voyage from Germany to America.* Kalona, Ia.: Jacob F. Swartzendruber.
Guth, Hermann
1986 *The Amish-Mennonites of Waldeck*

and Wittgenstein. Elverson, Pa.:
Mennonite Family History.
1987   "Preacher Johannes Nafzinger of
Essingen, Germany," *MFH* 6 (October):
129-31.
Haas, J. Craig.
1992   *Readings from Mennonite Writings,
New and Old.* Intercourse, Pa.: Good
Books.
Hall, Clarence W.
1962   "The Revolt of the Plain People,"
Reader's Digest (November): 74-78.
Harder, Leland, ed.
1985   *The Sources of Swiss Anabaptism:
The Grebel Letters and Related Documents.*
Scottdale, Pa. and Kitchener, Ont.: Herald
Press.
Hartzler, H. Harold
1991   *Amishman Travels Around the World:
The Life of Jonathan B. Fisher.* Elverson,
Pa.: Mennonite Family History.
Hartzler, Jonas S.
1921   *Mennonites in the World War, or
Nonresistance Under Test.* Scottdale, Pa.:
Mennonite Publishing House.
Hartzler, Jonas S. and Daniel Kauffman
1905   *Mennonite Church History.* Scottdale,
Pa.: Mennonite book and Tract Society.
Hartzler, Jonathan K.
1902   "Fifty Years in the Amish Mennonite
Churches of Pennsylvania," *HT* (June):
163, 164.
Haury, David A.
1981   *Prairie People: A History of the
Western District Conference.* Newton,
Kans.: Faith and Life Press.
Headings, Valentine J., Jr.
1959   "A History of the Old Order Amish
Mennonite Sunday School at East Center
Congregation, Hutchinson, Kansas," *MHB*
20 (April): 7.
Helmuth, Orva
1961   "History of the Arthur Amish
Mennonite Church," *MHB* 22 (October): 3, 4.
Hershberger, Guy F.
1951   *The Mennonite Church in the Second
World War.* Scottdale, Pa.: Herald Press.
Hertzler, Enos
1985   *Time Out for Paraguay.* Gordonville,
Pa.: Gordonville Print Shop.
Hess, Anna M. and Linda Lucille Fry
1983   "Leola, PA, Conestoga Church of the
Brethren," S.v. in *The Brethren
Encyclopedia,* ed. by Donald F.
Durnbaugh, 2: 737.
Hiller, Harry H.
1968/1969   "The Sleeping Preachers: An
Historical Study of the Role of Charisma in
Amish Society," *Pennsylvania Folklife* 18
(Winter): 19-31.
***Historical Statistics of the United
States: Colonial Times to 1970***
1975   Washington, D.C.: United States
Department of Commerce, Bureau of the
Census.
Homan, Gerlof D.
1990   "The Burning of the Mennonite

Church, Fairview, Michigan, in 1918,"
MQR 64 (April): 99-112.
**"Honduras: Spanish School by Amish
for Local Natives"**
n.d.   unpublished paper, Heritage Historical
Library, Aylmer, Ontario.
Horst, Irvin B.
1982   "Dordrecht Confession of Faith: 350
Years," *PMH* 5 (July): 2-8.
1988   trans. and ed. *Mennonite Confession
of Faith, ...* Lancaster, Pa.: Lancaster
Mennonite Historical Society.
Hostetler, Harvey
1912   ed., *The Descendants of Jacob
Hochstetler, the Immigrant of 1736.* Elgin,
Ill.: Brethren Publishing House.
Hostetler, Beulah Stauffer
1992   "The Formation of the Old Orders,"
MQR 66 (January): 5-25.
Hostetler, John A.
1948   "The Life and Times of Samuel Yoder
(1824-1884)," *MQR* 22 (October): 226-41.
1951   *Annotated Bibliography on the Old
Order Amish.* Scottdale, Pa.: Mennonite
Publishing House.
1955   "Old World Extinction and New World
Survival of the Amish: A Study of Group
Maintenance and Dissolution," *Rural
Sociology* 20 (September-December):
212-19.
1964   "Memoirs of Shem Zook," *MQR* 38
(July): 280-99.
1974   *Hutterite Society.* Baltimore: The
Johns Hopkins University Press.
1975   "The Cultural Context of the
Wisconsin Case," in *Compulsory Education
and the Amish: The Right Not to be
Modern,* ed. by Albert N. Keim. Boston:
Beacon Press.
1977   "Old Order Amish Survival," *MQR* 51
(October): 352-61.
1980   *Amish Society,* third ed. Baltimore:
The Johns Hopkins University Press. A
fourth edition will be released in 1993.
1983   "Amish," S.v. in *The Brethren
Encyclopedia,* ed. by Donald F.
Durnbaugh, I: 25, 26.
1989   ed., *Amish Roots: A Treasury of
History, Wisdom, and Lore.* Baltimore: The
Johns Hopkins University Press.
**Hostetler, John A. and Gertrude Enders
Huntington**
1992   *Amish Children: Education in the
Family, School, and Community,* second ed.
New York: Harcourt, Brace, Jovanovich
College Publishers.
Hudson, Winthrop S.
1965   *Religion in America.* New York:
Charles Scribner's Sons.
Huntington, Abbie Gertrude Enders
1956   "Dove at the Window: A Study of an
Old Order Amish Community in Ohio."
Dissertation presented to the faculty of the
Graduate School of Yale University.
Janzen, William and Frances Greaser
1990   *Sam Martin Went to Prison: The Story
of Conscientious Objection and Canadian*

Military Service. Winnipeg, Man. and Hillsboro, Kans.: Kindred Press.

Jones, Stanley L.
1964 *The Presidential Election of 1896.* Madison: University of Wisconsin Press.

Juhnke, James C.
1979 *A People of Mission: A History of General Conference Mennonite Overseas Missions*. Newton, Kans.: Faith and Life Press.
1989 *Vision, Doctrine, War: Mennonite Identity and Organization in America, 1890-1930.* The Mennonite Experience in America, volume three. Scottdale, Pa. and Waterloo, Ont.: Herald Press.

Kaiser, Grace H.
1986 *Dr. Frau: A Woman Doctor Among the Amish*. Intercourse, Pa.: Good Books.

Kauffman, J. Howard and Leland Harder
1975 *Anabaptists Four Centuries Later: A Profile of Five Mennonite and Brethren in Christ Denominations.* Scottdale, Pa. and Kitchener, Ont.: Herald Press.

Kauffman, S. Duane
1979 "Miscellaneous Amish Mennonite Documents," 2 *PMH* (July): 12-16.
1991 *Mifflin County Amish and Mennonite Story, 1791-1991.* Belleville, Pa.: Mifflin County Mennonite Historical Society.

Kaufman, Stanley A. with Leroy Beachy
1991 *Amish in Eastern Ohio.* Walnut Creek, Oh.: German Cultural Museum.

Keene, Carolyn
1955 *The Witch Tree Symbol.* New York: Simon and Schuster, Inc.

Keim, Albert N.
1975 ed., *Compulsory Education and the Amish: The Right Not to be Modern.* Boston: Beacon Press.
1990 *The CPS Story: An Illustrated History of Civilian Public Service.* Intercourse, Pa.: Good Books.
1993 "Military Service and Conscription," in *The Amish and the State*, ed. by Donald B. Kraybill, Baltimore: The Johns Hopkins University Press.

Keim, Albert N. and Grant M. Stoltzfus
1988 *The Politics of Conscience: The Historic Peace Churches and America at War, 1917-1955.* Scottdale, Pa. and Kitchener, Ont.: Herald Press.

Klaassen, Walter
1981a *Anabaptism: Neither Catholic Nor Protestant*, revised ed. Waterloo, Ont.: Conrad Press.
1981b ed., *Anabaptism in Outline: Selected Primary Sources.* Scottdale, Pa. and Kitchener, Ont.: Herald Press.

Kline, David
1986 "No-Till Farming and Its Threat to the Amish Community," *Festival Quarterly* 13 (Fall): 7-10.
1990 *Great Possessions.* San Francisco: North Point Press. Essays by an Ohio Amish farmer.

Kline, Edward A.
n.d.a *A Sure Path for Mankind.* Baltic, Oh.: Amish Brotherhood Publications.
n.d.b *A Theology of the Will of Man and Some Practical Applications for the Christian Life.* Baltic, Oh.: Amish Brotherhood Publications.

Klippenstein, Lawrence
1979 ed., *That There Be Peace: Mennonites in Canada and World War II.* Winnipeg, Man.: Conscientious Objectors Reunion Committee.

Klopfenstein, Joseph
1984 Elizabeth Horsch Bender, trans. "An Amish Sermon," *MQR* 58 (July): 296-317.

Klopfenstein, Perry A.
1984 *Marching to Zion: A History of the Apostolic Christian Church of America, 1847-1982.* Fort Scott, Kans.: Sekan Printing Co.

Krabill, Russell
1991 "The Coming of the Amish Mennonites to Elkhart County, Indiana," *MHB* 52 (January): 1-5.

Kraybill, Donald B.
1987 "At the Crossroads of Modernity: Amish, Mennonites, and Brethren in Lancaster County in 1880." *PMH* 10 (January): 2-20.
1989 *The Riddle of Amish Culture.* Baltimore: The Johns Hopkins University Press.
1990 *The Puzzles of Amish Life.* Intercourse, Pa.: Good Books.
1993 ed. *The Amish and the State.* Baltimore: The Johns Hopkins University Press.

Kraybill, Donald B. and Donald R. Fitzkee
1987 "Amish, Mennonites, and Brethren in the Modern Era," *PMH* 10 (April): 2-11.

Kriebel, H. W.
1910 *Seeing Lancaster County from a Trolley Window.* Lititz, Pa.: Express Printing Company.

Krehbiel, Christian
1961 *Prairie Pioneer: The Christian Krehbiel Story.* Newton, Kans.: Faith and Life Press.

Lageer, Eileen.
1979 *Merging Streams: Story of the Missionary Church.* Elkhart, Ind.: Bethel Publishing Co.

Landing, James E.
1969 "The Old Order Amish in Mexico," *MHB* 30 (October): 6, 8.

Landis, Ira D.
1955 "Amish Aid Society," S.v. in *ME*, 1: 89, 90.

Lapp, Christ S.
1991 *Pennsylvania School History, 1690-1990.* Gordonville, Pa.: Christ S. Lapp.

Lapp, Fern E.
1963 *History of Weavertown Church.* n.p.: Anna Mary Yoder.

Lehman, James O.
1969 *Sonnenberg—A Haven and a Heritage: A Sesquicentennial History of the Swiss Mennonite Community of Southeastern*

Wayne County, Ohio. Kidron, Oh.: Kidron Community Council, Inc.

1978 *Creative Congregationalism: A History of the Oak Grove Mennonite Church in Wayne County, Ohio.* Smithville, Oh.: Oak Grove Mennonite Church.

1990 *Uncommon Threads: A Centennial History of Bethel Mennonite Church.* West Liberty, Oh.: Bethel Mennonite Church.

Leith, John H.

1982 ed., *Creeds of the Churches: A Reader in Christian Doctrine from the Bible to the Present,* third ed. Louisville, Ky.: John Knox Press.

Lind, Hope Kauffman

1990 *Apart and Together: Mennonites in Oregon and Neighboring States, 1876-1976.* Scottdale, Pa. and Waterloo, Ont.: Herald Press.

Lindholm, William C.

1993 "The National Committee for Amish Religious Freedom," in *The Amish and the State,* ed. by Donald B. Kraybill, Baltimore: The Johns Hopkins University Press.

Loewen, Howard John

1985 *One Lord, One Church, One Hope, and One God: Mennonite Confessions of Faith in North America, An Introduction.* Elkhart, Ind.: Institute of Mennonite Studies.

Loomis, Charles P.

1979 "A Farm Hand's Diary," *MQR* 53 (July): 235-56.

Lord, Walter

1960 *The Good Years: From 1900 to the First World War.* New York: Harper and Row.

Lugibihl, Walter H.

1950 *Missionary Church Association.* Berne, Ind.: Economy Printing Concern.

Luthy, David

1971 "The Amish Division of 1693," *FL* 4 (October): 18-20.

1972a "An Amishman's City," *FL* 5 (February): 23-25.

1972b "The Arrest of an Amish Bishop—1918," *FL* 5 (March): 23-27.

1972/1973 "New Names Among the Amish," *FL* 5 (August/September): 31-35; (October): 20-23; (November): 21-23; 6 (February): 13-15; (June): 13-15.

1973 "The Amish in Europe," *FL* 6 (March): 10-14; (April): 16-20.

1974 "Old Order Amish Settlements in 1974," *FL* 7 (December): 13-16

1975 "A Survey of Amish Ordination Customs," *FL* 8 (March): 13-17.

1978a "Concerning the Name Amish," *MHB* 39 (April): 5.

1978b "Forced to Sell Their Farms," *FL* 11 (January): 19, 20.

1978c "A History of *The Budget*," *FL* 11 (June): 19-22; (July): 15-18.

1979 "Songbooks Used in Beachy Amish Churches," *FL* 12 (March): 20, 21.

1980a "Old Records," *FL* 13 (December): 23-25.

1980b "The Origin of Amish Tourism in Lancaster County, Pennsylvania," *FL* 13 (November): 31-34.

1980c "'White' Jonas Stutzman," *FL* 13 (February): 19-21.

1981a "Amish Meetinghouses," *FL* 14 (August/September): 17-22.

1981b "A History of *Die Ernsthafte Christenpflicht*," *FL* 14 (February): 19-23.

1981c "Replacing the *Ausbund*," *FL* 14 (November): 21-23.

1982 "An Amish View of the Panic of 1893 and the Election of 1896," *FL* 15 (May): 23-26.

1984a "A History of Raber's Bookstore," *MQR* 58 (April): 168-78.

1984b "An Important Pennsylvania Broadside of 1812," *PMH* 7 (July): 1-4.

1984c "Significant Books for Amish and Mennonites: A Brief Summary," *PMH* 7 (January): 6

1984/1985 "Lost Names Among the Amish," *FL* 17 (April): 21-25; (May): 21-25; (June): 21-25; (August/September): 23-27; (October): 22-27; (November): 21-25; 18 (January): 17-21.

1985 *Amish Settlements Across America.* Aylmer, Ont.: Pathway Publishers.

1986 *The Amish in America: Settlements That Failed, 1840-1960.* (Aylmer, Ont. and Lagrange, Ind.: Pathway Publishers). Includes descriptions of settlements which dissolved as well as those which failed to remain Old Order Amish. Thoroughly researched and full of biographical, historical and annecdotal material.

1988a "Amish Beginnings: Three Centuries of Migration," *MFH* 7 (July): 110-16.

1988b "Henry Lapp: Amish Folk Artist and Craftsman," *PMH* 11 (October): 2-6.

1988c "Two Waves of Amish Migration to America," *FL* 21 (March): 20-24.

1989a "The Graber Family Comes to America," *FL* 22 (April): 21-24.

1989b "Two Amish Writers: The Zook Brothers, David and Shem," *FL* 22 (November): 19-22; (December): 19-21.

1991a "Amish Folk Artist: Barbara Ebersol (1846-1922)," *PMH* 14 (April): 2-7.

1991b "Martin Bornträger and His Descendants," *FL* 24 (March): 19-21.

1991c "The Origin and Growth of Amish Tourism in Northern Indiana," *FL* 24 (October): 21-23.

1992 "Amish Settlements Across America: 1991," *FL* 25 (April): 19-24.

n.d. "The Origin and Growth of Tourism in the Three Largest Amish Settlements in Pennsylvania, Ohio, and Indiana." unpublished paper, Heritage Historical Library, Aylmer, Ontario.

McCauley, Daniel and Kathryn McCauley

1988 *Decorative Arts of the Amish of Lancaster County.* Intercourse, Pa.: Good Books.

MacMaster, Richard K.

1979   et al., *Conscience in Crisis: Mennonites and Other Peace Churches in America, 1739-1789, Interpretation and Documents.* Scottdale, Pa. and Kitchener, Ont.: Herald Press.
1985   *Land, Piety, Peoplehood: The Establishment of Mennonite Communities in America, 1683-1790.* The Mennonite Experience in America, volume one. Scottdale, Pa. and Kitchener, Ont.: Herald Press.
Martin, Helen Reimensnyder
1904   *Tillie, a Mennonite Maid: A Story of the Pennsylvania Dutch.* New York: The Century Company.
1905   *Sabina: A Story of the Amish.* New York: The Century Publishing Company.
Mast, C. Z.
1952   "Imprisonment of Amish in Revolutionary War," *MHB* 13 (January): 6, 7.
Mast, C. Z. and Robert E. Simpson
1942   *Annals of the Conestoga Valley in Lancaster, Berks, and Chester Counties, Pennsylvania . . . .* Elverson, Pa. and Churchtown, Pa.: C. Z. Mast and Robert E. Simpson.
Mast, J. Lamar and Lois Ann Mast
1982   *As Long as Wood Grows and Water Flows: A History of the Conestoga Mennonite Church.* Morgantown, Pa.: Conestoga Mennonite Historical Committee.
Mast, John B.
1950a ed., *Facts Concerning the Beachy A. M. Division of 1927.* Myersdale, Pa.: Menno J. Yoder.
1950b trans. and ed., *The Letters of the Amish Division of 1693-1711.* Oregon City, Oreg.: Christian J. Schlabach.
Material Accompanying the Ausbund
1987   Aylmer, Ont. and Langrange, Ind.: Pathway Publishers.
Menno Simons
1956   John Christian Wenger, ed. *The Complete Writings of Menno Simons, c.1496-1561.* Scottdale, Pa. and Kitchener, Ont.: Herald Press.
Mennonite Yearbook
1905- currently published by Scottdale, Pa.: Mennonite Publishing House.
"Mennonites on the Move"
1968   *MRJ* 9 (October): 44.
Meyers, Thomas J.
1990   "Amish," S.v. in *ME*, 5: 20-22.
1991   "Population Growth and Its Consequences in the Elkhart-Lagrange Old Order Amish Settlement," *MQR* 65 (July): 308-21.
1993   "Education and Schooling," in *The Amish and the State* ed. by Donald B. Kraybill, Baltimore: The Johns Hopkins University Press.
Miller, Harvey J.
1959   "Proceedings of Amish Ministers Conferences," 1826-1831," *MQR* 33 (April): 132-42.
Miller, Ivan J.

1985   *History of the Conservative Mennonite Conference, 1910-1985.* Grantsville, Md.: Ivan J. and Della Miller.
Miller, J. Virgil
1976   "Amish Mennonites in Northern Alsace and the Palatinate in the Eighteenth Century and Their Connection with Immigrants to Pennsylvania," *MQR* 50 (October): 272-80.
Miller, John S.
1971   "A Statistical Survey of the Amish Settlers in Clinton Township, Elkhart County, Indiana, 1841-1850." Unpublished manuscript at the Mennonite Historical Library, Goshen, Indiana.
Miller, L. A.
1955a "Amish Mennonite Publishing Association," S.v. in *ME*, 1: 92.
Miller, Levi D.
1970   "Another Sleeping Preacher," *MHB* 31 (April): 5, 6.
Miller, Levi P.
n.d.   *Teaching Emphases That Hinder Discipleship.* Baltic, Oh.: Amish Brotherhood Publications.
Miller, Thomas
1955b "Buchanan County," S.v. in *ME*, 1: 460.
Mook, Mayrice A.
1955   "An Early Amish Colony in Chester County, Pennsylvania," *MHB* 16 (July): 1-3.
Murray, John F.
1981   "Blank/Plank Ancestry of the Amish Mennonite Tradition," *PMH* 4 (July): 13-19.
Neff, Christian
1957   "Ibersheim Resolutions," S.v. in *ME*, 3: 2.
1959   "Offenthal Conference," S.v. in *ME*, 4: 21, 22.
Neff, Christian and Nanne van der Zijpp
1957   "Napoleon I," S.v. in *ME*, 3: 812.
Nussbaum, Stan
1976/1977   *You Must Be Born Again: A History of the Evangelical Mennonite Church.* Fort Wayne, Ind.: Evangelical Mennonite Church.
Ohio Amish Directory: Holmes County and Vicinity
1973   Ervin Gingerich, comp. Baltimore: Division of Medical Genetics, The Johns Hopkins University School of Medicine.
Olshan, Marc A.
1993   "The National Amish Steering Committee," in *The Amish and the State*, ed., by Donald B. Kraybill, Baltimore: The Johns Hopkins University Press.
Oyer, John S.
1984   "The Strasbourg Conferences of the Anabaptists," *MQR* 58 (July): 218-29.
Oyer, John S. and Robert S. Kreider
1990   *Mirror of the Martyrs: Stories of Courage, Inspiringly Retold, of Sixteenth Century Anabaptists Who Gave Their Lives for Their Faith.* Intercourse, Pa.: Good Books.
Oyer, Mary
1944   "Music in the Amish Church," *MHB* 5

(March): 3, 4.

Page, Doris L. and Marie Johns
1983   *The Amish Mennonite Settlement in Butler County, Ohio.* [Trenton, Oh.: Trenton Historical Society].

Pannabecker, Samuel Floyd
1968   *Faith in Ferment: A History of the Central District Conference.* Newton, Kans.: Faith and Life Press.
1975   *Open Doors: The History of the General Conference Mennonite Church.* Newton, Kans.: Faith and Life Press.
Peace, War, and Military Service: A Statement of the Position of the Mennonite Church
1937   Resolutions adopted by the Mennonite General Conference at Turner, Oregon. August.

Peachey, Titus and Linda Gehman Peachey
1991   *Seeking Peace.* Intercourse, Pa.: Good Books.

Pellman, Rachel T. and Kenneth Pellman
1984   *The World of Amish Quilts.* Intercourse, Pa.: Good Books.
1990   *A Treasury of Amish Quilts.* Intercourse, Pa.: Good Books.

Pfeffer, Leo
1975   "The Many Meanings of the Yoder Case," in *Compulsory Education and the Amish: The Right Not to be Modern,* ed. by Albert N. Keim. Boston: Beacon Press.

Place, Elizabeth
1993   "Annotated Legal Cases," in *The Amish and the State,*" ed. by Donald B. Kraybill, Baltimore: The Johns Hopkins University Press.

Raber, Ben J.
1930- comp., *Der Neue Amerikanische Kalender.* Baltic, Oh.: Raber's Bookstore. Since 1970 the Almanac has also been issued under the title *The New American Almanac.*
"Real Life Pictures of the Amish of Southeastern Pennsylvania"
1949   n.p.: H. C. Thorbahn.

Renno, John R.
[1976] A Brief History of the Amish Church in Belleville. Danville, Pa.: John R. Renno.

Ressler, Martin E.
1986   "American Continuance of European Origins in Mennonite, Hutterite, and Amish Music Functions," *PMH* 9 (January): 6-10.
The Revelation of Barbara Stutzman, Deceased, to All Mankind
n.d.   n.p. copy at the Mennonite Historical Library, Goshen, Indiana.

Roth, Lorraine and Marlene J. Grant
1986   "Canadian Amish Mennonite Roots in Pennsylvania," *PMH* 9 (April): 13-17.

Ruth, John L.
1975   Conrad Grebel, Son of Zurich. Scottdale, Pa. and Kitchener, Ont.: Herald Press.
1976   *'Twas Seeding Time: A Mennonite*

View of the American Revolution. Scottdale, Pa. and Kitchener, Ont.: Herald Press.
1985   *A Quiet and Peaceable Life,* revised ed. Intercourse, Pa.: Good Books.

S., E.
1980   "The Doctrine Most Churches Shun," *FL* 13 (May): 9-12. An explanation of the doctrine of social avoidance.

Savells, Jerry
1990   "Social Change Among the Amish in Eight Communities," *PMH* 13 (July): 12-16. The communities were located in Georgia, Indiana, Iowa, Ohio, Pennsylvania and Tennessee.

Sawatzky, Harry Leonard
1971   *They Sought a Country: Mennonite Colonization in Mexico with an Appendix on Mennonite Colonization in British Honduras.* Berkeley: University of California Press.

Schabalie, John Philip [Schabaelje, Jan Philipsz.]
1975   *The Wandering Soul, or Conversations of the Wandering Soul with Adam, Noah, and Simon Cleophas.* Baltic, Oh.: Raber's Book Store. First edition was 1635 in Dutch.

Schelbert, Leo
1985   "Pietism Rejected: A Reinterpretation of Amish Origins," in Frank Trommler and Joseph G. McVeigh, eds. *America and the Germans: An Assessment of a Three-Hundred-Year History, vol. 1: Immigration, Language, Ethnicity.* Philadelphia: University of Pennsylvania Press.

Scherer, Karl
1974   "The Fatherland of the Pennsylvania Dutch," *MRJ* 15 (July): 25-29.

Schlabach, Ervin
1978   *A Century and a Half with the Mennonites at Walnut Creek.* Walnut Creek, Oh.: Walnut Creek Mennonite Church.
1981   *The Amish and Mennonites at Walnut Creek.* Millersburg, Oh.: Ervin Schlabach.

Schlabach, Theron F.
1980   *Gospel Versus Gospel: Mission and the Mennonite Church, 1863-1944.* Scottdale, Pa. and Kitchener, Ont.: Herald Press.
1988   *Peace, Faith, Nation: Mennonites and Amish in Nineteenth-Century America.* The Mennonite Experience in America, volume two. Scottdale, Pa. and Kitchener, Ont.: Herald Press.

Schrag, Martin H.
1974   *The European History (1525-1874) of the Swiss Mennonites from Volhynia.* North Newton, Kans.: Swiss Mennonite Cultural and Historical Association.

Schwemer, R. and Harold S. Bender
1956   "Frankfurt Parliament," S.v. in *ME*, 2: 376, 377.

Schwieder, Elmer and Doroth Schwieder

1975 *A Peculiar People: Iowa's Old Order Amish.* Ames, Ia.: The Iowa State University Press.

Scott, Stephen E.
1981 *Plain Buggies: Amish, Mennonite, and Brethren Horse-Drawn Transportation.* Intercourse, Pa.: Good Books.
1986 *Why Do They Dress That Way?* Intercourse, Pa.: Good Books.
1988 *The Amish Wedding and Other Special Occasions of the Old Order Communities.* Intercourse, Pa.: Good Books.
1991 ["Information About the Groups Originating from the New Order Division Among the Lancaster County Amish,"] unpublished paper, personal papers of Stephen E. Scott.
1992 *Amish Houses and Barns.* Intercourse, Pa.: Good Books.

Scott, Stephen E. and Kenneth Pellman
1990 *Living Without Electricity.* Intercourse, Pa.: Good Books.

Seaton, Beverly
1980 "Helen Reimensnyder Martin's 'Caricatures' of the Pennsylvania Germans," *The Pennsylvania Magazine of History and Biography* 104 (January): 86-95.

Seguy, Jean
1973 Michael Shank, trans. "Religion and Agricultural Success: The Vocational Life of the French Anabaptists from the Seventeenth to the Nineteenth Centuries," *MQR* 47 (July): 179-224.
1977 *Les Assemblees anabaptistes-mennonites de France.* The Hague: Mouton.
1980 Mervin Smucker, trans. "The Bernese Anabaptists in Sainte-Marie-aux-Mines," *PMH* 3 (July): 2-9.
1984 "The French Anabaptists: Four and One-Half Centuries of History," *MQR* 58 (July): 206-17.

Shetler, Sanford G.
1963 *Two Centuries of Struggle and Growth, 1763-1962: A History of Allegheny Mennonite Conference.* Somerset, Pa.: Allegheny Mennonite Conference.

Smith, C. Henry
1929 *The Mennonite Immigration to Pennsylvania in the Eighteenth Century.* Norristown, Pa.: Pennsylvania German Society.
1962 *Mennonite Country Boy: The Early Years of C. Henry Smith.* Newton, Kans.: Faith and Life Press.

Smith, C. Henry and Cornelius Krahn
1981 *Smith's Story of the Mennonites*, fifth edition revised and enlarged. Newton, Kans.: Faith and Life Press.

Smith, Willard H.
1983 *Mennonites in Illinois.* Scottdale, Pa. and Kitchener, Ont.: Herald Press.

Smucker, Donovan E.
1977 ed. The Sociology of Canadian Mennonites, Hutterites, and Amish: A Bibliography with Annotations. Waterloo, Ont.: Wilfred Laurier University Press.
1991 ed. The Sociology of Mennonites, Hutterites and Amish: A Bibliography with Annotations, Volume II, 1977-1990. Waterloo, Ont.: Wilfred Laurier University Press. Heavily weighted toward Canadian sources.

Smucker, Mervin R.
1988 "How Amish Children View Themselves and Their Families: The Effectiveness of Amish Socialization," *Brethren Life and Thought* 33 (Summer): 218-36.

Sommer, Pierre and John A. Hostetler
1957 "Ixheim," S.v. in *ME*, 3: 58.

Stahly, Jerold A.
1989 "The Montbeliard Amish Move to Poland in 1791," *MFH* 8 (January): 13-17. Stahly followed this article with other MFH pieces which traced the stories of individual families who had been a part of the migration and later immigration.

"Statement in 1939 Concerning the Position of Non-resistance signed by Old Order Amish bishops . . ."
1939 original copy at the Heritage Historical Library, Aylmer, Ont.

Steering Committee
1966-1972 *Minutes of Old Order Amish Steering Committee.* vol 1. Gordonville, Pa.: Gordonville Print Shop.
1973-1980 *Minutes of Old Order Amish Steering Committee.* vol. 2. Gordonville, Pa.: Gordonville Print Shop.
1981-1986 *Minutes of Old Order Amish Steering Committee.* vol. 3. Gordonville, Pa.: Gordonville Print Shop.

Steiner, Sam
1990 "Ammann, Jakob," S.v. in *ME*, 5: 22.

Steinfeldt, Bernice
1937 *The Amish of Lancaster County: A Brief, but Truthful Account of the Actual Life and Customs of the Most Unique Class of People in the United States.* Lancaster, Pa.: Arthur G. Steinfeldt.

Steinmeier, Dorothy E.
1967 "Overlooked Indiana," *Travel: The Magazine That Roams the Globe* 127 (June): 28-33.

Stoll, Joseph
1966 "Introducing a New Paper," *AP* 1 (January): 1, 2.
1969 "An Amishman's Diary—1864, Notes from the Diary of John E. 'Hans' Borntrager," *FL* 2 (September): 34-39.
1970 "The Autumn Months of 1918—A Time of Tragedy," *FL* 3 (March): 24-26.
1972 "The Amish Settlement at Guaimaca, Honduras," *TD* 4 (October): 200, 196-99.
1974 "The Amish Church of Montbeliard, France (Founded 1713)," *TD* 6 (January): 19-23; (February): 48, 44-47.
1975 "Who Shall Educate Our Children," in *Compulsory Education and the Amish: The Right Not to be Modern*, ed. by Albert N. Keim, Boston: Beacon Press.
1987 "An Early Amish Lawsuit, 1861," *FL* 20 (August/September): 23-28.

Stoll, Joseph and Luthy, David
1973 "An Amish Church in France," *FL* 6 (December): 13-16.
Stoltzfus, Amos J.
1984 *Golden Memories*. Gordonville, Pa.: Pequae Publishers.
Stoltzfus, Grant M.
1954 "History of the First Amish Mennonite Communities in America," *MQR* 28 (October): 235-62.
1969 *Mennonites of the Ohio and Eastern Conference from the Colonial Period in Pennsylvania to 1968*. Scottdale, Pa.: Herald Press.
Stoltzfus, Nicholas
1981 comp. *Nonresistance Put to Test*. Aylmer, Ont.: Pathway Publishing Service.
Stoltzfus, Victor E.
1973 "Amish Agriculture: Adaptive Strategies for Economic Survival of Community Life," *Rural Sociology* 38 (summer): 196-206.
1977 "Reward and Sanction: The Adaptive Continuity of Amish Life," *MQR* 51 (October): 308-18.
Stucky, Solomon
1981 *The Heritage of the Swiss Volhynian Mennonites*. Waterloo, Ont.: Conrad Press.
Supreme Court of the United States
1972 *State of Wisconsin, Petitioner, v. Jonas Yoder, Adin Yutzy, and Wallace Miller. On Writ of Certiorari to the Supreme Court of Wisconsin*. [May 15], No. 70-110.
Swartzendruber, A. Lloyd
1950 "Samuel D. Guengerich," *MHB* 11 (October): 1, 3.
Swartzendruber, William
1977 et al., *Upper Deer Creek Conservative Mennonite Church Centennial Anniversary*. n.p.: Upper Deer Creek Conservative Mennonite Church.
The Swiss-Germans in South Dakota (From Volhynia to Dakota Territory), 1874-1974
1974 Freeman, S.D.: Pine Hill Press.
Swope, Wilmer D.
1969 "Nebraska Amish Mennonites and War Bonds in World War I," 30 *MHB* (January): 4, 5.
Teichroew, Allan
1979 ed., "Military Surveillance of Mennonites in World War I," *MQR* 53 (April): 95-127.
Thomas, Bill
1968 "Ohio's Amish Country," *Travel: The Magazine that Roams the Globe* 129 (April): 52, 53, 62, 63.
Thomson, Dennis L.
1993 "Canadian Government Relations," in *The Amish and the State*, ed. by Donald B. Kraybill, Baltimore: The Johns Hopkins University Press.
Troyer, Henry and Lee Willoughby
1984 "Changing Occupational Patterns in the Holmes County, Ohio, Amish Community," pp. 52-80 in Werner Enninger, ed. *Internal and External Perspectives on Amish and Mennonite Life*. Essen: Unipress.
The Truth in Word and Work: A Statement of Faith by Ministers and Brethren of Amish Churches of Holmes Co., Ohio, and Related Areas
1983 Baltic, Oh.: Amish Brotherhood Publications.
Umble, John S.
1933 "Amish Mennonites of Union County, Pennsylvania," *MQR* 7 (April): 71-96; (July): 162-90.
1939 ed., "Amish Ordination Charges," *MQR* 13 (October): 233-50.
1941a ed., "Amish Service Manuals," *MQR* 15 (January): 26-32.
1941b *Ohio Mennonite Sunday Schools*. Goshen, Ind.: Mennonite Historical Society.
1946 ed., "Catalog of an Amish Bishop's Library," *MQR* 20 (July): 230-39.
1947 "Why Congregations Die," *MHB* 8 (October): 1-3.
1948 ed., "Memoirs of an Amish Bishop," *MQR* 22 (April): 94-115.
1954 "An Early Amish Formulary," *MQR* 34 (January): 57-60. 1962 Certificates," *MQR* 36 (January): 88, 89.
1963 *One Hundred Years of Mennonite Sunday Schools in Logan County, Ohio*. West Liberty, Oh.: South Union Mennonite Church.
1964 "The Background and Origin of the Ohio and Eastern Amish Mennonite Conference," *MQR* 38 (January):
United States Department of Commerce Bureau of the Census
1941 *Religious Bodies: 1936*. Washington, D.C.: Government Printing Office.
Unruh, John D.
1952 *In the Name of Christ: A History of the Mennonite Central Committee and Its Service, 1920-1951*. Scottdale, Pa.: Herald Press.
Varry, Dominique
1984 "Jacques Klopfenstein and the Almanacs of Belfort and Montbeliard in the Nineteenth Century," *MQR* 58 (July): 241-57.
Wagler, David
1991 "Our Forefathers Left the Church," *FL* 24 (March): 40, 32-34.
n.d. *Are All Things Lawful?* Aylmer, Ont.: Pathway Publishers. An Amishman discusses automobile ownership.
Wagler, David and Roman Raber
1986 *The Story of the Amish in Civilian Public Service*. North Newton, Kans.: Bethel Press. A reprint of the original 1945 edition with an expanded directory of Amish who served in CPS.
Warkentin, Abe
1987 *Strangers and Pilgrims*. Steinbach, Man.: Die Mennonitische Post/Derksen Printers, Ltd.
Weaver, J. Denny.
1987 *Becoming Anabaptist: The Origin and Significance of Sixteenth-Century*

Anabaptism. Scottdale, Pa. and Kitchener, Ont.: Herald Press.

Weaver, William B.
1926 *History of the Central Conference Mennonite Church.* Danvers, Ill.: William B. Weaver.

Weber, Harry F.
1931 *Centennial History of the Mennonites of Illinois, 1829-1929.* Goshen, Ind.: Mennonite Historical Society.

Wenger, John Christian
1937 *History of the Mennonites of the Franconia Conference.* Telford. Pa.: Franconia Mennonite Historical Society.
1961 *The Mennonites in Indiana and Michigan.* Scottdale, Pa.: Herald Press.
1966 *The Mennonite Church in America, Sometimes Called Old Mennonites.* Scottdale, Pa.: Herald Press.

Wenger, Samuel S.
1981 "Nicholas Stoltzfus in Europe and America," *PMH* 4 (April): 15-17.

Williams, George H.
1962 *The Radical Reformation.* Philadelphia: Westminster Press.

Yoder, Don
1968/1969 "Trance-Preaching in the United States," *Pennsylvania Folklife* 18 (Winter): 12-18.

Yoder, Elmer S.
1987a *The Beachy Amish Mennonite Fellowship Churches.* Hartville, Oh.: Diakonia Ministries.
1990 *I Saw It in* The Budget. Hartville, Oh.: Diakonia Ministries.

Yoder, Harvey
1966 "*The Budget* of Sugarcreek, Ohio, 1890-1920" *MQR* 40 (January): 27-47.

Yoder, John Howard
1954 "Mennonites in a French Almanac," *ML* 9 (October): 154-56.
1955 "Bitscherland," S.v. in *ME*, 1: 349.
1956 "France," S.v. in *ME*, 2: 359-62.
1961 *The Christian and Capital Punishment.* Newton, Kans.: Faith and Life Press.
1973 trans. and ed., *The Schleitheim Confession.* Scottdale, Pa. and Kitchener, Ont.: Herald Press. Written in 1527.

Yoder, Joseph
1940 *Rosanna of the Amish.* Huntington, Pa.: Yoder Publishing Company.

Yoder, Mary Elizabeth
1971 "Amish Settlers and the Civil War," *FL* 4 (March): 26-28.

Yoder, Paton
1979a *Eine Würzel: Tennessee John Stoltzfus.* Lititz, Pa.: Sutter House.
1979b "Tennessee" John Stoltzfus and the Great Schism in the Amish Church, 1850-1877," *PMH* 2 (July): 17-23.
1985 "The Preaching Deacon Controversy Among the Nineteenth-Century American Amish," *PMH* 8 (January): 2-9.
1987b "The Structure of the Amish Ministry in the Nineteenth Century," *MQR* 61 (July): 280-97.
1987c *Tennessee John Stoltzfus: Amish Church-Related Documents and Family Letters.* Lancaster, Pa.: Lancaster Mennonite Historical Society.
1991 *Tradition and Transition: Amish Mennonites and Old Order Amish, 1800-1900.* Scottdale, Pa. and Waterloo, Ont.: Herald Press. The major interpretation of the time period, thoroughly researched and based on primary sources.

Yoder, Paton and Silas J. Smucker
1990 *Jonathan P. Smucker, Amish Mennonite Bishop.* Goshen, Ind.: Silas J. Smucker.

Yoder, Paul M.
1964 et al., *Four Hundred Years with the Ausbund.* Scottdale, Pa.: Herald Press.

Yoder, Sanford C.
1959 *The Days of My Years.* Scottdale, Pa.: Herald Press.

Yousey, Arlene R.
1987 *Strangers and Pilgrims: A History of Lewis County Mennonites.* Croghan, N.Y.: Arlene R. Yousey.

Zijpp, Nanne van der
1956 "Groningen," S.v. in *ME*, 2: 592-95.
1957 "Kampen," S.v. in *ME*, 3: 141, 142.

Zook, Lee J.
1993 "Slow Moving Vehicles," in *The Amish and the State*, ed. by Donald B. Kraybill, Baltimore: The Johns Hopkins University Press.

Zürcher, Isaac
1992 "Hans Reist and the 'Vale of Anabaptists,'" *MQR* 66 (July): 426, 427.

Index

164, 172, 189, 192, 198, 216
Buchanan County, 220, 221, 257, 259-261
Davis County, 102, 115, 121, 173
Hazelton, 249, 257-259
Johnson County, 122, 161, 199, 220
Kalona, 199, 282
Lee County, 102, 106
Washington County, 173, 220
Iowa-Nebraska (Mennonite) Conference, 169
Irish Creek Amish settlement, 56
Italy, 240
Ixheim Amish congregation (last in Europe), 182, 183

J

Jackson, Andrew (1767-1845), 115
Japan, 240
Joder, Joseph (1797-1887), 119, 147-150, 173
Johns, Daniel J. (1850-1942), 165
Jutzi, George, 114

K

Kansas, 157, 164, 210, 216, 221, 242
Bucklin, 225
Ford County, 228
Reno County, 192, 243
Kauffman family, 56
Kauffman, Christian (1810-1846), 99
Kauffman, Elizabeth Yoder (1804-1877), 99
Kauffman, Isaac (1718-1802), 72
Kauffman, John D. (1847-1913), 161
Kauffman, S. Duane, 117
Kaufman, Isaac (1806-1886), 159
Kenagy, Jacob, 109
Kentucky, 284
Louisville, 224
King family, 56
King, Aaron (1899-1986), 232
King, John P. (1827-1887), 153, 159
King, Samuel B. (1798-1876), 113
Kinsinger, Andrew S. (b. 1920), 256
Kinsinger, Peter, 97
Klopfenstein family, 86
Klopfenstein, Jacques (1763-1843), 84, 85
Korean war, 248
Krabill, Russell, 106
Kraybill, Donald B., 277, 282
Krehbiel, Henry J. (1865-1940), 173
Kurtz, Jonathan (1848-1930), 165

L

L'Anabaptiste ou Le Cultivateur Par Experience (The Anabaptist, or The Experienced Farmer), 84
Lais, John (1849-1894), 157
Lais, Susanna Plank (1860-1936), 157
Lambright, Jacob, 189
Lancaster, Pennsylvania, Chamber of Commerce and Industry, 279
Lantz family, 56
Lantz, Christian (b. c. 1751), 117

Lantz, Hans (d. 1789), 65, 73
Lapp, Henry (1862-1904), 208
Lensen, Jan, 47
Lensen, Mercken Schmitz, 47
Lincoln, Abraham (1809-1865), 119, 121
Lindholm, Rev. William C., 261, 262
Litwiller, Peter (1809-1878), 114
Lobwasser, Ambrosias, 83
Long, Noah, 168
Lorraine, 44, 49, 80, 181, 182
Bitsche, 182
Louisiana Purchase, 90
Louisiana
New Orleans, 95
Lower Deer Creek Amish congregation, 220
Lugbüll, Hans (1760-1835), 82
Luther, Martin (1483-1546), 7, 8
Lutheran Church, 53, 189, 198, 203
Luthy, David, 211
Luxembourg, 87, 182
Luyken, Jan (1649-1712), 16

M

Manitoba, 230
Mark Hellinger Theatre, 279
Martin, Helen Reimensnyder, 214
Martyrs Mirror, 16, 82
Maryland, 170
Garrett County, 199, 233
Hagerstown, 243
Saint Mary's County, 233, 267
Mast, David (1798-1869), 96
Mast, Jacob (1738-1808), 105
Mast, John "Johnny P.", (1826-1888), 159
Maurer, Christopher (1813-1872), 95
Maurer, Joseph (c. 1815-1867), 95
McKinley, William (1843-1901), 210-212
Medicare Insurance, 272
meetinghouses, 53, 58, 108, 109, 146, 168, 170, 176, 190, 199, 220, 227, 235, 269
Menno Simons (c. 1496-1561), 15, 17, 252
Mennonite Central Committee, 179
Mennonite Hospital, 176
Mennonite World Conference, 183, 241
Mennonites, 15, 16, 18-20, 24-26, 46, 48, 49, 60, 65, 74, 77, 80, 88, 97, 107, 109, 116, 121, 164, 165, 182, 185, 202, 205, 223, 226, 236, 239, 243, 268
General Conference Mennonite church, 170, 172, 173, 175, 187
"old" Mennonites, 168-170, 172
Dutch, 16, 49, 60, 83
Mennonite Church (MC), 172
Old Order Mennonites, 190, 191, 196
Russian Mennonites, 172
Methodist Church, 68
Mexico, 240
Nuevo Leon, 230
Paradise Valley, 230
Meyers, Thomas J., 276, 277, 284
Michigan, 210, 216, 242, 284
Atrim County, 166
East Tawas, 261
Pigeon, 170
migration in North America, Old Order

About the Author

Steve Nolt has an active interest in Mennonite and Amish history. He has worked at the Hans Herr House, a Mennonite museum in Lancaster County, Pennsylvania; the Mennonite Historical Library, Goshen, Indiana; and The People's Place, Intercourse, Pennsylvania.

Steve graduated from Goshen (Indiana) College with a degree in history. He has attended Associated Mennonite Biblical Seminaries, Elkhart, Indiana, and Eastern Mennonite Seminary—Lancaster (Pennsylvania) Campus. He is completing a masters degree in the field of church history.

He has published a number of articles in the field of Mennonite history. He is a contributing editor for the *Mennonite Historical Bulletin,* an editorial advisor for *Pennsylvania Mennonite Heritage,* and an active member of the Lancaster Mennonite Historical Society.

In 1992 Steve married Rachel Miller, of Engadine, Michigan. They live near Willow Street, Pennsylvania.